Doing Labor Activism in South China

How did labor NGOs come into existence in contemporary China? How do labor activists act – or not act – when the limits of state tolerance are unclear? With a focus on labor NGOs in South China and Western funding agencies, this book sets out to address these questions by investigating the dynamics of state control in post-socialist China since the 1970s, in which rapid economic and social transformations have cultivated an environment of uncertainty.

Taking uncertainty as an analytical space, productive of emergent practices and discourses, this book draws on original fieldwork and interviews to study the lived experiences of different actors throughout the labor NGO community, the foreign donors trying to bring about change, and the networks of social relationships being strategically reconfigured.

Doing Labor Activism in South China offers an ethnography of the Chinese state that reveals an intimate and complicit modality of self-governing, demonstrating how neoliberal ideas are at once represented by international development and deflected in grassroots development. It will be useful to students and scholars of Social Anthropology and Urban Ethnography, as well as Political Science and Chinese Studies more generally.

Darcy Pan is a social anthropologist whose research focuses on the state, labor, infrastructure, area studies specific to China, technology and urban development. She is a postdoctoral research fellow in the department of Social Anthropology at Stockholm University, Sweden. Her most recent work has been published in the *Handbook of Dissident and Protest in China* (2019).

Routledge Contemporary China Series

For more information about this series, please visit: https://www.routledge.com/Routledge-Contemporary-China-Series/book-series/SE0768

Doing Labor Activism in South China

The Complicity of Uncertainty

Darcy Pan

Routledge
Taylor & Francis Group

LONDON AND NEW YORK

First published 2020
by Routledge
2 Park Square, Milton Park, Abingdon, Oxon OX14 4RN

and by Routledge
52 Vanderbilt Avenue, New York, NY 10017

Routledge is an imprint of the Taylor & Francis Group, an informa business

British Library Cataloguing-in-Publication Data
A catalogue record for this book is available from the British Library

Library of Congress Cataloging-in-Publication Data
Names: Pan, Darcy, author.
Title: Doing labor activism in South China : the complicity of uncertainty / Darcy Pan.
Description: Abingdon, Oxon ; New York, NY : Routledge, 2020. | Series: Routledge contemporary China series | Includes bibliographical references and index.
Identifiers: LCCN 2020007721 (print) | LCCN 2020007722 (ebook) | ISBN 9780367406752 (hardback) | ISBN 9780367810092 (ebook)
Subjects: LCSH: Labor movement—China. | Labor unions—China. | Non-governmental organizations—China. | China—Economic policy—1949– | China—Economic conditions—1949–
Classification: LCC HD8734 .P35 2020 (print) | LCC HD8734 (ebook) | DDC 331.8809512—dc23
LC record available at https://lccn.loc.gov/2020007721
LC ebook record available at https://lccn.loc.gov/2020007722

ISBN: 978-0-367-40675-2 (hbk)
ISBN: 978-0-367-81009-2 (ebk)

Typeset in Times New Roman
by codeMantra

Printed in the United Kingdom
by Henry Ling Limited

Contents

Acknowledgments

This book is based on my PhD dissertation, which was completed in 2016 in the Department of Social Anthropology at Stockholm University. The research on which my PhD study is based was generously funded by grants from Forum for Asian Studies, Helge Ax:son Johnson Foundation, the Swedish Society for Anthropology and Geography, and the Department of Social Anthropology, Stockholm University. They funded the different stages of my fieldwork in 2012–2013. Scholarship from the Sweden-America Foundation gave me the opportunity to spend one year in the Department of Anthropology at Yale University from 2014 to 2015 to focus on writing my dissertation.

In China and Hong Kong, I am truly grateful to all the people whom I met and spent time with, many of whom have become good friends. Nearly all of them have been given pseudonyms in this study. I hope that the perspective I offer will in some way repay their interest and kindness. I thank Anthony Spires at the University of Melbourne for inspiring discussions at the early stage of my fieldwork.

In Taiwan, I am grateful for Chih-jou Jay Chen at Academia Sinica and Hsing-chung Wang at Soochow University for helping me make contacts in Guangzhou at the early stage of my fieldwork.

In the Department of Social Anthropology at Stockholm University, Johan Lindquist has been my mentor since I began my graduate education. He has read and commented on several versions of this study and continuously shown confidence in me and this project, and pushed me to broaden and deepen my understanding of and engagement with contemporary issues in anthropology and social theory. I cannot express enough my gratitude to him for being a guide and an interlocutor for so many years. As my second advisor, Anette Nyqvist has offered her unwavering support and has had faith in me and has given me invaluable comments as I wrote and revised the study. Along with these people, I have been sustained by conversations with Ulf Hannerz, Helena Wulff, Shahram Khosravi, Mark Graham, Renita Thedvall, Paula Uimonen, and Dolly Kikon. I am also indebted to the graduate students and the administrative staff at the department. I thank Hege Høyer Leivestad, Peter Skoglund, and Lina Lorentz for guiding and helping me with the practicalities.

I was affiliated with the Asia Research Institute at National University of Singapore during the summer of 2010. I thank Brenda Yeoh for the invitation which allowed me to conduct some preliminary fieldwork in the region. I am also grateful for Melody Lu, Lai An-Eng, Lan Anh, Cheryll Alipio, Shu-yi Pearl Wang, and Mika Toyota for inspiring conversations and support. I would also like to extend my gratitude to all the administrative staff at the Asia Research Institute for making my visit so comfortable and memorable. During the winter of 2010, I had the opportunity to do some coursework at the Institute of Social and Cultural Anthropology at University of Oxford. I am grateful for Xiang Biao's invitation and letting me be part of the stimulating research environment.

I spent the academic year 2014–2015 in the Department of Anthropology at Yale University. I am grateful for the Sweden-America Foundation for funding my stay. I would like to thank Erik Harms for inviting me and allowing me to be part of the stimulating and vibrant academic environment. I would also like to thank the administrative staff Marlene Cullen for helping me settle and get situated as smoothly as possible in the beginning of my arrival. I am hugely indebted to Paul Kockelman who has generously read the early version of several chapters and offered comments and ideas that have been crucial in shaping the direction of the study. I am also grateful for Helen Siu who has shared her expertise in Chinese studies and offered practical guidance of teasing out the conceptual issues in my own work. I would also like to thank Kalyanakrishnan Sivaramakrishnan who kindly shared with me his expertise in development studies and offered some constructive suggestions in the early stage of my writing.

I am also indebted to Graham Jones in the Department of Anthropology at Massachusetts Institute of Technology for helping me think through some of the issues and the structure of the study. I would also like to convey my heartfelt gratitude and sincere appreciation to Michael Herzfeld at Harvard University who was the discussant of the final discussion of my doctoral thesis. He has given me invaluable and inspiring comments that have made the last stage of writing up a truly rewarding experience. I cannot thank him enough.

This book would not have seen the light of the day without the support of my friends who have believed in me and supported me through these years. I thank Jennifer Lindsay for excellent copyediting of my dissertation. I would also like to thank Alan Lindsay for being a great teacher and friend in supporting my writing for so many years.

Finally, I want to express my deepest gratitude to my family, including my cat August, who have been supportive in many different ways, and through all different phases of my life.

A note on names, translations, and currency issues

All translations of textual and spoken materials from Chinese to English that appear in this book were done by the author. The Pinyin System for Romanizing Chinese characters is used throughout the text. In an effort to ensure the safety and security of my informants living and working in mainland China and Hong Kong, I have changed the names of the people and organizations and have left references that could identify them out of the bibliography. Therefore, all the Chinese names of individuals, organizations, and factories are pseudonyms, if not otherwise specified. The personal names are written as they would be in Chinese; that is, the family name is followed by the first name. The names of the provinces and cities are real names, while the names of districts and villages are pseudonyms in order to protect the identity of the individuals and organizations where I conducted fieldwork. In this book, I have chosen and translated certain terms and phrases from Chinese to English because they are specific Chinese terms and have specific meanings in the contexts where they were uttered and used. I have included the Chinese characters together with the English translations in order to ensure that their meanings are not compromised too much by translation.

The official currency of the PRC is the renminbi and is abbreviated RMB. Throughout this study I will use primarily the renminbi and the U.S. dollar, and, unless otherwise noted, the rate was 6.66 RMB per dollar during the time of my fieldwork.

Introduction

"Any new gossip?" Mandy asked with a mischievous smile. It was a February afternoon in 2013 in the office of the Chinese Workers' Front (CWF), a Hong Kong-based nongovernmental labor organization (hereafter referred to as labor NGO). This was Mandy's way of checking how my research had been going and if I was willing to share any information I had obtained from the labor NGOs I had been working with, some of which were CWF's partners. Mandy was the coordinator for CWF's projects in mainland China[1] and the main contact person for their partner NGOs there. She tried to maintain contact with each partner on a daily basis, mainly by phone and email, and also conducted on-site visits to partners at least once a month. Additional visits would be scheduled if the donors were in town and wanted to visit the organizations they support. I had been going to CWF for the past few months to either meet with staff or participate in workshops, and on this day I was meeting Mandy to talk about CWF's projects in China.

Mandy was always keen to know more about these NGOs so that she could, as she put it, "manage the projects better." In response, I told Mandy one new piece of information about myself that I had recently heard from a labor NGO staff member. The director of the labor NGO where I was conducting fieldwork at the time had given my resumé to the local police. Mandy let out a light laugh and said calmly,

> I am not surprised at all. I know he has been giving information [to the state security agents]. He even gives away information about the workers. Whose side is he on? I understand that you need to give information but you need to have a bottom line (*dixian*). Don't you think? You can't just give whatever they ask for.

Mandy continued,

> You know CWF is a bit sensitive (*mingan*). But we can still carry out our work in China. It requires some skill (*jiqiao*). Some things need to be kept secret and some things need to be compromised. We can compromise so that's not a problem. But it is hard to trust [people] because

you don't always know what's going on [between the NGOs and the government]. It's very ambiguous (*hen aimei*).

It seemed I had touched on a topic that Mandy felt strongly about and she felt compelled to express her opinion. Sounding both frustrated and demoralized, Mandy noted that the lack of transparency of CWF's partners was a serious issue. She said,

> Many NGOs use government surveillance as a shield to justify the fact that they can't share all the information with their partners. This makes it very convenient [for these NGOs] to keep some information to themselves. It's a really big issue for us. I feel that in the mainland (*neidi*), the more slippery [labor NGOs] get around better (*yu huatou hun de yu hao*) because they know how to handle and mingle (*zhouxuan*) with different people. I thought about quitting my job because I didn't want to deal with people like that every day.

Suddenly one of Mandy's colleagues knocked on the door and popped in to say that there was a phone call for her. Left alone in the conference room, I was somewhat struck by how Mandy's words were palpably tinged with jaded professionalism, mission fatigue, and even some cynicism, revealing a gloomy outlook for the development of labor NGOs in China.

This book examines the workings of Chinese state power by exploring how development projects supporting labor activism are implemented in a restrictive political climate in which the limits of state tolerance are uncertain. Focusing on labor NGOs in both mainland China and Hong Kong, and their foreign donors, this study aims to illustrate how the Chinese state is embedded and enacted at the margins of the nation-state in which practices, discourses, and relationships are created, reinforced, and maintained (Das & Poole 2004: 3), and how the effect of state power is not all-encompassing but uneven, which, in turn, creates an ambiguous boundary between state and society and thus a contingent space of activism. More specifically, I am concerned with two sets of empirical questions: The first deals with the social, political, and economic conditions under which labor activists and NGOs have emerged in South China. How did labor NGOs come into existence in an authoritarian regime? What do the labor NGOs do? What role does the international community play in the development and survival of the labor NGOs in China? How do international funds trickle down to these labor NGOs? The second focuses on the political and economic processes that have made political space available to labor NGOs in contemporary China. What are these processes and what effects do they have? How do the labor NGOs engage with these processes while trying to build the labor movement and induce social change? How do the labor NGOs carry out their work when the boundaries of state tolerance of labor activism are often uncertain and ambiguous? Essentially, these two sets of questions address the relationship between trust and power: How do labor activists establish trust relationships and negotiate power among them, and contend with state control under the uncertain circumstances fostered by the Chinese state?

With the aim of exploring the dynamics of state control and the specific workings of state power in contemporary China, I treat uncertainty as an analytical and ethnographic space that is (re)productive of emergent practices, discourses, and modes of existence that strategically configure and reconfigure social relationships among different actors while masking and unmasking the state. It is in such a space that I situate and study the lived experiences of everyday life and relationships among a group of labor NGOs in Guangdong Province and Hong Kong, and Western funding agencies that try to bring about change in post-socialist China where rapid economic and social transformations since the 1970s have unleashed diverse social forces and cultivated an environment of uncertainty in social, political, and moral terms (Liu 2000; Ku 2003; Oxfeld 2010; Heilmann & Perry 2011). More specifically, I investigate how a social realm—a contested boundary between state and society—located in the margins of the state has emerged in the midst of uncertainty. By "social" I mean those "not-to-be-compartmentalized dimensions of the human experience" (Shue 1988: 27). It is in this social realm that I examine how variously positioned subjects mobilize around the idea of the state, which, in turn, leads to articulations and practices of dealing with the state. The state becomes an enabler whereby certain kinds of knowledge, practices, relationships, and networks are made possible and necessary. As such, this social realm is also a space of intimacy (cf. Herzfeld 2016) where different ways of engaging in complicity between the state and social actors can be explored. I thus examine the ways in which uncertainty is (re)productive of knowledge and practices whereby labor activists not only effectively self-censor but also skillfully map the gray zone between relatively safe and unacceptably risky choices.

Foregrounding the uncertainty about the boundaries of permissible political action allows me to shift my analysis of the agency of the subaltern groups from critical moments of resistance to the ways in which "the conceptual boundaries of the state are extended and remade in securing survival or seeking justice in the everyday" (Das & Poole 2004: 20). I move beyond the common story of state control through coercion and regulation, and look into the ripple effect of how uncertainty affects the agency of those in the margins. How does one gauge the distance from the state when there are limits of knowing and acting? What are the ways of gathering knowledge so as to come to a degree of certainty in the midst of uncertainty? How does uncertainty affect and shape subjectivity? How does one conduct ethnographic fieldwork under uncertain conditions and write an ethnography about these limits of knowing and acting which in turn become the constraints of the ethnographer's knowing and writing?

This study treats the state as an idea that is constantly being imagined, evoked, articulated, embodied, and negotiated by these NGOs and funding agencies. As such, the state as an idea has tangible effects on the actors, the institutions, and the relationships between them (Abrams 1988 [1977]; Mitchell 1991, 1999; Taussig 1992, 1997; Sharma & Gupta 2006). Labor NGOs are a critical site of investigation to illuminate a specific form of organizational arrangement, born of interactions between a variety of domestic and foreign actors as well as with the state (Trouillot 2003). With a focus on the ways in which the partnerships among these organizations are formed and Western funds trickle down to the labor NGOs in mainland China, this study illustrates how the state is constitutive of and constituted in the network of relationships among these labor NGOs and foreign funding foundations. These relationships become the lived experiences of the ongoing processes of state formation or the state as a "structural effect" (Mitchell 1991), and comprehending them is crucial to a more nuanced understanding of the changing state-society relationship in contemporary China. More importantly, by focusing on how the state as an idea is embedded and enacted in networks of relationships among different actors in the labor community, this study offers an ethnography of the Chinese state which illustrates a modality of self-governing in which neoliberal ideas, represented by international development, are reconfigured and deflected in grassroots development.

Background

After the death of Mao Zedong in 1976, Deng Xiaoping launched a set of radical and comprehensive economic programs to reinvigorate the country's economy. Deng's programs were characterized by a decentralization of economic authority and limited introduction of market mechanisms. During his "Southern Inspection" (*nanxun*) tour in the special economic zones in 1992, Deng reiterated the importance of boosting the country's economic development and stated that "development is the absolute principle" (*fazhan cai shi ying daoli*). Deng's selective and pragmatic approach has paid off: China has enjoyed remarkable economic growth that has astonished the world, although this growth is uneven and more beneficial to cities and coastal areas than to rural regions. As economic reforms intensified, the 1990s saw a widespread privatization and bankruptcy of state-owned enterprises, pension and welfare reforms, and a rush of global capital, as well as deepened economic polarization and inequalities.

Since the mid-1990s, labor unrest has been on the rise and described as a source of political and social instability (Lee 2007: 228). Precarious working conditions such as long hours, wage arrears, lax enforcement of health and safety standards, lack of labor contracts, limited access to medical insurance and retirement, and poor housing have led to increasing labor protests and strikes across China. This has been particularly notable in Guangdong, home to a large population of peasants-turned-workers who leave their rural homes and flock to the coast of South China, where labor-intensive, export-oriented, and light industry has concentrated and labor exploitation is prevalent (Chan 2001; SACOM 2005). These migrants are often referred to as *mingong*, peasant workers or *liudong renkou*, meaning floating population, which consists of people who "float and move, implying that they are not, and will not become, a permanently settled group" (Solinger 1999: 15). Because peasant-turned-workers move to seek employment, they are also commonly referred to as migrant workers, which is the term used in this study.

In the wake of economic reforms, China has been undergoing significant political, economic, and social transformations. China has endured the Tiananmen Uprising, outlasted both Eastern European and Soviet variants of communism, and weathered ethnic riots in 2008 and 2009 (Heilmann & Perry 2011). Regardless of numerous predictions of its impending demise and the widely shared anticipation of a commensurate political liberalization (Chang 2001; Gilley 2004; Pei 2006; Shirk 2007), China's Communist Party continues to be in power in the wake of astounding economic progress. What intrigues as well as confounds many China observers is not only the continued absence of liberal democratic institutions in the country but also the fact that the Chinese Communist regime has become increasingly adept at managing challenges posed by leadership succession, popular unrest, administrative reorganization, legal institutionalization, and the integration with the global economy. As political scientist Andrew Nathan acknowledges, "One of the puzzles of the post-Tiananmen period has been the regime's apparent ability to rehabilitate its legitimacy" (Nathan 2003: 13).

Without doubt, the discrepancy between economic growth and political liberalization in China comes at a great cost. Ordinary Chinese citizens are still deprived of civil liberties. The absence of political restraints has contributed to cadre corruption, labor exploitation, poor protection of consumers, environmental degradation, and increasing social inequality. In spite of these numerous problems, the Chinese Communist regime continues to govern, which raises the question of legitimacy, a subject to be addressed in Chapter 2. When discussing Chinese politics, one is readily reminded of stories of heavy-handed repression and violence. The "interplay of repression and resistance" (Heilmann & Perry 2011: 4) animates and dominates the popular imagination of the political situation in China. But these stories do not reveal a more nuanced face of the Chinese Communist regime. Coercion is not a staple of daily political life. As Stern and Hassid point out, the number of people that are in effect severely punished or imprisoned makes up fewer than 1% of the activists in China. So, the question is, What keeps the other 99% in line? (Stern & Hassid 2012). How does the Chinese state secure compliance from the governed? I suggest that foregrounding the uncertainty of the political life in post-socialist China can shed light on these questions.

Thinking through uncertainty

In this book, I use uncertainty to include situations of ambiguity, indeterminacy, and contradictions as well as tensions and contingencies that arise from such situations. Uncertainty is inextricably entangled with human existence and figures as a powerful motivation in our striving for knowledge. Uncertainty prompts us to try to predict the future so as to hopefully generate more certainty when confronted with the unknown (Nowotny 2015). Anthropological theory has long privileged the discovery of order and regularities of everyday life (Radcliffe-Brown 1922; Malinowski 1944; Lévi-Strauss 1963 [1958]; James 1995; Geertz 2000 [1973]; Benedict 2005 [1934]). Since the 1980s, there has been a gradual theoretical shift to address the shortcomings of structuralist approaches in linguistics and social sciences (Derrida 1976, 1978, 1994, 1997; Foucault 1984, 1992 [1978], 2002 [1969], 2002 [1970]; Ortner 1984; Sahlins 1985; Moore 1987; Deleuze 1994; Das 1995; Niehaus 2013). This broad theoretical shift reflects a loss of confidence in the explanatory sufficiency of the capacity and coherence of structures, that is, encompassing systems, durable social forms, regular occurrences, and everyday practices. It has become apparent that while a focus on regularities and consistency can shed light on some areas of social life, it also obscures and ignores other irregular, transitory, uncertain, anomalous, or ambiguous forms, practices, and events. More importantly, this theoretical imbalance prevents us from contemplating the "substantial areas of normative indeterminacy" (Moore 1987: 729) and developing social theory of irregularity, unpredictability, precariousness, inconstancy, and fickleness—in other words, a social theory of uncertainty.

Some scholars have addressed this conceptual imbalance and underscored the productivity of uncertainty and indeterminacy. Bruno Latour (2005) accentuates and uses uncertainties to name strategies that assemble and disassemble research sites and forge research practices because he wants to curb social scientists' inclinations to cling to stable stories. Questioning the common view that writing fixes and secures relations among people, things, and places, Matthew Hull's work on the materiality of bureaucracy in urban Pakistan illustrates how indeterminacy and equivocation can be generated from the mediation of documents (2012; cf. Riles 2006). In line with the recent turn to the ambiguous, indeterminate, and unpredictable, I foreground uncertainty in my study so as to further explore ongoing discourses, events, practices, and processes of negotiating with, dismantling, or creating rules, orders, temporalities, and spatialities.

Uncertainty is often associated with and translated into the language of risk and danger in anthropological thought and practice (Cancian 1980; Cashdan 1990; Adams 1997; Rosa 1998; Boholm 2003). Earlier approaches to risk, notably those framed in terms of culture (Douglas & Wildavsky 1982) and modernization (Beck 1992; Giddens 2000), have positivistic inclinations, as risk, danger, and uncertainty are treated as things that can be observed, perceived, calculated, and dealt with. Thus, they are often lumped together as observable objects. In contrast, Niklas Luhmann (1993) considers risk not as an object in a first-order observation but as a concept in a second-order observation. By differentiating between two levels of observation in a system, Luhmann distinguishes risk from danger, as the former is contingent on the system whereas the latter is caused by forces outside of the system (1993: 21–28). Crucial to Luhmann's treatment of risk and danger is his focus not on the quality or quantity of dangers in the world but on "the mode of observing risk as conceptually inherent to modern systems and how each decision or abstention from decision concerning the future determines risk" (Samimian-Darash & Rabinow 2015: 3). As it will become clear later in the book, this distinction made by Luhmann bears great relevance to my discussion of how Chinese labor NGOs deal with state surveillance while implementing development projects of labor activism funded by Western organizations. Under the restrictive political conditions, the ways in which Chinese labor activists conduct themselves closely hinge on how they view the Chinese state, which, in turn, sets the parameters of their activism work so that they can gauge and diminish risk, and try to work in a way that will not be deemed as an affront to the state.

Predicated on how the Chinese state and the associated potential risk are perceived, the parameters of these NGOs' work give rise to knowledge, practices, tactics, and strategies created with the hope to mitigate risk and estimate the appropriate distance from the Chinese state. This is similar to what Limor Samimian-Darash and Paul Rabinow's emphasis of how certain knowledge and practices are circulated and made available to deal with risk, danger, and uncertainty, which should be treated as distinct concepts both analytically and anthropologically (Samimian-Darash & Rabinow 2015: 1). This is because "the world is increasingly being populated by forms, practices, and events of uncertainty that cannot be reduced to risk" (ibid.). Considering uncertainty as a distinct concept, according to Samimian-Darash and Rabinow, directs the analytical and anthropological attention to "emergent problem spaces" (ibid.) that consider the understanding of, representation of, and response to the problems at hand which then allow us to examine what and how forms of governing and modes of subjectivity have developed.

Drawing attention to "emergent problem spaces" makes an analytical shift from the control of risk to the management of uncertainty. With the control of risk, the emphasis is placed on technologies designed to identify, prevent, and control risk—in other words, making risk governable, and, as such, a mode of governance (Rose 1999 [1989], 2008 [1999]). In contrast, the management of uncertainty relies on technologies that focus on precaution and preparedness. Technologies of uncertainty rely on past information to make predictions about future events and propose which preparedness practices in response. Technologies of uncertainty thus lay emphasis on the ways in which observations about uncertainty are made and come to circulate in the contemporary world and thus constitute a new problematic field for which certain policies and practices emerge as solutions (Samimian-Darash & Rabinow 2015: 3). As such, uncertainty can be viewed as a productive and constitutive concept that can be mobilized to generate and facilitate discourses, forms, and practices. Following Luhmann and Limor Samimian-Darash and Paul Rabinow, this book analyzes the relationship between Chinese labor NGOs and the state through the prism of uncertainty so as to open up an analytical space in which how Chinese labor NGOs manage and negotiate the uncertain limits of state-sanctioned activism can be examined. By doing so, I hope to illustrate and understand the often-elusive state-society dynamics that are deeply enmeshed within historical, political, and social fabrics.

That uncertainty should be treated as a productive concept instead of a problem, an irregularity, or a misfortune to be faced, avoided, or solved is also highlighted in recent research on the subject of governance in China. Researchers of Chinese politics have been turning to such words as uncertainty (Link 2002; Hassid 2008; Yang 2009: 188; Dillon 2011; Heilmann & Perry 2011; Stern & Hassid 2012), ambiguity (O'Brien & Li 2006: 63; McNally 2011), and ambivalence (deLisle 2004; Shue 2004: 41; O'Brien & Li 2006: 31; Levy 2007: 47; Yang 2008: 131; Lee 2010: 51; Xu & Pu 2010: 164) to delineate the "dual, almost schizophrenic nature" (Litzinger 2007: 298; cf. Taussig 1992) of the Chinese state. Many of these studies focus their attention on how the uncertainty and ambiguity of the Chinese government's policy and guidelines create a prevalent sense of indeterminacy, arbitrariness, and insecurity that work as a "control mechanism" or "regime of uncertainty" to keep the majority of the population in line (Hassid 2008: 415; see also Stern & Hassid 2012; Pan 2019).[2]

This body of literature not only shows that uncertainty is a common characteristic of Chinese politics but also serves as an important point of entry to understand the specific workings of state power. It shows that uncertainty becomes a technology of power that is productive and generative of a certain kind of order when used skillfully. Inherent in this use of the notion of uncertainty is that information or signals that are being transmitted and conveyed by the Chinese state are unclear and incomplete and thus subject to interpretation (Perry 2002; Stern & O'Brien 2012) whereby modes of observation of uncertainty can be extrapolated. Chinese activists have to grapple with "correctly" reading mixed signals, which provide clues to assess opportunities and threats. Addressing the mixed signals of the Chinese state, Stern and Hassid argue, allows us to move beyond "some well-patrolled forbidden zones" and see how "the state speaks with many, contradictory voices" (Stern & O'Brien 2012: 177). It also allows us to unsettle the visual metaphor of the state as an observer watching from a singular perspective (Scott 1998) that often leads to the assumption that there is a unity of state representations and falls short of illustrating "how such unity is achieved (or not) through coordination in practice" (Hull 2012: 166).

Taking the notion of uncertainty as the theoretical point of departure for this book, I study political life in contemporary China by investigating how labor NGOs, individual activists, and donors manifest a certain mode of being, acting, and knowing in contemporary China. In this book, the notion of uncertainty serves both analytical and methodological purposes. I will develop the methodological parameters in Chapter 1. Here, following Luhmann (1993), I treat uncertainty as an analytical concept to understand the political, social, and economic conditions under which these labor NGOs operate. This opens up an analytical and ethnographic space where the dynamics between state control, practices of self-censorship, and performances of labor activism can be conceptualized as a relationship fraught with and generative of negotiations with, mediations of, and enactments of discourses, relationships, and practices. With this analytical move, I explore what forms and practices of gauging the limits of state tolerance have emerged in shaping and conditioning the relationships between the labor NGO sector (labor NGOs, donors, labor scholars, and media) and the state. These forms and practices are illustrated by informal ways of communication such as gossip, rumor, and storytelling, and practices of activism and secrecy, which are often characterized by a tactful balancing and situational act between the state, labor NGOs, and donors. It is true that informality, gossip, rumor, and secrecy are not unique to China. These informal ways of communication and practices exist in both liberal democracies and authoritarian regimes. But as my study shows, these informal practices become imperative to the existence and survival of Chinese labor NGOs when they operate in a political landscape where uncertainty is a technology of state power. The extent to which the Chinese state deliberately and quite successfully deploys and allows uncertainty, ambiguity, and arbitrariness to seep into its making and implementation of policies and regulations is unparalleled among other authoritarian countries. This makes uncertainty an important point of entry into an understanding of contemporary Chinese politics. While uncertainty serves as the analytical lens to situate and anchor this study, the informal communication practices of gossip, rumor, and secrecy are the heuristic and ethnographic moments and spaces where uncertainty is experienced, conveyed, and discussed. In the chapters that follow, I will illustrate ethnographically how such forms and practices, which are enactments of how uncertainty is observed and managed, are played out and can be understood as epistemological mediations of trust in situations of uncertainty when the permitted boundaries of activism are unclear.

Notions of the state

At the center of the domain of uncertainty is the idea of the Chinese state, which often evokes an opaque, skeletal, ghostly, and monolithic image (Nettle 1968: 559; Shue 1988: 17). The ambiguous perception of the Chinese state opens up an ethnographic space in which we can conceptualize how different relationships and subjectivities are cultivated, formed, mobilized, and managed against the unclear idea about the state. Anthropological interest in the state has increased considerably since the beginning of the 1990s as shown by a number of recent publications (Mitchell 1991; Taussig 1992, 1997;

Hansen & Stepputat 2001; Ferguson & Gupta 2002; Trouillot 2003; Das & Poole 2004; Geertz 2004; Elyachar 2005; Yang 2005; Sharma & Gupta 2006; Gupta 2012; Hull 2012). These publications can be viewed in light of the "cultural turn" in the study of the state (Steinmetz 1999), which attempted to address the issue of how to determine appropriate approaches and levels to study the state. In the 1940s, Radcliffe-Brown had already argued against taking the state as an empirical object of study and urged researchers to direct attention to more concrete forms of political organizations, relations, and individuals (Radcliffe-Brown 1987 [1940]: xxiii).

In contrast to Radcliffe-Brown's call to abandon the state as the object of study, Philip Abrams directed the analytical attention to the idea of the state and described the state-idea as an ideological project that legitimates subjection, a claim to domination, and a mask that hides the institutionalization of political power in the state system (Abrams 1988 [1977]; see also Sharma & Gupta 2006: 46). Abrams's analysis of the state-idea as an ideological project has been influential and led many anthropologists to treat the state as more than just a functional bureaucratic apparatus—a productive site where the state itself is culturally and symbolically constructed and represented. Abrams's conceptualization paints an utterly disturbing picture of the state and reality that prompts Michael Taussig to call it "a thoroughly nervous Nervous System" (Taussig 1992: 113). In line with Abrams's emphasis on the processes whereby the power of the state is exercised, Timothy Mitchell raises a slightly different question of the significance and effects of sustaining the uncertain distinction between the state and society (1991: 89). To mark the boundary between the state and society is an exercise of power that has consequences.

> The line between state and society is not the perimeter of an intrinsic entity, which can be thought of as a free-standing object or actor. It is a line drawn internally, *within* the network of institutional mechanisms through which a certain social and political order is maintained.
>
> (Mitchell 1991: 90, emphasis in original)

The ways in which the state-society distinction, which is uncertain and always contested, are produced and maintained become a mechanism that generates resources of power (ibid.).

A good number of anthropological studies have illustrated and discussed the ways and processes in which such constructions and representations take place (Bayart 1993 [1989]; Joseph & Nugent 1994; Cohn 1996; Bernal 1997; Coronil 1997; Nugent 1997; Taussig 1997; Comaroff 1998; Scott 1998; Ferguson & Gupta 2002; Trouillot 2003). Several analytical concepts have been developed to understand these processes such as "the spatialization of states" (Ferguson & Gupta 2002) and "state effects" (Trouillot 2003). These studies have all illustrated analytical as well as empirical endeavors to move beyond the reification of the state. While doing so, however, they have also fallen short of demonstrating the actual workings of the state, more specifically, the particular workings of state power.

In the modern Chinese state, the issue of state power and governance has been discussed in terms of "state involution" (Duara 1987; Siu 1989a, 1989b; Murphy 2007). Although these studies have dealt with different periods of state-making in modern Chinese history, they have all shared a basic line of thinking that, regardless of an appearance of the construction of formal rationality, the formation of a modern state from the republican era onward failed to result in an efficient and transparent state bureaucracy. It is a language of order that is inherited largely from the modern European state (Das & Poole 2004: 5). Following Duara (1987), many of these studies borrow the concept of "involution" from Geertz's study of Javanese wet rice agriculture (1969 [1963]). According to Geertz, involution is a process through which a social or cultural pattern persists and fails to transform itself into a new pattern even after it has reached a definitive form. Implicit in the notion of "state involution" is a Eurocentric presumption that views the state as well as society to be where they should not be or have failed to be where they should be. It indicates a linear way of thinking about development and implies an attribution of backwardness. As such, the notion of "state involution" also reinforces the treatment of the state and society as separate entities. Not only does the notion of "state involution" run the risk of reifying the state-society relationship, but it also postulates the state-society relationship in an overly simplistic dichotomy between formal and informal structures (Duara 1987: 132–133; Siu 1989a, 1989b; Lu 2000; Murphy 2007). Hence, it fails to consider the interactional dynamics and processes that are jointly defining contemporary Chinese society.

In order to move away from the reification of state-society relationship and to capture the dynamics of such a relationship, I turn to the idea of uncertainty. This book deals with the subject of uncertainty in Chinese politics and discusses how it creates and shapes a complicit relationship between the Chinese state and labor NGOs. As discussed in the previous section, uncertainty is conceptualized as a technology of power that is generative and constitutive in the sense that it gives rise to discourses, informal communication practices, tactics, and strategies that help the NGOs to deal with the Chinese state. Here, the work of Abrams and Mitchell is relevant to my analysis of the state-society relationship in South China. Abrams's theory of the state-idea as an ideological project opens up an analytical space where one can discuss the discursive work of how the state is conceived, experienced, talked about, and acted on. By describing the state as a "spurious object of sociological concern" (Abrams 1988 [1977]: 63), Abrams urges that our understanding of the state cannot be further advanced unless it is acknowledged that the state is illusory referencing Marx and Engels—"the state constitutes the 'illusory common interest' of a society" (Marx & Engels 1965: 42 in Abrams 1988 [1977]: 64, emphasis in original). Abrams directs our attention to the word "illusory" and points out that the state is illusory not because it is some reality or entity hidden behind a mask but because it is the mask. The ideological power of the state is exerted through the state's active work of masking and mystifying itself. As such, the key task to study state, according to Abrams, is to unravel the ways in which the state is masked and mystified and thus "illusory" (ibid.: 72).

In the Chinese context, one specific way for the Chinese state to exercise its ideological power is through the technology of uncertainty. The shifting boundaries of state-sanctioned activism is a very crucial part of the mysti-fication of the Chinese state leaving the labor NGOs in a constant state of anxiety and frustration. Moreover, the uncertain limits of state tolerance about labor activism consequently lead to particular discourses and forms of practices that the labor NGOs employ to deal with the state, which illus-trates how state power is exercised through the elusive boundary between the state and society. The uncertainty about the state—what the state wants, knows, and thinks—brings into sharp focus where the state appears to be both as a material force and an ideological construct (Mitchell 1991). More importantly, the uncertainty about the state tolerance becomes a power-ful force that keeps the parameters of the NGO work in flux. These shift-ing parameters and the consequent practices to manage them—a form of self-censorship—are the specific work of state power. So through the idea of uncertainty, I show how this internal line between the state and society is drawn as Mitchell suggested. It is in the midst of uncertainty that one can start to discern the actual contours of the amorphous state and understand how state power works.

Hence, drawing on Abrams (1988 [1977]) and Mitchell (1991) in my theoret-ical discussion of uncertainty, I examine how the Chinese state is perceived, experienced, utilized, and mobilized by subjects located in the margins of the state. It is through the uncertainty at the margins of the Chinese state that I investigate the contingencies where boundaries and processes are instigated so as to facilitate certain relationships, distinct identities, and a particular mode of thinking, acting, and being. In these processes, the state and society are often treated as disparate and fixed entities so as to contin-gently justify and sustain certain discourses, forms, and practices. Rather than taking this distinction for granted, my analytical focus is to inquire into how the reification has come about and what effects and functions it has and serves because such contingent reification is the core of what makes the state-society relationship in contemporary China so dynamic and fraught with tension.

Intimacy and complicity

How does one locate and tease out such processes of contingent reifica-tion against the uncertainty of and about the state? I suggest that these contingent processes are to be located by studying a variety of practices, both discursive and performative, that have emerged from the domain of uncertainty. In my study, I trace how practices such as gossip, humor, irony, storytelling, *guanxi* (social relations), and secrecy are employed to gather and share information, apprehend incidents, and decipher signals from the state, as well as create and manage relationships in the labor community. These practices are studied in various social situations and encounters such as training workshops, staff meetings, outreach visits, office gossip, social media, mealtimes, and tea breaks. Simultaneously constituted by and constitutive of the associations of people, organizations, places, issues, and things with specific regard to the Chinese state, these practices are employed by labor activists to try to govern themselves in such a way to exist and operate without upsetting the Chinese state. In other words, these practices are exercised to navigate through the domain of uncertainty pivoted on the idea of the Chinese state.

Drawing inspiration from Pierre Bourdieu (1977, 1990), I see practice as a skillful manipulation of time and space that simultaneously acts in the present and draws on shared understandings from the past. My focus, however, is not to unearth and describe an internalized and unreflexive "habitus" but to illustrate the constant and reflexive manipulation of social options that results from a continual modification of and interplay between the temporal and spatial conditions, thus constituting "a practice of everyday life" (de Certeau 1984). Not only does this notion of practice allow me to discuss the temporal and spatial aspects of state control, but it also illustrates how the practices adopted by my research subjects articulate and embody sites of intimacy and complicity that have emerged from the domain of uncertainty. They are intimate because they are not readily available to the outsider; they are complicit because they are a necessary entailment of the state, a necessary component of the regime (Das & Poole 2004: 4).

By "intimacy," I refer to the implicit knowledge and practices that constitute the sites that are straddling the line between official and vernacular, center and periphery, formal and informal, public and private, and inside and outside (Shryock 2004: 10–16). Michael Herzfeld has devoted much of his work to problematizing these distinctions, particularly with the concept of "cultural intimacy," defined as "the recognition of those aspects of an officially shared identity that are considered a source of external embarrassment but that nevertheless provide insiders with their assurance of common sociality" (2016: 7). The kind of intimacy is predicated on the presence of an outsider whose opinions and judgments are crucial to dictating what kind of value the common sociality can have (Shryock 2004: 10). While Herzfeld focuses on the emotional reaction of embarrassment, I would like to extend the idea of cultural intimacy to moments of self-recognition that trigger feelings of pride, superiority, empathy, solidarity, complicity, bitterness, and victimhood (cf. Shryock 2004: 11).

What is crucial in these moments is the acknowledgement of "an external observer whose opinion is imagined *and imagined to matter*" (Shryock 2004: 11, emphasis in original). As such, intimacy is understood against a background that foregrounds the experience of difference and "orients that experience toward the task of ranking, comparing, accommodating, impressing, persuading, or excluding an 'audience' of real and imaginary onlookers" (ibid., emphasis in original). Intimacy is not only the outcome of a response to the presence of the state but also a response to power (Kiossev 2002: 165–190). It is this extended understanding of intimacy that I employ in my analysis and in which I locate the sites of intimacy in the webs of relationships as well as discursive and performative practices of self-representation in the community of labor NGOs, workers, donors, and the Chinese state. More importantly, these practices are "ultimately dual, consisting *both* of what the outside observer can see *and* of the actors' understanding of what they are doing. The duality, not the intentionality alone, sets the problem for social science" (Pitkin 1972: 261, emphasis in original). Hence, the knowledge of the sites of intimacy and the practices employed to demarcate their boundaries have to be shared and expressed implicitly within the community in order to keep these sites productive of sociality and solidarity, which, in turn, is open for manipulation and creates a "community of complicity" (Steinmüller 2013).

To investigate the ways in which these practices and their intended functions are manifested in these meetings and encounters is also to understand how identity politics and the discourse of rights are played out among these actors who often need to strategically position themselves in relation to one another. In other words, these social situations call forth particular performative practices to form and communicate such identities as a "rights defender," a "social service provider," a "rule-abiding citizen," and a "victim of state violence." When the limits of state tolerance are unclear, the performance, negotiation, and sometimes reinforcement of the stereotypes of these different identities can become an essential survival strategy for these actors.

For labor NGOs and activists, the labor invested to gauge the limits of state tolerance can be examined by their use of certain words, their understanding of abstract concepts, and their everyday practices of enacting, reinforcing, or distancing the work that these words and concepts do, which, in turn, produce specific logics, engender discernible political effects, and regulate political behavior. I do not suggest that there are hidden and predetermined logics waiting to be uncovered and thus can lead us to predict and know the actors' intentions. Quite the contrary, my use of "logics" signifies how words, concepts, and practices make sense in specific contexts. The intelligibility of logics "comes from the ways in which language and institutions are embedded in a social world of iterative actions and performative practices" (Wedeen 2008: 15). Understood as actions repeated over time, practices are learned, reproduced, and subjected to risk because their iteration creates possibilities for intervention, action, improvisation, and subversion (de Certeau 1984; Butler 1993, 1997; Bourdieu 1977, 1990, 1991). For practices to be intelligible to others, they are dependent on contexts in the sense that they presuppose rules, norms, and conventions shared; freedom exercised; and responsibility entailed.

The practices described and discussed in this study are pivoted on the idea of *mingan* (敏感), which is usually translated as "sensitive" in English. In the context of this study, *mingan*, according to my research subjects, almost always refers to what is so politically sensitive as to engender unwanted risks and consequences. To gauge the limits of state tolerance of labor activism is to perceive and articulate the idea of *mingan* properly in order to maintain the appropriate distance from the state; it is also to strategically capitalize on the idea of *mingan* in order to, for example, create new partnerships. All of this is what I call the politics of *mingan*, which is the subject of Chapter 4. The ability to estimate and take advantage of the boundaries of the politically permissible embodies a kind of tacit knowledge (Polanyi 1958, 1966; Scott 1990) that is acquired through hands-on experiences and informal interactions among different actors. In this sense, tacit knowledge is also a type of intimate knowledge that is shared and circulated informally against formally instituted censorship. This type of knowledge leads to certain day-to-day practices, which are essential to the survival and development of the labor NGOs and is often mediated through gossip, rumor, humor, and irony. Moreover, to be able to adequately negotiate the politics of *mingan* is also an exercise of discretion. Lilith Mahmud discusses how the logic and practice of discretion is an important element of the world of Freemasons in contemporary Italy, which is frequently depicted as the quintessential Western secret society. Mahmud says that "[d]iscretion required an understanding that objects are at the same time in plain sight and hidden from the view [...] but only the correctly conjured public has the knowledge necessary [...] to decipher, to participate, to see" (Mahmud 2014: 30). In Chapter 4, I situate the politics of *mingan* in a workshop where the labor NGOs and donors met and discuss how the notion of *mingan* is played out, enacted, and received by a specific public that is in the know.

In the prefatory description of my meeting with Mandy, her commentary on her work touches upon the politics of *mingan* and indicates that some tacit knowledge and practices are required for her to manage projects and partnerships with the labor NGOs in mainland China. One such practice is the performance of secrecy. As Mandy noted, her Hong Kong-based NGO is so sensitive that certain things need to be kept secret. Her words crystalize the nexus between the politics of *mingan* and the practice of secrecy, revealing how these labor NGOs and foreign donors try to manage relationships with one another when dealing with government surveillance. As such, the practice of secrecy, which will be discussed in Chapter 5, embodies a space of intimacy in which discretion and complicity are exercised to uphold its boundaries by determining, for example, what things should be kept secret and how they are circulated within the labor community. I argue that the performative practice of secrecy, particularly public secrecy, is not only a practice of navigating through government surveillance but, more crucially, an essential performative practice of fostering trust among these social actors and of understanding the workings of state power.

Outline of the chapters

Chapter 1 addresses the methodology of this study and how I locate and study the field of uncertainty through multisited fieldwork and fieldwork as a research design process. I discuss the notions of NGO and civil society and how they are used and analyzed in my study. I also describe and reflect on the conditions of my fieldwork, the processes of negotiating access to and locating the field, and my own positionality. Against the backdrop of an authoritarian regime where civil liberties are limited and state surveillance is in operation, I discuss how I have come to use gossip as an ethnographic practice to manage my relationships with my interlocutors.

In Chapter 2, I give an account of the historical context of the emergence of labor NGOs in South China. It describes how an ethos of uncertainty, ambiguity, and indeterminacy has arisen in the wake of the economic reforms introduced in the late 1970s that have created the political, economic, and legal circumstances under which the labor NGOs emerged. Accompanying the economic growth was an increasing number of social organizations in the post-Mao era. By focusing on how labor NGOs struggle to become economically viable, I discuss the involvement of the international community via the mediation of Hong Kong labor groups. The political system will be described in particular with regard to the state secrets system and state surveillance in China.

In Chapter 3, I discuss how the notion of uncertainty is manifested in the day-to-day work of the labor NGOs and their relationships with their partners in Hong Kong as well as with the state. I show how uncertainty can be conceptualized as a notion that is productive in making certain relationships and practices possible. These relationships and practices occupy an analytical and ethnographic space, which is constitutive of the ways in which governance works in China and can be understood through such concepts as intimacy, complicity, secrecy, and *mingan*, which will be closely examined ethnographically in the ensuing chapters.

In Chapter 4, I discuss the local understanding and usage of the concept of *mingan* which is not only used as a guiding principle in the day-to-day work of the NGOs but is also a constitutive part of the uncertainty of the political environment. *Mingan* is conceptualized as a productive notion whereby impressions can be managed and resources can be mobilized. I use the example of a workshop in Beijing in which the NGOs tried to mobilize around and capitalize on the notion of *mingan* when interacting with foreign funding agencies.

With the notion of secrecy, Chapter 5 discusses the partnerships among the labor NGOs in mainland China and Hong Kong. Despite the fact that the practice of secrecy is very much informed by state surveillance, I argue that the performance of secrecy is not so much about managing their relationship with the Chinese state as it is with managing the relationships among the NGOs. Secrecy is productive in the sense that it is utilized to foster sociality, solidarity, and, most important of all, trust among these NGOs.

In Chapter 6, I discuss the implementation of a development program in order to show specifically how the aforementioned skills, practices, and knowledge of navigating the uncertain political terrains are applied in a particular context. Two ethnographic examples (two labor NGOs) are used in this chapter, which serve as contrasting examples to illustrate the success as well as failure in carrying out the program. The chapter ends with an ethnographic anecdote that shows that despite acquiring the necessary skills and doing the right things as perceived by the NGOs themselves, the NGOs still encountered harassment from the government. With this, this chapter brings the reader back to the notion of uncertainty and further reinforces the uncertain conditions under which these NGOs exist. In the conclusion, I return to the notions of uncertainty, intimacy, and complicity, and discuss how they affect my production of knowledge about the labor community in South China. More importantly, I argue how these notions provide an entry point to a more nuanced understanding of the workings of the Chinese state.

Notes

1 In this study, I use "mainland China" and "the mainland" interchangeably; both specifically refer to the geographical area under the direct jurisdiction of the People's Republic of China and exclude the Special Administrative Regions of Hong Kong and Macau. The distinction is important in the context of this study. There are two terms in Chinese for "mainland": One is *dalu* (大陆), which means continent, and the other is *neidi* (内地), which means inland or inner land.
2 In his study of the Chinese Communist Party's Central Publicity Department (CPD), Hassid (2008) argues that CPD has absolute power to determine what is appropriate media coverage. What is frustrating for the Chinese news workers is that what qualifies as appropriate news coverage is not always clear. In fact, all too often the boundaries of suitable news stories are so vague and arbitrary that many media workers have to exert critically more self-censorship in order to stay within the vaguely defined boundaries of state tolerance.

Bibliography

Abrams, Philip. 1988 [1977]. Notes on the difficulty of studying the state. *Journal of Historical Sociology* 1 (1): 58–89.

Adams, John. 1997. "Cars, cholera, cows, and contaminated land: virtual risk and the management of uncertainty." In *What risk?* edited by Roger Bate. Oxford: Butterworth-Heinemann, pp. 285–314.

Bayart, Jean-Francois. 1993 [1989] *The state in Africa: the politics of the belly.* New York: Longman.

Beck, Ulrich. 1992. *Risk society: toward a new modernity.* New York: Sage Publications.

Benedict, Ruth. 2005 [1934]. *Patterns of culture.* Boston, MA: Houghton Mifflin.

Bernal, Victoria. 1997. Colonial moral economy and the discipline of development: the Gezira scheme and "Modern" Sudan. *Cultural Anthropology* 12 (4): 447–479.

Boholm, Åsa. 2003. The cultural nature of risk: can there be an anthropology of uncertainty? *Ethnos* 68 (2): 159–178.

Bourdieu, Pierre. 1991. *Language and symbolic power.* Translated by Gino Raymond and Matthew Adamson. Cambridge, MA: Harvard University Press.

———1990. *The logic of practice.* Translated by Richard Nice. Cambridge: Polity Press.

———1977. *Outline of a theory of practice.* Translated by Richard Nice. Cambridge: Cambridge University Press.

Butler, Judith. 1997. *Excitable speech: a politics of the performative.* New York: Routledge.

———1993. *Bodies that matter: on the discursive limits of "sex."* New York: Routledge.

Cancian, Frank. 1980. "Risk and uncertainty in agricultural decision making." In *Agricultural decision making: anthropological contributions to rural development,* edited by Peggy F. Barlett. Orlando, FL: Academic Press, pp. 161–176.

Cashdan, Elizabeth. ed. 1990. *Risk and uncertainty in tribal and peasant economies.* Boulder, CO: Westview Press.

Chan, Anita. 2001 *China's workers under assault: the exploitation of labor in a globalizing economy.* New York: M.E. Sharpe.

Chang, Gordon G. 2001. *The coming collapse of China.* New York: Random House.

Cohn, Bernard S. 1996. *Colonialism and its forms of knowledge: the British in India.* Princeton, NJ: Princeton University Press.

Comaroff, John L. 1998. Reflections on the colonial state, in South Africa and elsewhere: factions, fragments, facts, and fictions. *Social Identities* 4 (3): 321–361.

Coronil, Fernando. 1997. *The magical state: nature, money, and modernity in Venezuela.* Chicago: University of Chicago Press.

Das, Veena. 1995. *Critical events: an anthropological perspective on contemporary India.* Delhi: Oxford University Press.

Das, Veena, and Deborah Poole, eds. 2004. *Anthropology in the margins of the state: comparative ethnographies.* Santa Fe: School of American Research Press.

De Certeau, Michel. 1984. *The practice of everyday life.* Berkeley: University of California Press.

Deleuze, Gilles. 1994. *Difference and repetition.* Translated by Paul Patton. London: Athlone.

deLisle, Jacques. 2004. Atypical pneumonia and ambivalent law and politics. *Temple Law Review* 77: 193–245.

Derrida, Jacques. 1997. *The politics of friendship.* Translated by George Collins. London: Verso.

———1994. *Specters of Marx: The state of the debt, the work of mourning, and the new international.* Translated by Peggy Kamuf. New York: Routledge.

———1978. *Writing and difference.* Translated by Alan Bass. London: Routledge.

———1976. *Of grammatology.* Translated by Gayatri Chakravorty Spivak. Baltimore, MD: Johns Hopkins University Press.

Dillon, Nara. 2011. "Governing civil society: adapting revolutionary methods to serve post-communist goals." In *Mao's invisible hand: the political foundations of adaptive governance in China*, edited by Sebastian Heilmann and Elizabeth J. Perry. Cambridge, MA: Harvard University Asia Center, pp. 138–164.

Douglas, Mary, and Aaron Wildavsky. 1982. *Risk and culture: an essay on the selection of technical and environmental dangers*. Berkeley: University of California Press.

Duara, Prasenjit. 1987. State involution: a study of local finances in North China, 1911–1935. *Comparative Studies in Society and History* 29 (1): 132–161.

Elyachar, Julia. 2005. *Markets of dispossession: NGOs, economic development, and the state in Cairo*. Durham, NC: Duke University Press.

Ferguson, James, and Akhil Gupta. 2002. Spatializing states: toward an ethnography of neoliberal governmentality. *American Ethnologist* 29 (4): 981–1002.

Foucault, Michel. 2002 [1969]. *The archaeology of knowledge*. Translated by A. M. Sheridan Smith. London: Routledge.

——2002 [1970]. *The order of things: an archaeology of the human sciences*. London and New York: Routledge.

——1992 [1978]. *The history of sexuality*. Vol. 2: *the use of pleasure*. Translated by Robert Hurley. New York: Penguin Books.

——1984. *The Foucault reader*. Edited by Paul Rabinow. New York: Pantheon.

Geertz, Clifford. 2004. What is a state if it is not a sovereign? Reflections on politics in complicated places. *Current Anthropology* 45 (5): 577–593.

——2000 [1973]. "Deep play: notes on the Balinese cockfight." In *The interpretation of cultures*. New York: Basic Books, pp. 412–453.

——1969 [1963]. *Agricultural involution: the processes of ecological change in Indonesia*. Berkeley: University of California Press.

Giddens, Anthony. 2000. *Runaway world: how globalization is reshaping our lives*. New York: Routledge.

Gilley, Bruce. 2004. *China's democratic future: how it will happen and where it will lead*. New York: Columbia University Press.

Gupta, Akhil. 2012. *Red tape: bureaucracy, structural violence, and poverty in India*. Durham, NC: Duke University Press.

Hansen, Thomas Blom, and Finn Stepputat, eds. 2001. *States of imagination: ethnographic explorations of the postcolonial sate*. Durham, NC and London: Duke University Press.

Hassid, Jonathan. 2010. *Pressing back: the struggle for control over China's journalists*. PhD dissertation, University of California, Berkeley.

——2008. Controlling the Chinese media: an uncertain business. *Asian Survey* 48 (3): 414–430.

Heilmann, Sebastian, and Elizabeth J. Perry, eds. 2011. *Mao's invisible hand: the political foundations of adaptive governance in China*. Cambridge, MA: Harvard University Asia Center.

Herzfeld, Michael. 2016. *Cultural intimacy: social poetics and the real life of states, societies, and institutions*. New York: Routledge.

Hull, Matthew S. 2012. *Government of paper: the materiality of bureaucracy in urban Pakistan*. Berkeley: University of California Press.

James, Wendy, ed. 1995. *The pursuit of certainty: religious and cultural formulations*. London: Routledge.

Joseph, Gilbert M., and Daniel Nugent, eds. 1994. *Everyday forms of state formation: revolution and the negotiation of rule in rural Mexico*. Durham, NC: Duke University Press.

Kiossev, Alexander. 2002. "The dark intimacy: maps, identifications, acts of identifications." In *Balkan as metaphor: between globalization and fragmentation*, edited by Dušan I. Bjelić and Obrad Savić. Cambridge, MA: MIT Press, pp. 165–190.

Ku, Hok Bun. 2003. *Moral politics in a South China village: responsibility, reciprocity, and resistance*. Lanham, MD: Rowman & Littlefield.

Latour, Bruno. 2005. *Reassembling the social: an introduction to actor-network-theory*. Oxford: Oxford University Press.

Lee, Ching Kwan. 2010. "Workers and the quest for citizenship." In *Reclaiming Chinese society: the new social activism*, edited by You-tien Hsing and Ching Kwan Lee. London and New York: Routledge, pp. 42–63.

——2007. "Is labor a political force in China?" In *Grassroots political reform in contemporary China*, edited by Elizabeth J. Perry and Merle Goldman. Cambridge, MA: Harvard University Press, pp. 228–252.

Lévi Strauss, Claude. 1963 [1958]. *Structural anthropology*. London: Allen Lane.

Levy, Richard. 2007. "Village elections, transparency, and anti-corruption: Henan and Guangdong provinces." In *Grassroots political reform in contemporary China*, edited by Elizabeth J. Perry and Merle Goldman. Cambridge, MA: Harvard University Press, pp. 20–47.

Link, Perry. 2002. China: the anaconda in the chandelier. *New York Review of Books*. Available at: www.nybooks.com/articles/2002/04/11/china-the-anaconda-in-the-chandelier/ accessed December 11, 2015.

Litzinger, Ralph. 2007. "In search of the grassroots: hydroelectric politics in Northwest Yunan." In *Grassroots political reform in contemporary China*, edited by Elizabeth J. Perry and Merle Goldman. Cambridge, MA: Harvard University Press, pp. 282–299.

Liu, Xin. 2000. *In One's own shadow: an ethnographic account of the condition of post-reform rural China*. Berkeley: University of California Press.

Lu, Xiaobo. 2000. *Cadres and corruption: the organizational involution of the Chinese Communist Party*. Stanford: Stanford University Press.

Luhmann, Niklas. 1993. *Risk: a sociological theory*. New York: Aldine de Gruyter.

Mahmud, Lilith. 2014. *The brotherhood of Freemason sisters: gender, secrecy, and fraternity in Italian Masonic lodges*. Chicago: University of Chicago Press.

Malinowski, Bronislaw. 1944. *A scientific theory of culture and other essays*. Chapel Hill: University of North Carolina Press.

Marx, Karl and Friedrich Engels. 1965. *The German ideology*. London: Lawrence & Wishart.

McNally, Christopher A. 2011. China's changing *guanxi* capitalism: private entrepreneurs between Leninist control and relentless accumulation. *Business and Politics* 13 (2), article 5: 1–29.

Mitchell, Timothy. 1999. "Society, economy, and the state effect." In *State/Culture: state formation after the cultural turn*, edited by George Steinmetz. Ithaca, NY: Cornell University Press, pp. 76–97.

——1991. The limits of the state: beyond statist approaches and their critics. *The American Political Science Review* 85 (1): 77–96.

Moore, Sally Falk. 1987. Explaining the present: theoretical dilemmas in processual ethnography. *American Ethnologist* 14 (4): 727–736.

Murphy, Rachel. 2007. The paradox of the state-run media promoting poor governance in China: case studies of a party newspaper and an anti-corruption film. *Critical Asian Studies* 39 (1): 63–88.

Nathan, Andrew J. 2003. Authoritarian resilience. *Journal of Democracy* 14 (1): 6–17.

Nettle, J. P. 1968. The state as a conceptual variable. *World Politics* 20 (4): 559–592.

Niehaus, Isak. 2013. Confronting uncertainty: anthropology and zones of the extraordinary. *American Ethnologist* 40 (4): 651–660.

Nowotny, Helga. 2015. *The cunning of uncertainty*. Cambridge: Polity.

Nugent, David. 1997. *Modernity at the edge of empire: state, individual, and nation in the northern Peruvian Andes, 1885–1935*. Stanford: Stanford University Press.

O'Brien, Kevin J., and Lianjiang Li. 2006. *Rightful resistance in rural China*. New York: Cambridge University Press.

Ortner, Sherry B. 1984. Theory in anthropology since the sixties. *Comparative Studies in Society and History* 26 (1): 126–166.

Oxfeld, Ellen. 2010. *Drink water, but remember the source: moral discourse in a Chinese village*. Berkeley: University of California Press.

Pan, Darcy. 2019. "Thinking like a state: doing labor activism in South China." In *Handbook of protest and resistance in China*, edited by Teresa Wright. Cheltenham, UK: Edward Elgar Publishing, pp. 151–165.

———2016. *Laboring through uncertainty: an ethnography of the Chinese state, labor NGOs, and development*. PhD dissertation, Stockholm University.

Pei, Minxin. 2006. *China's trapped transition: the limits of developmental autocracy*. Cambridge, MA: Harvard University Press.

Perry, Elizabeth J. 2002. *Challenging the mandate of heaven: social protest and state power in China*. New York: M. E. Sharpe.

Pitkin, Hanna Fenichel. 1972. *Wittgenstein and justice: on the significance of Ludwig Wittgenstein for social and political thought*. Berkeley: University of California Press.

Polanyi, Michael. 1966. *The tacit dimension*. Chicago: University of Chicago Press.

———1958. *Personal knowledge: towards a post-critical philosophy*. London: Routledge & Kegan Paul.

Radcliffe-Brown, A.R. 1987 [1940]. "Preface." In *African political systems*, edited by Meyer Fortes and E. E. Evans-Pritchard. London: Routledge & Kegan Paul, Associated Book Publishers Ltd, pp. xi–xxiii.

———1922. *The Andaman islanders: a study in social anthropology*. Cambridge: Cambridge University Press.

Riles, Annelise. ed. 2006. *Documents: artifacts of modern knowledge*. Ann Arbor: University of Michigan Press.

Rosa, Eugene A. 1998. Metatheoretical foundations for post-normal risk. *Journal of Risk Research* 1(1): 15–44.

Rose, Nikolas. 2008 [1999]. *Powers of freedom: reframing political thought*. Cambridge: Cambridge University Press.

———1999 [1989]. *Governing the soul: the shaping of the private self*. London and New York: Free Association Books.

SACOM. 2005. Looking for Mickey Mouse's conscience: a survey on working conditions of Disney supplier factories in China. Available at: http://sacom.hk/wp-content/uploads/2008/07/disney.pdf accessed September 15, 2015.

Sahlins, Marshall. 1985. *Islands of history*. Chicago: University of Chicago Press.

Samimian-Darash, Limor, and Paul Rabinow. 2015. "Introduction." In *Modes of uncertainty: anthropological cases,* edited by Limor Samimian-Darash and Paul Rabinow. Chicago: University of Chicago Press, pp. 1–9.

Scott, James C. 1998. *Seeing like a state: how certain schemes to improve the human condition have failed.* New Haven, CT: Yale University Press.

———1990. *Domination and the arts of resistance: hidden transcripts.* New Haven, CT: Yale University Press.

Sharma, Aradhana, and Akhil Gupta, eds. 2006. *The anthropology of the state: a reader.* Oxford: Blackwell Publishing.

Shirk, Susan L. 2007. *China: fragile superpower.* New York: Oxford University Press.

Shryock, Andrew, ed. 2004. *Off stage on display: intimacy and ethnography in the age of public culture.* Stanford: Stanford University Press.

Shue, Vivienne. 2004. "Legitimacy crisis in China?" In *State and society in 21st century China: contention and legitimation,* edited by Peter Hays Gries and Stanley Rosen. New York: Routledge, pp. 24–49.

———1988. *The reach of the state: sketches of the Chinese body politic.* Stanford: Stanford University Press.

Siu, Helen F. 1989a. *Agents and victims in South China: accomplices in rural revolution.* New Haven, CT: Yale University Press.

———1989b. Socialist peddlers and princes in a Chinese market town. *American Ethnologist* 16 (2): 195–212.

Solinger, Dorothy J. 1999. *Contesting citizenship in urban China: peasant migrants, the state, and the logic of the market.* Berkeley: University of California Press.

Steinmetz, George, ed. 1999. *State/Culture: state-formation after the cultural turn.* Ithaca, NY: Cornell University Press.

Steinmüller, Hans. 2013. *Communities of complicity: everyday ethics in rural China.* New York: Berghahn Books.

Stern, Rachel E., and Jonathan Hassid. 2012. Amplifying silence: uncertainty and control parables in contemporary China. *Comparative Political Studies* 45 (10): 1230–1254.

Stern, Rachel E., and Kevin J. O'Brien. 2012. Politics at the boundary: mixed signals and the Chinese state. *Modern China* 38 (2): 174–198.

Taussig, Michael. 1997. *The magic of the state.* New York: Routledge.

———1992. *The nervous system.* New York: Routledge.

Trouillot, Michel-Rolph. 2003. *Global Transformations: anthropology and the modern world.* New York: Palgrave Macmillan.

Wedeen, Lisa. 2008. *Peripheral visions: publics, power, and performance in Yemen.* Chicago: University of Chicago Press.

Xu, Bin, and Xiaoyu Pu. 2010. Dynamic statism and memory politics: a case analysis of the Chinese war reparations movement. *The China Quarterly* 201: 156–175.

Yang, Guobin. 2009. *The power of the Internet in China: citizen activism online.* New York: Columbia University Press.

———2008. "Contention in cyberspace." In *Popular protest in China,* edited by Kevin J. O'Brien. Cambridge, MA: Harvard University Press, pp. 126–143.

Yang, Shu-Yuan. 2005. Imagining the state: an ethnographic study. *Ethnography* 6 (4): 487–516.

1 Locating uncertainty

In recent decades, there has been increased interest in addressing the problem of the limits of the "field" as well as the empirical, theoretical, ethical, and, not the least, emotional challenges that fieldworkers are bound to encounter (Marcus 1995; Gupta & Ferguson 1997a, 1997b; Tsing 2005; Kalir 2006; Cerwonka & Malkki 2007; Rabinow et al. 2008; Faubion & Marcus 2009). In relation to these discussions, two programmatic statements by George Marcus have been the most notable methodological development and relevant to my own fieldwork in China: multisited fieldwork (Marcus 1995) and fieldwork as a research design process (Marcus 2009: 1–34). My study is centered on five labor NGOs both in mainland China and Hong Kong, so multisited fieldwork is a necessary methodological strategy. Given the politically sensitive nature of my research project, my fieldwork experience also becomes a research design process in which I had to, for example, adopt the practice of gossip to negotiate access and locate the field of my study, which could only be made visible conceptually and ethnographically in the process of fieldwork.

At the center of my study is the notion of uncertainty, which serves as an analytical tool for locating "emergent problem spaces" (Samimian-Darash & Rabinow 2015: 1) in which I examine how labor NGOs negotiate and manage uncertainty of the limits of state tolerance. In this chapter, I want to address how the notion of uncertainty serves a methodological purpose in this study. I trace, examine, and reflect on the conditions as well as the processes in which I negotiated access to and situated the field of this study as well as my own positionality as an ethnographer. With a focus on how I used gossip as an ethnographic practice, I demonstrate a processual view on fieldwork and conceptualize fieldwork as a process that invariably involves contending, intervening, improvising, and bridging the theoretical as well as the empirical.

Situating the field

I conducted ethnographic fieldwork predominantly in the province of Guangdong in South China (see Figure 1.1), the very first site of economic experimentation under economic reform initiated by Deng Xiaoping.

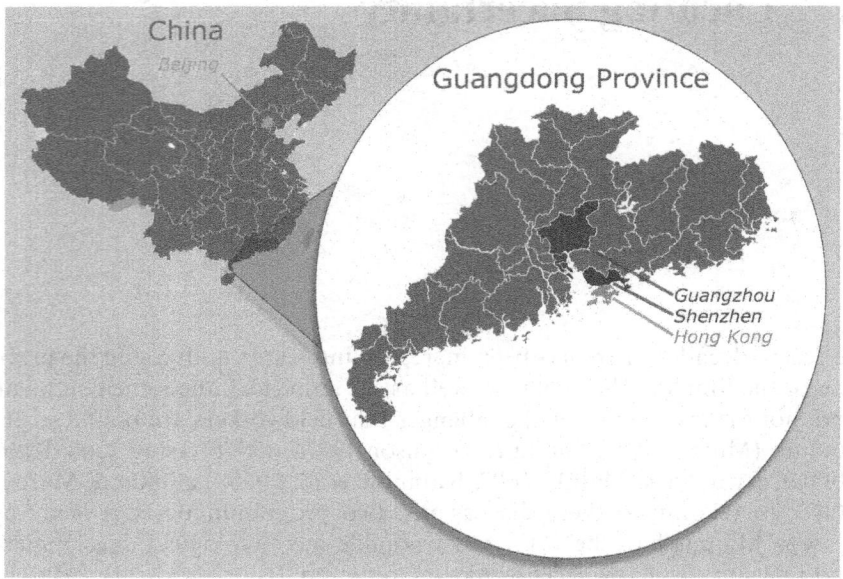

Figure 1.1 Map graphic by Jonathan Howell, using the following maps via Wikimedia Commons: China—By Wlongqi—Own work, CC-BY-SA-3.0, https://commons.wikimedia.org/w/index.php?curid=19242509 accessed August 10, 2016. Guangdong Province—By NordNordWest/Wikipedia, CC-BY-SA-3.0-DE, https://commons.wikimedia.org/wiki/File:China_Guangdong_location_map.svg accessed August 10, 2016. From: http://creativecommons.org/licenses/by-sa/3.0/de/legalcode accessed August 10, 2016.

Known as "socialism with Chinese characteristics," Deng's program set out to allow a market mechanism to grow within a socialist territory. Adopting a pragmatic attitude toward national development, Deng refused to follow the Maoist doctrine, characterized as scientific socialism, that any economic strategy should be justified by the doctrines of Marx and Engels before being put into practice. Deng and the Party legitimized their reform program by noting that the reorganization of the economy followed the natural laws of the market and thus is rational and scientific, which serves to achieve the socialist ends of national economic prosperity, social stability, and prestige in the global arenas of economy and politics. In order to restore the national economy after the ten catastrophic years of the Cultural Revolution, Deng believed that socialist development should be approached practically and flexibly with realistic goals. Deng's main concern was the concrete outcomes of implementing any economic strategy.

The reform program started with a focus on foreign direct investment and export-oriented manufacturing. China's leadership first established four special economic zones in four cities (Shantou, Shenzhen, Zhuhai, and

Xiamen) in the provinces of Guangdong and Fujian, located in the southern corner of the country. Guangdong and Fujian were used by the central state as a site of economic experimentation or "a testing stone thrown in the dark to get a reaction for determining what should be done next" (Lin 1997: 59). Not only do the experiments clearly demonstrate the pragmatic approach of Deng's reform program, but they also demonstrate that Chinese leadership did not have a clear and detailed blueprint for implementing the economic reforms (Naughton 1995: 5). This also created a condition as well as ethos of uncertainty where economic, social, and legal parameters were in flux, a topic to be discussed in Chapter 3. The experiments in Guangdong and Fujian have been so successful that they have changed the positions of Guangdong and Fujian in the hierarchy of provincial significance, from backwater places to the first provinces in China under reform to receive foreign investment. Moreover, the success in Guangdong and Fujian has also led to a series of special open cities and development zones that have gradually expanded the scope of the economic reforms. The success of these two provinces as sites for production of exports and accumulation of capital has paved the way for the special economic zone model to develop into an urban formula in China (Bach 2011, 2017).

Compared to other regions in China, the Pearl River Delta region, the main fieldsite of this study, is distinguished by its leading role in attracting foreign capital investment and export production. The definition of what this region encompasses geographically has gone through several changes. The first official definition of this region came in 1985 when the delta was officially announced as an open economic region to be offered preferential treatment to foreign investors. According to this official definition, the Pearl River Delta included four municipalities (Foshan, Jiangmen, Zhongshan, and Dongguan) and 13 counties (Doumen, Bao'an, Zengcheng, Panyu, Nanhai, Shunde, Gaoming, Heshan, Xinhui, Taishan, Kaiping, Enping, and Sanshui) (Lin 1997: 79). In 1987, another new definition of the delta came about and its geographic area was expanded further to include three more municipalities (Qingyuan, Huizhou, and Zhaoqing) and eight counties (Huaxia, Chonghua, Huiyang, Huidong, Boluo, Gaoyao, Sihui, and Guangning) (Lin 1997: 80).

It should be noted that both the 1985 demarcation and the 1987 designation of the Pearl River Delta were made mainly for the purpose of attracting foreign investment. No administrative authorities were set up to govern this region. More crucially, neither Guangzhou, which has traditionally been the main economic center of the delta, nor Shenzhen and Zhuhai, two special economic zones, were included in the 1985 and 1987 official definitions of the delta since they had already been granted special power and status to manage foreign economic affairs (Lin 1997: 80). However, some scholars think it is inappropriate to separate Guangzhou, Shenzhen, Zhuhai and even Hong Kong and Macao from the Pearl River Delta (Lin 1997), a stance shared in this study. As such, in this study, the Pearl River Delta region refers to the areas specified in both the 1985 and 1987 definitions as well as Guangzhou, Shenzhen, Zhuhai, Hong Kong, and Macao.

As one of the most populous and agriculturally productive regions in China, the Pearl River Delta has long been the country's southern gateway for foreign trade and sea transportation. This region was chosen as the first target of the central government's reform program partly due to its geographic isolation in relation to the political center of Beijing and the economic hub of Shanghai. Its remoteness is further accentuated by the presence of high mountains, which physically separate the delta from the vast territory of the country (Lin 1997: 83).

With the advancement of modern telecommunications and transportation, these high mountains may not pose a major concern. However, the physical barrier of the mountains has been a crucial element in shaping the historical development of the region (ibid.). As geographer George C. S. Lin notes,

> It is such remoteness that has given the local people considerable flexibility in seeking development, and, in some circumstances, the possibilities of rebellion or revolution, as evidenced by the 1910 republican revolution led by a delta native, Dr. Sun Yat-sen.
>
> (ibid.)

Indeed, the ability to strategically deploy the geographical as well as political positions of remoteness into an advantage has resulted in some crucial revolutionary movements in China in the twentieth century that had important bases of activism in the coastal cities of southern China and networks of support among the overseas Chinese, not least Guangzhou (Cartier 2008 [2001]: 143–175). In a similar vein, the geographic remoteness of the Pearl River Delta has allowed the labor NGOs, activists, and foreign donors to navigate more flexibly through policy space where they can maneuver to find space for activism. This is an important historical and geographic context against which the high concentration of labor NGOs in the Pearl River Delta and their connections with the international community, particularly in and via Hong Kong, are to be understood.

The NGO form

As I wrote this chapter in 2015, nongovernmental organizations (NGOs) have already been a highly visible feature across many societies and become increasingly normalized as key players in national and global politics (Pan 2016). NGOs have been around for at least two centuries (Davies 2014), but from the late 1980s, a global associational explosion with a particular enthusiasm for NGOs as a form of organizing and acting collectively started to captivate the imagination of researchers and policymakers (Fisher 1997: 440). Two reasons account for this keen interest. The first has to do with the political transformation that had taken place in Eastern Europe and Latin America where the idea of civil society was reexplored by activists. NGOs were seen as part of a growing civil society that could engage with the state (Fisher 1997; Schuller & Lewis 2014). In this post-Cold War context, NGOs were valued to be able to contribute to the democratizing processes (Huntington 1991; Fisher 1997: 444). The second reason is the rise of the so-called new public management in advanced capitalist countries that supported the rolling back of the state and public services. In other words, there was a paradigm shift in governance toward more flexible forms of "good governance" promoted by international development agencies such as the World Bank that favored NGOs as important private actors within the wider neoliberal restructuring (Fisher 1997: 444; Schuller & Lewis 2014: 1). NGOs have been hailed as a "magic bullet" that will simply find its target and cure the ills that have befallen the development processes (Edward & Hulme 1996: 3–16).

NGOs are now well established as an institutional form that works with a whole range of diverse issues and areas concerning development, humanitarian aid, human rights, labor rights, women's welfare and empowerment, health, and environment. It seems as if every agenda and political project has a corresponding NGO. The proliferation and diversity of NGOs around the globe has led many to interrogate the nature and functioning of NGOs, the impact NGOs have on nations and states, and, ultimately, the role of NGOs in shaping global and local configurations of power and inequality. Interestingly, despite their diversity and heterogeneity, NGOs are viewed as a unified phenomenon whether they are taking up some aspects of the state or corporations. Nevertheless, it is also precisely the expansion and diversity of NGOs that has complicated efforts to comprehend and theorize such an institutional form (Bernal & Grewal 2014; Lewis & Schuller 2017). As such, some scholars also suggest that discussions on NGOs should focus not so much on the assessments of the work done by NGOs as on the nature of the NGO as a form of organizing, that is, "the NGO form" (Bernal & Grewal 2014: 6–11).

The scholarship on NGOs remains divided. A large body of literature sees NGOs as an instrumental and apolitical tool that can be wielded to achieve various development goals. NGOs are imagined to have the ability to transfer training and skills that educate and help individuals and communities to compete in markets, to provide social welfare services to people who are marginalized by the markets, and to advance democratization and the growth of civil society (Frantz 1987; Fowler 1991; Fisher 1997; Mehra 1997). For some scholars, NGOs are civil society organizations that emerge in opposition to the state and provide important checks to state power (Bratton 1989; Clarke 1998). In this perspective, NGOs are viewed as an important alternative to the state under some circumstances such as reducing the costs of developing countries' institutional weaknesses (World Bank 1991). Some researchers also contend that NGOs are best understood as agents or consequences of neoliberalism and play an active role in expanding globalization processes and forming part of a "contemporary neoliberal aid regime" (Schuller 2009: 84).

More critical perspectives on the relationship between NGOs and development have emerged since the early 2000s. Some scholars view NGOs as being coopted by neoliberal institutions (Kamat 2004), others place NGOs within the transnational circuit of neoliberal power (Grewal 2005), and still others see NGOs as being caught in a double bind negotiating relations with funding agencies, governments, and neoliberal processes while trying to work with the disenfranchised communities that they intend to serve. In an even more political register, some development critics emphasize NGOs' potential for posing challenges to as well as bringing forth transformations of relationships of power. Here, NGOs are seen to be able to engage in a struggle for moral and political autonomy from the state, political parties, and the interests of the development industry (Friedman 1992; Lind 1992). In this view, NGOs and activists are not deemed as part of a growing civil society that engages with the state but as part of a critical process in creating and shaping alternative discourses and practices that can transform the state and society. The appropriate role of NGOs, according to this perspective, is to seek alternatives to development rather than be development alternatives, and to be critical of the so-called democratization processes and neoliberal development agendas (Fisher 1997: 445).

Thus, debates about the role and impact of NGOs are deeply connected to theories of the state, globalization, and neoliberalism. A central issue of contention in discussions about globalization and neoliberalism is whether NGOs strengthen or weak state power, which is essentially predicated on the divergent views of whether there are distinct boundaries between the private and public, and civil society and state. Predominantly from classical liberalism, the aforementioned scholarship hinges on the essentialization of the analytical categories of civil society and NGOs regardless of the varying critical stances toward development. The idea of civil society is understood as "that segment of society that interacts with the state, influences the state, and yet is distinct from the state" (Chazan 1992: 281). With its origins in European political thought, the notion of civil society has been conceptualized in two distinct ways: in terms of individual rights, citizenship, and civil liberties on the one hand, and in terms of intermediate associations and groups on the other. Implicit in both of the conceptualizations of civil society is the clear boundary between state and society. The category of NGO is a shorthand for a wide range of formal and informal organizations that fulfill various functions and purposes as described earlier.

In contrast to classical liberal theory, a poststructuralist view to the state blurs the divide between the state and civil society, and the private and public. This approach adopts a more dynamic view on these contested boundaries and focus more on the everyday practices of NGOs; their strategies for existence, survival, and performance; and their internal politics as well as external struggles with donors and communities they intend to work for. My approach to labor NGOs in South China is more in line with this perspective because treating NGOs and civil society as essentialized categories obscures the diversity found in different contexts and on different levels, which is particularly so in the context of China.

Observers of China have debated the possibility of a renewed development of a social realm between the state and family in post-socialist China. Central to this line of thinking, mostly born of Habermas's theory of the public sphere (1989), is to connect the rise of a market economy with an emergence of "civil society" where contractual ties and interaction between economic actors challenge relations to the family and the state. While the understanding of civil society in the Habermasian sense is fairly rigid and thus lacks explanatory sufficiency, to use the idea of civil society primarily developed from the Western historical experience to understand China is also fraught with the danger of imposing one interpretative framework on a different social and historical context (Wakeman 1993; Yang 1994; Gries & Rosen 2004; Béja 2006).

The distinct state-society divide inherent in the Western notion of civil society proves to be particularly problematic in the Chinese context (Flower & Leonard 1996: 199–221) because oftentimes the relationship between the state and social organizations are symbiotic (Spires 2011). Nevertheless, this is not to say that the discussions of civil society and the state are not relevant to what is happening in contemporary China. Quite to the contrary, this is to highlight how the notion of civil society is highly contested and unstable, and can take on various meanings and shapes in different contexts. The same can be said about the term NGO. Given the fact that there is so little agreement about what NGOs are and what they should be, some scholars contend that NGOs are best understood through an articulation of what they are not (Bernal & Grewal 2014: 7), namely, they are not the state. All this is to show that the category of NGO is not only hard to determine but also inherently unstable (Lewis & Schuller 2017). But this instability is also productive, as it allows for an exploration of how the meaning of NGO varies and is appropriated across contexts and how these different meanings may shift over time (ibid.). Moreover, with the focus on the instability of the category of NGO rather than on its rigid definition, it also opens up a space where the ways in which different interests and ideas interact can be examined and shed light on the broader transformations in society.

In a way, my study of labor NGOs in South China contributes to these broader discussions about NGOs and civil society. And yet, I do not just study NGOs but also study with and within NGOs. Ultimately, my ethnographic fieldwork with and within labor NGOs allows me to explore the affordances and constraints of the NGO as a form of organizing in the Chinese context. The conceptually ambiguous category of NGOs becomes even more capricious when state surveillance is omnipresent and uncertainty about the limits of state-sanctioned activism is rampant. My study of and with labor NGOs in China thus becomes a lens through which I interrogate the relationship between state power and forms of resistance and subjugation, which eventually shapes a complicit coexistence of the Chinese state and labor NGOs.

The NGOs of my study predominantly work with labor-related issues, which are usually closely linked with issues of workers' rights, employment conditions, and human rights in general. There are two kinds of labor NGOs in my study. The first is the grassroots labor NGOs in mainland China. By grassroots labor NGOs, I mean the labor NGOs that are neither government creations nor offshoots of some government agency looking to push cadres into early retirement. The labor NGOs in my study were all created and led by migrant workers themselves. More specifically, these NGOs are classified by the Chinese government as social organizations (*shehui zuzhi*) or civil organizations (*minjian zuzhi*), which refer to a range of nongovernmental groups and noncommercial enterprises, whether registered or not (Ma 2006: 1). My interlocutors often call themselves either *shehui zuzhi* or *minjian zuzhi*. They also use the English term NGO to describe their organizations, which is an influence from their interaction with the Hong Kong labor NGOs. In Chapter 3, I will talk more about the registration and the categories of social organizations in China where it shows how the labor NGOs in my study have utilized the administrative category such as private enterprises while negotiating their legal and social status as nonprofit organizations. The second type of labor NGOs in this study is the intermediary NGOs. By intermediary NGOs, I refer to the NGOs that act as the intermediary between the labor NGOs in mainland China and Western foundations in terms of channeling the funds as well as transferring knowledge and skills of managing an NGO and implementing development projects on the ground. The labor NGOs operating in Hong Kong fall into this category.

Negotiating access

I arrived in Guangdong in the summer of 2012. Initially, I had wanted to be based in the city of Shenzhen due to its large number of migrant workers, high concentration of labor NGOs, and geographic proximity to Hong Kong. However, months before I was to start my fieldwork in September 2012, the Chinese government launched an unprecedented large-scale crackdown on labor NGOs in Shenzhen, many of which were forced to shut down their operations and relocate. The crackdown sent a shockwave throughout the province. The labor NGOs that were not the direct target of the government crackdown also chose to keep a low profile and discontinued many of their services and activities. Under such circumstances, the last thing these NGOs wanted was a researcher asking to do ethnographic fieldwork with them. "*Xianzai bu fangbian*" (It is not convenient right now) was one response I often got when I requested to work with the labor NGOs in Shenzhen.

As a result, I moved to the city of Guangzhou, provincial capital of Guangdong, where the labor NGOs were still in operation but kept a low profile by suspending some of their activities. In light of my unsuccessful experiences of accessing the labor NGOs in Shenzhen, I decided to use an indirect approach and reached out to a labor scholar at Sun Yat-sen University in Guangzhou who has good connections with some labor NGOs in Guangzhou. It was through his help that I was put in touch with Green Grass Workers' Service Center (hereafter referred to as Green Grass), a labor NGO that has been operating since the late 1990s. At the request of the director of Green Grass, I submitted a resumé, a brief summary of my research project, and what I planned to do at Green Grass. After an interview with the director, I was allowed to volunteer as a *shixisheng* (intern), a term commonly used by the labor NGOs to refer to researchers doing research projects with the organizations. As it turned out, Green Grass served as an important node in my fieldwork from which I was to locate individuals and organizations that are both constituted and constitutive of the processes that have been transforming Chinese society. Through Green Grass, I was connected with other labor NGOs in the neighboring cities of Guangzhou, and more importantly, was later connected with its partner organization in Hong Kong and foreign donors.

Along with Green Grass, I conducted multisited fieldwork in three other labor NGOs in Guangdong Province: South Mountain Migrant Workers' Center (hereafter referred to as South Mountain), Little Flower Women Workers' Center (hereafter referred to as Little Flower), and Blue Sky Social Work Service Center (hereafter referred to as Blue Sky). These three labor NGOs were all connected with Green Grass in a number of ways. The directors of these three labor NGOs all used to be migrant workers themselves, were injured at work, and received assistance from Green Grass to claim financial compensation from their respective employers. They all started as volunteers at Green Grass before they went to set up their own respective NGOs with financial support from Western donors. Both South Mountain and Blue Sky started as branch offices of Green Grass in two neighboring cities of Guangzhou. However, the director of Blue Sky decided to leave Green Grass and became independent due to the internal politics in Green Grass, where some staff members were not satisfied with the organization's leadership. Blue Sky became independent just a few months before I started my fieldwork in Guangzhou. At the time of writing, South Mountain is closed down and has been closed since April 2014, six months after I finished fieldwork and left China.[1] Distinct from the other two NGOs, Little Flower was set up as an NGO independent from Green Grass, but the director of Little Flower meets with the director of Green Grass regularly to consult on organizational matters as well as organize activities together.

These labor NGOs offer similar services to migrant workers. They hold regular legal training workshops to disseminate knowledge about labor laws; they assist workers by offering free legal advice and drafting legal documents to file complaints against their employers as well as to bring cases to court. My tasks in these NGOs were very similar, usually involving a lot of documentation, such as documenting staff meetings and legal training sessions and writing and translating project proposals as well as contacting foreign foundations and conducting outreach activities. I spent different amounts of time in these labor NGOs: six months at Green Grass, three months at Little Flower, three months at South Mountain, and six months at Blue Sky. At the time of my fieldwork, Green Grass, Little Flower, and South Mountain were partners and worked closely together; as a result, during the first six months of my fieldwork I was moving among these NGOs, and my time was divided among them.

These labor NGOs all had connections of varying degrees to the Hong Kong-based labor NGO Chinese Workers' Front (CWF) where I conducted fieldwork for three months in the summer of 2013. They were all partners with the CWF, which acted as the intermediary that channeled foreign funds to them as well as managed and supervised projects. Blue Sky was at first a partner of CWF, but the partnership was terminated when it left Green Grass and became independent. Despite the lack of formal partnership, Blue Sky was still invited by CWF to participate in workshops. During my time at CWF, my main task was to translate coaching material on collective bargaining from English to Chinese, which was later used in their trainings of the labor NGOs in China. I was also allowed to attend their staff meetings and training workshops.

Apart from doing fieldwork with these labor NGOs, I also spent one month at Shenzhen-based Wei Min Law Firm, where I was allowed to sit in on the meetings between the lawyers and workers as well as given access to the legal documents of previous and ongoing labor disputes that the law firm had handled or was handling at the time. This law firm was an important partner of the labor NGOs that I worked with both in mainland China and Hong Kong. It provided free legal consultation to the workers referred by the labor NGOs, and the lawyers also represented the workers in court for a relatively low cost and sometimes pro bono if the worker's financial situation was really critical. I got to meet Chen Yishen, one of the founders of Wei Min Law Firm, at a legal training workshop organized by Green Grass. Chen Yishen is a well-known lawyer in China whom a staff member at Green Grass described as someone "*houtai henying*" (well-connected). Therefore, having been able to be connected to him and his law firm through my internship at Green Grass facilitated the progress of my fieldwork, especially with regard to gaining access to more sensitive organizations such as CWF in Hong Kong.

I conducted participant observation at these labor NGOs. I went with the staff to meet with the workers and participated in their activities, such as workshops and social gatherings. I carried out semi-structured interviews with the NGO staff and the migrant workers whenever they had some free time. Given the politically sensitive nature of their work, doing structured and taped interviews was almost always met with great hesitation and suspicion. Hence, I would phrase "doing interviews" in a casual way, such as *"liao yi liao"* (having a chat) to make it sound less formal to my interlocutors (Spires 2007: 33). In addition to conducting ethnographic fieldwork in these organizations, I also participated in labor-related workshops that took place in Shenzhen, Guangzhou, and Beijing. At these workshops, I met and talked with labor NGOs from parts of China other than Guangdong, labor scholars, trade union officials, lawyers, foreign donors, and foreign government officials. These meetings gave me not only a better sense of the kind of actors that are involved in labor-related issues in China but also important and contextualized knowledge of the complex political and economic terrains through which the labor NGOs as well as researchers like me have to navigate. During the period in which I conducted my fieldwork, I met and interviewed twenty-five staff members from thirteen labor NGOs in mainland China and three labor NGOs in Hong Kong as well as nine representatives from nine foreign funding agencies, which included foreign embassies. I also interviewed fifteen migrant workers, five of whom were very actively involved in two cases of collective action assisted by Green Grass when I was doing fieldwork at the organization.

During my fieldwork, I was moving between these different labor NGOs, which were all connected to one another. While trying to understand the work of each organization, I was also trying to trace and make sense of the different sets of relationships among the NGOs, the state, the donors, and the workers that were imaginable as well as conducive to their existence and connections. Instead of merely focusing on how these labor activists strategize resistance against the state, I am more interested in understanding the internal politics of these relationships that are embedded in this particular sociopolitical space, which, in turn, is significantly determined by the authoritarian state. Sherry Ortner (1995) points out that the limitation of many studies of resistance lies in their focus on the relationship between the dominant and the subordinate. Such a focus of analysis, according to Ortner, tends to exude "an air of romanticism" (1995: 177) and ignores the different forms of internal conflict among the subaltern. Ortner emphasizes that

> [i]f we are to recognize that resistors are doing more than simply opposing domination, more than simply producing a virtually mechanical *re*-action, then we must go the whole way. They have their own politics— not just between chiefs and commoners or landlords and peasants but within all the local categories of friction and tension [...].
> (1995: 176–177, emphasis in original)

The focus on the relationships and connections between these organizations and individuals allows me to observe and theorize a political space that is fraught with tension, competition, and suspicion, all of which are manifestations of the political and economic risks and calculations that these individuals and organizations have to grapple with in the Chinese context. Such an ethnographic strategy leads me to make apparent and describe "a reconfigured space of multiple sites of cultural production" (Marcus 1995: 101) where I was able to ask different questions about resistance and move beyond the rigid dichotomy between resistance and domination as well as state and society. Instead, I raise questions about and illustrate the shape of the structural processes and modes of complicity with these processes among differently positioned subjects.

The position of the ethnographer

In an authoritarian regime where there are still many restrictions on freedom of speech and organizations, my study brings together at least two issues—labor and organization—that are politically sensitive and thus uneasy for the Chinese government. To complicate the matter, my Taiwanese nationality may have also made my research project even more politically sensitive and unwelcome given the political relations between Taiwan and the People's Republic of China (PRC). How does an ethnographer of Taiwanese nationality immerse herself in the field and navigate through a space that is both politically sensitive and constantly contested and threatened?

Before I started my fieldwork, I was concerned that I would have much more difficulty in finding people to talk with and establishing relationships with my research participants because of my Taiwanese citizenship. Taiwan's political relationship with the PRC is still fraught with tension. The PRC considers Taiwan a renegade province that must be united with the PRC, by force if necessary. Official PRC media outlets and officials often refer to Taiwan as China's Taiwan Province, which is a term that pro-independence Taiwanese strongly oppose. That cross-strait relations are still politically tense and marked by concerns of national security and espionage is tellingly illustrated by the fact that some academic institutions in Taiwan give Taiwanese students extra instructions and preparations before they leave for China to conduct scholarly research.

Thus, it was with some trepidation that I embarked on my first ethnographic fieldwork in China. Nevertheless, to my surprise, I did not encounter insurmountable difficulties in finding people to talk to and organizations to do research with. In fact, my Taiwanese identity was met with more curiosity than hostility from my interlocutors, who were more than ready to talk with me and ask me about Taiwan. That my speaking Mandarin with a Taiwanese accent was often commented on positively indicates a cordial curiosity as well as the sense that I am not totally an outsider for my interlocutors, most of whom do share the official PRC conviction that Taiwan is a province of China. Since most of my interlocutors were labor activists, they were curious about and impressed by the vibrant protest culture and the labor movement in Taiwan. More than once, some labor activists expressed their wish to visit Taiwan to glean valuable lessons for their own work in

China. Toward the end of my fieldwork, several labor NGO friends confided in me that they would have been more cautious if I were from mainland China as I could be sent by the Chinese government to spy on them.

Most of my research participants in Guangdong come from different parts of China, and many of them are bilingual in Mandarin and their home dialects. Some of them have picked up some Cantonese during their years of living in Guangdong. When I interacted with my research participants, we spoke Mandarin, including the Hong Kong-based labor NGO Chinese Workers' Front where the majority of the staff speaks Mandarin as their first language. Without a doubt, my fluency in Mandarin facilitated my fieldwork. This proved particularly important as when the political climate is uncertain and state surveillance is in action, information is often circulated and shared in informal settings and through informal communicative means such as gossip. Being able to directly grasp the informally mediated information without having to rely on interpreters plays a crucial role in the kind and quality of information gathered in this study.

Learning to gossip

As mentioned previously, central to this study is the notion of uncertainty through which I explore how labor NGOs in China navigate through the ambiguous political climate in post-socialist China. When dealing with the state entails so much uncertainty, obtaining useful information becomes important for gauging the limits of state tolerance, which is crucial to the survival of the labor NGOs in my study. Information becomes a boundary setter that creates, manages, and structures relationships that are often enmeshed in a hierarchy of credibility (cf. Stoler 1992). As such, how and what information is gathered and circulated becomes a way to think about the political space in which the labor NGOs and activists are differently positioned. How does one gain access to such a contested and contingent space where suspicion is the norm and where its contours cannot be presumed but are themselves a key discovery of ethnographic inquiry (Marcus 1997: 96)? In my study, I use gossip as an ethnographic practice to negotiate access to this domain of uncertainty and embed myself in a network of organizations and individuals, which, in turn, has an impact on how I obtain information and conduct my analysis.

Gossip is a phenomenon of everyday life that everyone has some experience with. Gossip is commonly defined as a type of informal communication between an individual and a small selected audience in a private setting. Popular understanding holds that gossip is idle talk, tittle-tattle, malicious tales, scandal, and rumor, and is often associated with a negative stereotype against women. Research on gossip in the disciplines of history, anthropology, linguistics, philosophy, communications theory, cultural theory, and literature shows that definitions of gossip are inevitably slippery, but most defines it as pejorative talk about an absent person and tends to focus on negatively evaluative and morally laden verbal exchanges about the conduct of absent third parties (Hannerz 1967: 36; Merry 1984: 275; Scott 1990: 142–143; Besnier 2009). Some scholars, however, point out that not all gossip is negative; "praise gossip" (Elias & Scotson 1994 [1965]), for instance, focuses on the achievement or admirable conduct of a member of a social group. Others emphasize understanding gossip as a process and that gossip can have a positive role for members of an organization, as it can communicate rules, values, and morals as well as maintain the exclusivity of the group (Noon & Delbridge 1993: 33).

Thus, a fundamental point of discussion in the literature on gossip lies in the tension between conceptualizing gossip as largely positive or negative. While some scholars view gossip as mainly a form of surveillance, or subjugation, and others consider gossip as largely creative, liberating, or subversive, many of them do acknowledge the merit of the opposite point of view (Smith 2009: 1002). As such, depending on its cultural context, gossip can be either creative or destructive, ethical or unethical. Viewed in such a double light, theories on the social function of gossip view gossip as a means of social control, a mechanism for preserving social groups, and a technique of information management (Bergmann 1993).

In anthropology, gossip is often treated as a research method rather than a subject of investigation. The everyday obviousness of gossip is almost routinely detected, acknowledged, and commented on. The usefulness of gossip in facilitating ethnographic fieldwork does not go unnoticed as Malinowski once emphasized the importance to take interest in the gossip of the village life, which would facilitate his life as an ethnographer in harmony with his surroundings (Malinowski 1932 [1922]: 7–8). And yet, gossip has largely been treated as a marginal phenomenon and has not been able to attract concentrated attention.

Moving beyond the view of gossip as merely a research method, some anthropologists have highlighted the cultural and analytical relevance of gossip in anthropology and argued that "[t]hrough gossip, people make sense of what surrounds them, interpreting events, people, and the dynamics of history" (Besnier 2009: 3). In the daily life of the communities that anthropologists study, gossip is not only ubiquitous but also closely intertwined with the ways in which anthropologists collect information, conduct themselves, and develop analyses (Van Vleet 2003). Since the content of gossip is intricately tailored to the identities of the audience, it is unavoidably affected by the presence of an observer (Merry 1984: 273). Therefore, when anthropologists hear gossip from their interlocutors, the information obtained is inevitably colored by how anthropologists are perceived by their interlocutors. The power dimensions implicated in anthropologists' relationship with their research participants can lead to situations in which gossiping, for anthropologists, can become "a way of winning favor and defeating rivals" (Merry 1984: 273). As such, anthropologists are usually excluded from naturally occurring, intimate, and private gossip sessions.

Moreover, the content of gossip is usually complex, and the information shared tends to be trimmed, shortened, scattered, and anecdotal. This means that one needs to have acquired a great amount of local and tacit knowledge in order to understand gossip. To understand gossip is to understand how culture and power work, as "[...] gossip reveals how native actors examine, use, and manipulate cultural rules in natural contexts" (Haviland 1977: 5).

In the Chinese context, the function of gossip is further complicated by concerns about surveillance and security. In authoritarian regimes, it is not uncommon that people use gossip to obtain and disseminate information for security and survival reasons. One famous poster of the Soviet propaganda shows a Russian woman with a red handkerchief wrapped around her head. With a serious expression, this woman puts her right index finger on her lips. In large bold letters beneath the woman it says, "Don't chatter!" On the top right corner of the poster runs a text also in red but a smaller font: "Be vigilant, in such days the walls eavesdrop. It is not far from chatter and gossip to treason" (Byran 2011). Similarly, emblematic of the Chinese surveillance machinery is the control mechanism of the *dang'an*, or personal file, that documents matters mundane and profane of the Chinese citizens. Typically, a personal file starts with the citizens' middle-school grades, then their adult lives, employment history, religious affiliations, psychological problems, and political affinities. Such information is gathered through comprehensive channels within the communist party. One learns to be cautious with one's classmates, teachers, friends, neighbors, and even relatives. One also tries to find out who one can trust or not. Shrouded in fear for one's safety and what goes into the file, the Chinese citizens, particularly activists, are accustomed to being cautious, especially with outsiders, and to finding ways of obtaining useful information. And gossip often becomes instrumentalized in serving these purposes.

Thus, the fieldwork conditions in China have led me to use gossip as an ethnographic practice not only to gather information but, more importantly, become a way of conducting myself and interacting with others in the field. I will now describe the process of how I began to learn to engage with this form of communication and how it gradually maps and shapes the contours of my fieldwork and content of my analysis.

In the first few months of my fieldwork, as I was learning about the work of these labor groups and how they carry out their work, I soon found myself fumbling through the way people talked and what they talked about in this community. Informal ways of talking such as reminiscing, personal anecdotes, badmouthing, and gossip dominated the conversations I had with these labor organizations and also occurred a few times among the members when I happened to be present and was temporarily ignored. These informal ways of talking opened up a channel whereby the internal tension among these people and organizations as well as the politics of my fieldwork could be studied.

For example, when I started my fieldwork at Green Grass, it was not long before I noticed the tension in the office as one of the staff members liked to criticize the director. The staff member's dissatisfaction was centered on the director's work ethic and how he dealt with the state security agents. In the beginning, I was mainly a passive listener when such gossip occurred for two main reasons. First, I was baffled by the unanimously critical and negative tone of such talk, which tended to be so critical that it used a lot of judgmental and emotionally charged words or phrases such as *"budui"* (wrong), *"bu daode"* (immoral), *"mei dixian"* (no bottom line), *"meiyou diqi"* (lack of confidence), or *"meiyou yuanze"* (lack of principles). At first, I was ready to discard these morally charged words and phrases as overly subjective and as nothing but small talk about some personal matter between the gossip instigator and the director that was not worthy of further scientific investigation. Second, all too often, these conversations were person-oriented and laden with evaluations and judgments of other people's and NGOs' work. In the beginning, I was confounded by the information acquired in these different types of talking because it was difficult for me to verify the information. My bewilderment also arose from the fact that oftentimes these conversations were context-bound and tended to leave out contextual details. Therefore, it was difficult to follow the gossip when my interlocutors made references to other people whom I did not yet know at the time.

My initial lack of knowledge of some of the "focal individuals" (Haviland 1977: 7) among these labor NGOs limited my interaction with these labor groups. I soon realized that my knowledge of these key individuals and organizations dictated how my interlocutors related to and would perceive me as a researcher with or without resources. The more I knew or at least appeared to know, the more detailed information I was likely to get from these labor groups. More significantly, I realized that I needed to talk like them; in other words, I needed to gossip. In retrospect, my entry into the field was a process of learning to engage and participate in gossiping.

Five months into my fieldwork, my research participants still kept me at arm's length and were very reserved when talking about their relationships with their partners in Hong Kong and sources of funding. The silence that existed from omitting these relationships spoke louder than what was gossiped to me. From a Foucauldian perspective, silences "are neither spoken nor heard: that is their power. They evade explicit meanings" (White 2000: 75). Asking biographical questions is often an indication of how well or poorly one knows an individual. While engaging in office gossip at Green Grass, I gradually realized that it was not always a good thing to reveal my ignorance (cf. Geertz 2000 [1973]; Marchand 2015). For example, in the beginning of my fieldwork, some of the most common questions I asked were: Who is that person? What does he or she have to do with Green Grass? The answer I would get often depended on the importance of the person in question. I soon discovered that the more important the person was, the more general the answer I would get from the NGO staff. This was how the

NGO staff maintained their relationship with me: by managing what kind of information I could acquire from them.

Navigating through the office gossip by trial and error, I realized that it would be helpful if I could be more careful and sometimes economic about my questions even when I didn't necessarily understand the gossip completely. I needed to, at least in the beginning, appear to be in possession of some information that was worth sharing. "[G]ossip is a valuable social commodity" (Rosnow 1977: 158) which can be viewed as "an instrumental transaction in which A and B trade small talk about C for something in return—more gossip, status, fun, money, social control, or any material or psychological stimulus capable of fulfilling preconditioned needs, wishes, and expectations" (Rosnow 1977: 158–159). I was trying to learn about the criterion applied to a newcomer such as "learning enough about everyone involved to know, at least most of the time, what to say to whom and what not to say" (Haviland 1977: 7).

With time, I had come to learn more about how these people and organizations were connected, some of the causes of their tension and conflicts, and a few past scandals. Later, I was perceived by my interlocutors to be a researcher who "knew a lot of things." This was related to me a few times when I was doing fieldwork at the Chinese Workers' Front in Hong Kong. One of the staff said to me, "XXX talked to me the other day and said that Yenjun [my Chinese name] seems to know a lot of things." During my fieldwork, I helped a labor NGO get a small amount of funding from a European foundation by putting in a few good words for them during my meeting with this foundation in Beijing. This incident was talked about among some of the labor organizations where I did fieldwork. The story was later circulated back to me when I was participating in a training workshop in Hong Kong. A female NGO worker walked up to me and said,

> I heard that you got funding for XXX. You know I am trying to set up this project to provide day care for migrant mothers who have to work and can't take care of their children. Maybe you could help us too. Say a few good words for us.

In retrospect, my entry into the field was a process of learning to engage and participate in gossiping. My process of learning to gossip illustrates how the restrictive political climate and the organizational context in China influence the research process, methodological adjustments, and innovations needed when doing fieldwork (Garsten & Nyqvist 2013a: 2). I underwent "a process of enskillment" (Elyachar 2011: 85) to learn and train myself how to talk with my interlocutors and to exercise discretion when obtaining and sharing information (Mahmud 2014: 21–45). Using gossip as an ethnographic practice has significant consequences for what and how information is gathered, analyzed, and interpreted; in other words, it becomes a conceptual and a research design process whereby a mode of knowing is developed and articulated. More importantly, it is an ethnographic practice that has emerged in the process of doing fieldwork where the political conditions are uncertain and precarious and thus pose limits of knowing and acting both for my interlocutors and myself.

Complicity in ethnography

In anthropology, to achieve rapport has long been favored and considered a mark of the ideal conditions of fieldwork and plays a significant role in assessing the quality of the research that anthropologists conduct. In one of perhaps the most influential essays on the subject of rapport, "Deep Play: Notes on the Balinese Cockfight," Clifford Geertz opens with an anecdote of his fieldwork experiences where he achieved rapport with the people he was studying through a circumstance of complicity as they ran from the police together (Geertz 2000 [1973]: 412–453). In comparison, my use of gossip as an ethnographic practice can be viewed as my attempt to establish rapport with my research participants. That I became a subject of informal talk in the field indicates, at the very least, that I had made myself known in a network of people and organizations that worked with labor issues. I was no longer just a researcher who came to collect data and left as soon as the task was completed. I was perceived to be someone with enough resources to be talked about. Some of the labor NGOs are well-known, so they are used to talking to researchers. Researchers with foreign connections are more welcome than the domestic ones because of the possibility of being connected to foreign organizations and thus funding. I had been asked more than once by some labor NGOs if I could organize something so that they could visit Sweden or the United States. Of course, I was not so naïve as to think that I had gained 100% trust from these labor organizations in South China and had been unconditionally included in the network of their personal relationships. But at least I had managed to talk myself into their network to the point where I was sometimes given permission to participate in their activities, including gossip.

However, using gossip as a means of field research does lead to some difficulties and moral quandaries, and lays bare the precarious position of the researcher. It has been documented that researchers who actively participate in gossip run the risk of being deemed negatively (Srinivas 1976), gaining limited access and partial information (Frankenberg 1957), or jeopardizing the research participants' degree of communicability (Bell 1968). Thus, it is necessary to consider not only the ethical but also the cognitive implications of complicity in ethnographic fieldwork and to reconsider the space and positioning of the relationship between the anthropologist and research participants (Marcus 1997: 87; Marcus 2000). To gossip is very much a trust-building activity for both parties with the hope of obtaining more information from each other. "Gossip is interested data" (Van Vleet 2003: 494). I was moving among a group of individuals and organizations that have partnerships. I found myself having to negotiate different levels of trust and this is largely done by carefully managing and imparting the information I have acquired when talking to different research participants. At times, I had to talk about things without giving away the biographical information of specific individuals when the issue of confidentiality was on the line. When dealing with new interlocutors, I would keep the conversation going as long as possible so that I could get an idea of how much my interlocutors knew about the topic in question. In other words, I had to be discreet so as to make a decision on how I could share information without having to compromise the trust I have from other interlocutors and their confidentiality. Interestingly, this was how my research participants treated me in the early stage of my fieldwork. But for them, the management of the information was not so much about ethical concerns as about hoping to obtain more information in return. They wouldn't tell me more unless I could show them that I had something to share, too. As I continued to move among these people and organizations, I learned to talk and perform like them so as to maintain the trust relationships without compromising my integrity as a researcher (cf. Favret-Saada 1990).

As such, while trying to establish trust with my research participants, I was also negotiating relationships of complicity in which, ironically, trust, instead of being an ontological requisite for relationship-building, could be strategically enacted. To use gossip as an ethnographic practice is to engage in a kind of complicity in the multisited fieldwork of my study. My complicity in my study was not only a way to learn about the social world of a group of individuals in a specific time and place but also an attempt to capture their articulation of the kinds of anxiety generated by the uncertainty of the circumstances, both local and global, in which they engage in activism. In the next chapter, I will discuss how the economic reforms and subsequent institutional transformations in China have given rise to such an uncertainty.

Conclusion

In this chapter, I discussed how the notion of uncertainty has shaped the methodological parameters of my study by focusing on my multisited fieldwork as a research design process in which I gradually carved out my ethnographic "field." Through learning how to gossip, I intervened and negotiated various power and trust relations in different sites of "the field," a kind of social-spatial movement (Cerwonka & Malkki 2007: 101). I had to deal with "shifting identifications amid a field of interpenetrating communities and power relations" (Narayan 1993: 671). In this sense, "the field" is "something one strategically works at" (Gupta & Ferguson 1997a: 37), which does not become a meaningful space, both empirically and theoretically, until someone discursively mediates in it. Michel de Certeau argues that space is never a given; space emerges from a process of meaning-making in which people actively create and negotiate relations (de Certeau 1984). To situate "the field" denotes processes of interventions and negotiations that shape the contour of fieldwork. A processual approach proves to be fruitful in my research, as it allows me to pay attention to issues of power, ideology, politics, and identity that can emerge in the domain of uncertainty (Garsten & Nyqvist 2013b: 241). Moreover, when the conditions of fieldwork are characterized by uncertainty, ambiguity, and indeterminacy, a processual approach to fieldwork helps keep my attention focused on the material gathered in the process. "[I]t encourages theoretical work at the level of material—the 'stuff' of fieldwork [...] and privileges found concepts that emerge from it. It also looks beyond the confines of its own production to response and revision" (Marcus 2009: 28, emphasis in original). This also adds a more dynamic perspective to the ongoing discussions about ethnographic knowledge production and rephrases the issue of authority by admitting that the worth of ethnographic fieldwork lies in heeding what people think, say, and do in "the field." It contributes to locating the discrepancies or "frictions" (Tsing 2005) between the theoretical and the empirical.

Thus, in my study, fieldwork is not only a methodological practice but also an important component in the broader process of research. Conceptually, by tracing the relationships between the labor NGOs and their foreign donors, I located their negotiations with the uncertainty of state tolerance of activism as an emergent subject deriving from as well as constituting a social reality. Methodologically, with the practice of gossip, my act of actively making associations between different organizations and relationships was ultimately constitutive in making that social reality visible. The process of situating "the field" of my fieldwork became crucial in my exploration of spaces and practices of intimacy and complicity, which often escape theory's ready-made prediction.

Note

1 The director of South Mountain was under a lot of pressure from the local police, who had gone so far as to harass his family in Shanxi Province in North China. He then decided to leave the NGO.

Bibliography

Bach, Jonathan. 2017. "They come in peasants and leaves citizens: urban villages and the making of Shenzhen." In *Learning from Shenzhen: China's post-Mao experiment from special zone to model city*, edited by Mary Ann O'Donnell, Winnie Wong, and Jonathan Back. Chicago: University of Chicago Press, pp. 138–170.

———2011. Modernity and the urban imagination in economic zones. *Theory, Culture & Society* 28 (5): 98–122.

Béja, Jean-Philippe. 2006. The changing aspects of civil society in China. *Social Research* 73 (1): 53–74.

Bell, Colin. 1968. *Middle class families: social and geographic mobility.* London: Routlege.

Bergmann, Jörg R. 1993. *Discreet indiscretions: the social organization of gossip.* New York: Aldine De Gruyter.

Bernal, Victoria, and Inderpal Grewal, eds. 2014. *Theorizing NGOs: states, feminisms, and neoliberalism.* Durham, NC: Duke University Press.

Besnier, Niko. 2009. *Gossip and the everyday production of politics.* Honolulu: University of Hawaii Press.

Bratton, Michael. 1989. The politics of government-NGO relations in Africa. *World Development* 17 (4): 569–587.

Byran, Anna. 2011. The Soviet poster collection. *Wright Museum of Art Beloit College.* Available at: https://pdfs.semanticscholar.org/bb6a/0164b227df2abc3fd c4406fb561e628216aa.pdf accessed April 5, 2020.

Cartier, Carolyn L. 2008 [2001]. *Globalizing South China.* Malden, MA: Blackwell. Available at: http://onlinelibrary.wiley.com.ezp.sub.su.se/book/10.1002/9780470712764 accessed February 4, 2016.

Cerwonka, Allaine, and Liisa H. Malkki, eds. 2007. *Improvising theory: process and temporality in ethnographic fieldwork.* Chicago: University of Chicago Press.

Chazan, Naomi. 1992. Africa's democratic challenge. *World Policy Journal* 9 (2): 279–307.

Clarke, Gerad. 1998. Non-governmental organizations (NGOs) and politics in the developing world. *Political Studies* 46 (1): 36–52.

Davies, T. 2014. *NGOs: a new history of transnational civil society.* New York: Oxford University Press.

De Certeau, Michel. 1984. *The practice of everyday life.* Berkeley: University of California Press.

Edwards, Michael, and David Hulme. 1996. "NGO performance and accountability: introduction and overview." In *Beyond the magic bullet: NGO performance and accountability in the post-Cold War world,* edited by Michael Edwards and David Hulme. West Hartford, CT: Kumarian Press, pp. 3–16.

Elias, Norbert, and John L. Scotson. 1994 [1965]. *The established and the outsiders: a sociological inquiry into community problems.* London: Sage.

Elyachar, Julia. 2011. The political economy of movements and gesture in Cairo. *Journal of the Royal Anthropological Institute* 17 (1): 82–99.

Faubion, James D., and George E. Marcus, eds. 2009. *Fieldwork is not what it used to be: learning anthropology's method in a time of transition.* Ithaca, NY: Cornell University Press.

Favret-Saada, Jeanne. 1990. About participation. *Culture, Medicine and Psychiatry* 14: 189–199.

Fisher, William F. 1997. Doing good? The politics and anti-politics of NGO practices. *Annual Review of Anthropology* 26: 439–464.

Flower, John, and Pamela Leonard. 1996. "Community values and state cooptation: civil society in the Sichuan countryside." In *Civil society: challenging Western models,* edited by Chris Hann and Elizabeth Dunn. London and New York: Routledge.

Fowler Alan. 1991. The role of NGOs in changing state-society relations: perspectives from Eastern and Southern Africa. *Development Policy Review* 9 (1): 53–84.

Frankenberg, Ronald. 1957. *Village on the border: a social study of religion, politics and football in a north Wales community.* London: Cohen and West.

Frantz, Telmo Rudi. 1987. The role of NGOs in the strengthening of civil society. *World Development* 15 (supplement 1): 121–127.

Friedman, John. 1992. *Empowerment: the politics of alternative development.* Cambridge MA: Blackwell.

Garsten, Christina, and Anette Nyqvist. 2013a. "Entries: engaging organizational worlds." In *Organizational anthropology: doing ethnography in and among complex organizations*, edited by Christina Garsten and Anette Nyqvist. London: Pluto Press.

———2013b. "Momentum: pushing ethnography ahead." In *Organizational anthropology: doing ethnography in and among complex organizations*, edited by Christina Garsten and Anette Nyqvist. London: Pluto Press.

Geertz, Clifford. 2000 [1973]. "Deep play: notes on the Balinese cockfight." In *The interpretation of cultures*. New York: Basic Books, pp. 412–453.

Grewal, Inderpal. 2005. *Transnational America: feminism, diasporas, neoliberalism.* Durham, NC: Duke University Press.

Gries, Peter Hays, and Stanley Rosen. 2004. "Introduction: popular protest and state legitimation in 21st century China." In *State and society in 21st century China: crisis, contention, and legitimation*, edited by Peter Hays Gries and Stanley Rosen. New York and London: Routledge.

Gupta, Akhil, and James Ferguson, eds. 1997a. "Discipline in practice: 'the field' as site, method, and location in anthropology." In *Anthropological locations: boundaries and grounds of a field science*, edited by Akhil Gupta and James Ferguson. Berkeley: University of California Press.

——— eds. 1997b. *Culture, power, place: explorations in critical anthropology.* Durham, NC and London: Duke University Press.

Habermas, Jürgen. 1989. *The structural transformation of the public sphere.* Cambridge: Polity Press.

Hannerz, Ulf. 1967. Gossip, networks and culture in a black American ghetto. *Ethnos* 32 (1–4): 35–60.

Haviland, John Beard. 1977. *Gossip, reputation, and knowledge in Zinacantan.* Chicago: University of Chicago Press.

Huntington, Samuel P. 1991. *The third wave: democratization in the late twentieth century.* Norman: University of Oklahoma Press.

Kalir, Barak. 2006. The field of work and the work of the field: conceptualizing an anthropological research engagement. *Social Anthropology* 14 (2): 235–246.

Kamat, Sangeeta. 2004. The privatization of public interest: theorizing NGO discourse in a neoliberal era. *Review of International Political Economy* 11 (1): 155–176.

Lewis, David, and Mark Schuller. 2017. Engagements with a productively unstable category: anthropologists and nongovernmental organizations. *Current Anthropology* 58 (5): 634–651.

Lin, George C. S. 1997. *Red capitalism in South China.* Vancouver: University of British Colombia Press.

Lind, Amy. 1992. "Power, gender and development: popular women's organizations and the politics of needs in Ecuador." In *The making of social movements in Latin America: identity, strategy, and democracy*, edited by Arturo Escobar and Sonia E. Alvarez. Boulder, CO: Westview.

Ma, Quisha. 2006. *Non-governmental organizations in contemporary China: paving the way to civil society?* London and New York: Routledge.

Mahmud, Lilith. 2014. *The brotherhood of Freemason sisters: gender, secrecy, and fraternity in Italian Masonic lodges*. Chicago: University of Chicago Press.

Malinowski, Bronislaw. 1932 [1922]. Argonauts of the Western Pacific. London: G. Routledge & Sons.

Marchand, Trevor H. J. 2015. "Managing pleasurable pursuits: utopic horizons and the arts of 'ignoring' and 'not knowing' among fine woodworkers." In *Regimes of Ignorance: anthropological perspectives on the production and reproduction of non-knowledge*, edited by Roy Dilley and Thomas G. Kirsch. New York: Berghahn Books.

Marcus, George E. 2009. "Introduction: notes toward an ethnographic memoir of supervising graduate research through anthropology's decades of transformation". In *Fieldwork is not what it used to be: learning anthropology's method in a time of transition*, edited by James D. Faubion and George E. Marcus. Ithaca, NY: Cornell University Press.

——— ed. 2000. *Para-sites: a casebook against cynical reason*. Chicago: University of Chicago Press.

———1997. The uses of complicity in the changing mise-en-scène of anthropological fieldwork. *Representations* 59: 85–108.

———1995. Ethnography in/of the world system: the emergence of multi-sited ethnography. *Annual Review of Anthropology* 24: 95–117.

Mehra, Rekha. 1997. Women, empowerment and economic development. *Annals of the American Academy of Political and Social Sciences* 554 (November 1997): 136–149.

Merry, Sally Engel. 1984. "Rethinking gossip and scandal." In *Toward a general theory of social control*, Vol. 1, edited by Donald Black. New York: Academic Press.

Narayan, Kirin. 1993. How native is a "native" anthropologist? *American Anthropologist* 95 (3): 671–686.

Naughton, Barry. 1995. *Growing out of the plan: Chinese economic reform, 1978–1993*. Cambridge: Cambridge University Press.

Noon, Mike, and Rick Delbridge. 1993. News from behind my hand: gossip in organizations. *Organization Studies* 14 (1): 23–36.

Ortner, Sherry B. 1995. Resistance and the problem of ethnographic refusal. *Comparative Studies in Society and History* 37 (1): 173–193.

Pan, Darcy. 2016. *Laboring through uncertainty: an ethnography of the Chinese state, labor NGOs, and development*. PhD dissertation, Stockholm University.

Rabinow, Paul, George E. Marcus, James D. Faubion, and Tobias Rees. 2008. *Designs for an anthropology of the contemporary*. Durham, NC and London: Duke University Press.

Rosnow, Ralph L. 1977. Gossip and marketplace psychology. *Journal of Communication* 27 (1): 158–163.

Samimian-Darash, Limor, and Paul Rabinow. 2015. "Introduction." In *Modes of uncertainty: anthropological cases*, edited by Limor Samimian-Darash and Paul Rabinow. Chicago: University of Chicago Press.

Schuller, Mark. 2009. Gluing globalization: NGOs as intermediaries in Haiti. *PoLAR* 32 (1): 84–104.

Schuller, Mark, and David Lewis. 2014. Anthropology of NGOs. *Oxford Bibliographies*. doi:10.1093/obo/9780199766567-0090 accessed March 16, 2016.

Scott, James. 1990. *Domination and the arts of resistance: hidden transcripts*. New Haven, CT: Yale University Press.

Smith, Hazel. 2009. The erotics of gossip: fictocriticism, performativity, technology. *Textual Practice* 23 (6): 1001–1012.

Spires, Anthony. 2011. Contingent symbiosis and civil society in an authoritarian state: understanding the survival of China's grassroots NGOs. *American Journal of Sociology* 117 (1): 1–45.

———2007. *China's unofficial civil society: the development of grassroots NGOs in an authoritarian state*. PhD dissertation, Yale University.

Srinivas, M. N. 1976. *The remembered village*. Berkeley: University of California Press.

Stoler, Ann Laura. 1992. "In Cold blood": hierarchies of credibility and the politics of colonial narratives. *Representations* 37: 151–189.

Tsing, Anna Lowenhaupt. 2005. *Friction: an ethnography of global connection*. Princeton, NJ: Princeton University Press.

Van Vleet, Krista. 2003. Partial theories: on gossip, envy and ethnography in the Andes. *Ethnography* 4 (4): 491–519.

Wakeman, Frederic. 1993. The civil society and public sphere debate: Western reflections on Chinese political culture. *Modern China* 19 (2): 108–138.

White, Luise. 2000. *Speaking with vampires: rumor and history in colonial Africa*. Berkeley: University of California Press.

World Bank. 1991. *World development report 1991: the challenge of development*. Washington, DC: World Bank/Oxford University Press.

Yang, Mayfair Mei-hui. 1994. *Favors and banquets: the art of social relationships in China*. Ithaca, NY: Cornell University Press.

2   Pragmatic state, precarious labor

The emergence of labor NGOs in China is closely connected with China's integration into the global economy. The economic reforms introduced in 1978 have transformed not only the contours of China's national economy but also its social and institutional landscapes where new interests, strata, needs, and possibilities have started to take shape. In this chapter, I describe the economic, social, and legal changes that China has undergone since the late 1970s and set the stage for our understanding of how these changes have fostered a domain of uncertainty in which labor NGOs carve out a contingent space of activism. Crucial to these changes is the gradual shift of the role and function of the Chinese state and how it exercises control. These changes challenge existing state categories such as the rural versus the urban, peasants and workers, and city and village, and confront various social groups to renegotiate the meanings of these categories as well as to reinterpret entrenched power structures that continue sustaining these discursive practices.

Since the 1970s, the Chinese government has avidly promoted a nationalist agenda of modernization and development that encourages a crass form of capitalism whereby the survival of the fittest and unbridled market choices are privileged (Siu 2007: 332). Such an agenda runs counter to the official ideology of the Chinese Communist Party (CCP)—Marxism in which one of its key tenets is the program for the working-class struggle for power against the new capitalist rulers. Ignoring the plain contradiction, the Chinese government continues to state that Marxism should guide all areas of its work while at the same time, the country is geared toward economic pragmatism under Deng Xiaoping's economic reforms launched in 1978. It seems that economic prosperity becomes the main if not the only reference point for determining and judging the strength of the country. The values of economic pragmatism are in direct contradiction with Marxism. And yet, economic pragmatism seems to have established its legitimacy by, ironically, resorting to the Marxism argument that the economy is the basis of the political superstructure. Although the country's economic achievements in the last four decades have laid a strong foundation for the values of economic pragmatism, they did not resolve the tensions arising from the competing ideologies. This has led to an ideological uncertainty where the conceptual boundaries such as rural vs. urban and labor power vs. value are in flux, and the national order of things seems contingent, especially in light of the unprecedented large-scale rural-urban migration creating new political and social formations that challenge the existing administrative resources and categories.

The emergence of labor NGOs in South China that began in the mid-1990s embodies such an ethos of uncertainty and a response to the increasing social needs of numerous peasants-turned-workers toiling away on factory floors in southern cities. South China is believed to have the highest concentration of labor-related organizations in the country (Chan 2013; Franceschini 2014). Moreover, with a focus on the expansion of China's security apparatus, I draw attention to how labor NGOs carve out a space of development in the midst of rapid social transformations where market reforms coexist with an authoritarian regime. This chapter is devoted to discussing how a space of uncertainty and contingency is created through these transformation processes leading to the development of the labor NGOs, and how these NGOs have tried to work with the uncertain conditions of their existence, which, in turn, have further facilitated their growth.

Capital, labor, and land

When the Chinese Communist Party (CCP) came to power in 1949, the regime instituted the distinction between rural and urban by focusing its limited resources on developing state-owned industries and nurturing a committed urban proletariat. Farmers were restricted to agricultural units based on collective land ownership and were excluded from state industrial sector (Siu 2007: 330). This rural-urban divide has been crucial in the CCP's efforts to strengthen central planning and public security. This divide has created administrative categories that exert social control, determine resource allocation, control mobility, and regulate entitlements for members of society. Under Deng's pragmatic reform program characterized by its *tacit laissez-faire* approach to develop the national economy, the central government removed its constraints on local economic development and allowed local governments and individuals the autonomy to make economic decisions while honoring the interest of the state (Lin 1997: 52). Some argued that reduced intervention from the central government also led to the development of a new mechanism of "local state corporatism" which played an important role in facilitating emergent capitalism in South China (Oi 1995: 1132). In other words, the reform program under Deng led to a shift in the role of the central government from interventionist to regulatory, which, in turn, resulted in space for local initiatives and global influence, as well as uneven advancement of the country's liberalization processes. Nevertheless, the intense processes of pursuing modernization and development have led to boundary transgressions that question existing state categories and deepen ideological uncertainty resulting from the interplay and reconfiguration of socialist institutions and market reforms.

The processes in South China have been particularly intense: Foreign capital, cheap labor, and natural resources have merged, leading to the country's unprecedented double-digit economic growth for three decades since the reform. As noted by Pun Ngai, the convergence of state power and global capital leads to new forms of control at both the societal and individual levels where "land and labor, nature and human life, are all marketed as commodities for sale, not merely by the 'capitalist' market but by the 'socialist' party-state" (2005: 5). With China joining the World Trade Organization in 2001, capital from manufacturing industries and high-tech and finance sectors continued to pour into China. This also led to criticism in the West that Chinese workers were stealing jobs from Western labor markets (Pun 2009: 154).

However, while the global economy was fueled by the surplus labor drawn from rural China, labor NGOs and academics have expressed concern that labor conditions in post-socialist China are generally precarious (Chan 2001; SACOM 2005) despite the increasing application of global codes of good conduct by transnational companies. "Globalization and price competition and the introduction of just-in-time production strategies by transnational corporations do not favor an improvement of labor relations in China" (Pun 2009: 155). What has emerged instead is a "dormitory labor regime" in which Chinese migrant workers are housed within or near factory compounds, which has become a *systemic* feature of global production processes" (Pun 2009: 157, emphasis in original). Pun distinctly locates these dormitory factories as a site where global capitalism and the legacies of state socialism converge and where workers as a social force, in and of themselves, are quietly resisting the existing order.

As noted by Pun, institutional legacies of state socialism dictated predominantly by the logic of the rural-urban divide still regulate life in China. The government continues to exert control over the population and economic development as well as employ repressive measures against independent labor organizations. The *hukou* system (household registration system), a mechanism for controlling the movement of the population, is still in place. An important feature of the *hukou* system is that it differentiates between urban and rural registration status. Although the central government has facilitated internal migration by partially relaxing some of the restrictions,[1] the fundamental principle of *hukou*, which links a person's birthplace to entitlements and benefits, is still in place.

The reform program has brought about an unprecedented rise in rural-urban migration in China and has had a significant impact on the social fabric of Chinese society. In the government's nationalist narrative of modernization and development, peasants are often equated with backwardness and treated as carriers of feudal practices and targets for political transformation despite "[d]ecades of Maoist rhetoric to appreciate the 'revolutionary potential' of peasants" (Siu 2007: 330). As a result, peasants-turned-workers, popularly known as *mingong* (民工) or migrant workers, encounter considerable prejudice from urban residents and are often viewed as the source of rising crime rates and judged to be uncivil and poorly educated. Furthermore, because of the *hukou* system, migrant workers in cities are denied equal access to housing, healthcare, welfare, social security, pensions, and education compared to urbanites (Solinger 1999; Zhang 2001; Pun 2009). As rural residents, migrant workers living and working in the city have no rights to urban privileges, nor do they have the right to make claims upon urban authorities. As such, many labor NGOs have come into existence to provide services for and act on behalf of migrant workers articulating their grievances and demands.

The rapid economic transformation in South China has occurred not only because of this region's ability to attract domestic and foreign investors but also because regulations on land-use conversion and environmental pollution have not been strictly enforced. Before reform, the Pearl River Delta (PRD), for example, had mainly been dominated by farms and small rural villages. Since the onset of the reform program, the delta has undergone rapid industrialization. Agriculture and farmland have given way to rural industry and small-scale, labor-intensive, and market-oriented manufacturing facilities. One of the places where I conducted fieldwork went through such a process of land-use transformation driven by the incentive of seeking higher profits and attracting foreign investment while labor exploitation was prevalent. It embodied the social and economic consequences of economic reforms.

The village of Tianlan is located in a district of Guangzhou, about a one-and-a-half-hour bus ride from the city center. When riding the bus into the village, instead of rice fields, one is greeted with factories and houses inhabited predominantly by migrant workers. Officially labeled a *chengzhongcun* (village in the city), Tianlan is one of those urban village enclaves that was engulfed by highways, shopping malls, and factory complexes as Guangzhou expanded into the surrounding countryside. Embodying the specific spatial configurations of power and practice in the context of China's transition to a market economy, such an urban village enclave is often viewed as a site of crime and disease that threatens a modern cityscape (Siu 2007: 330). The population of Tianlan consists of about 50,000 people with local registration status and approximately 80,000 migrant workers. Tianlan hosts manufacturing companies in industries such as food, electronics, shoes, toys, jewelry, and automobile components. While there are also quite a few locally run enterprises in the village, the majority of foreign investors come from Taiwan, Hong Kong, and Macau.

Tianlan is run by a village committee (*cun wei hui*), which manages public affairs and public welfare projects of the village, mediates disputes among villagers, helps maintain public order, and conveys the villagers' opinions and demands and brings their suggestions to the local and central government. A village committee does not have much standing in political representative power. Members of the village committee are directly nominated and elected by the villagers. As mentioned earlier, under the rule of the CCP, land cannot be privately owned in China. It must be owned publicly. In urban areas, the land is directly owned by the state; in rural and suburban areas, the land is owned by the village collective, usually through the villagers' collective economic organization or the village committee. As such, not only does the village committee own the land, but it can also decide what to do with it. Since the advent of economic reform, a lot of the land in places like Tianlan has been leased to investors to build factories.

Liu Kaihua, a staff member at Little Flower Women Workers' Center, a labor NGO based in Tianlan, explained to me the importance of the village committee: "The village committee has a lot of power. Not only are they in charge of leasing the land but also in charge of the recruitment and wages of the workers." She said that foreign investors usually hire local villagers to be the actual factory directors (see also Huang 1998: 201–202; Siu 2007; Bach 2010) who manage the factories. "The village committee decides who can be a factory director. It's usually those on the committee. They also help these factories to recruit workers [from among both villagers and migrant workers], usually workers on the production line. The wages paid to the workers have to go to the village committee first. Then they give out the wages to each worker hired in the factories. All the money in the village has to go through them. They really have a monopoly here. They are like *tuhuangdi* [local tyrant, despot]," said Liu Kaihua (Pan 2017: 140). *Tuhuangdi*, a term used in ancient China, refers to a warlord, a local tyrant, or an exploitative gentry that has a monopoly over the resources of an area.

The words of Liu Kaihua seem to have portrayed these "*tuhuangdi*" or villagers as having benefited considerably from economic development. Nevertheless, like migrant workers, these villagers are also subjected to popular disdain as they are associated with rurality. These villagers have been an integral part of China's rapid urban transformation processes, but they are also locked into the dichotomous administrative category of the rural-urban divide, despite the fact that they no longer engage in agricultural farming. They also lack the skills to navigate in the city, so they cling to their rural *hukou* that entitles them to village land by developing rental properties for factory manufacturers and migrant workers. They occupy an ambiguous space where no adequate administrative category can legitimately incorporate them into the Chinese state apparatus (Bach 2010: 428). In Tianlan, not only does the village committee provide housing for migrant workers and manage the factories, but it also hires its own security team (*baoan dui*) to keep order in the village, even though the ordinary police force, the Public Security Bureau, is stationed in the town (Pan 2017: 140).

The presence of *tuhuangdi* and *chengzhongcun* breaches the boundary between the urban and the rural and embodies an ambiguous space that is integral to the development of Guangzhou. Tianlan illustrates how this ambiguity is employed in the post-socialist era, where specific urban and social reconfigurations have emerged from the workings of globalization and appropriation of socialist legacies (Bach 2010: 422). It is through these reconfigurations that the village constitutes the city, providing the conditions for Guangzhou's growth and giving the village a different role than its symbolic status as a vestige of backwardness (Bach 2010: 433). In a complicit way, the village practices of using and managing land and labor "enabled the municipal government to avoid taking responsibility for social, economic, and infrastructural development in these villages" (Wang et al. 2009: 967).

With particular regard to labor relations in the village, Liu Kaihua noted sarcastically that "the labor laws are only for reference here." She gave me an example,

> "At a Japanese invested-factory, the boss says he wants to pay the workers 1800 RMB a month. But the real wage the worker receives is 1300 RMB. Where does the 500 RMB go? It goes to their [the village committee] pockets! Of course, the Japanese boss has no idea that this is going on." Liu Kaihua continued, "It is *henhei*.[2] The police know about these things and the security team. I am sure they talk and share information with each other. But for the sake of economic growth, the police usually just let the security team take care of things."[3]

According to Liu Kaihua, for the village committee, the most important thing is the profit generated by the factories and the economic growth of the entire town, so violations of labor laws are rampant, including excessive working hours, delayed wages, precarious working conditions, the lack of payments of benefits such as social security, the absence of employment contracts, and wrongful dismissal. The existence of Little Flower Women Workers' Center is an attempt to address these violations and the plight of migrant workers.

The emergence of labor NGOs

After the Revolution in 1949, the CCP tried to restore social order after years of conflict by banning organizations considered a threat and coopting others. More importantly, the Party established its own mass intermediary organizations such as the All-China Women's Federation, the All-China Federation of Trade Unions, and the Communist Youth League. These mass organizations are the links between the Party and defined constituencies such as women, workers, children, and youth, and act as a transmission belt relaying downward Party edicts and policy and reporting upward grassroots views and perceptions (Howell 2008: 172). The development of social organizations was limited, particularly so during the days of the Cultural Revolution. It was not until the late 1970s that the growth of mass organizations was resurrected, not only because economic reforms had reshaped the ways of organizing production and services but also because the central state, which had partially withdrawn from directly managing the economy, required new ways—for example, business associations—of mediating the relationship between the Party-state and the market (Howell 2008: 172). In effect, the market reforms have resulted in a rapid growth of various voluntary associations, such as nonprofits, philanthropies, and other intermediate organizations (Dillon 2011: 138–164). During the 1980s, business and professional associations increased rapidly and constituted the majority of more independent forms of association during this period (Wank 1995; Unger 1996).

The development of social organizations reached a peak in 1989 when independent student organizations, autonomous trade union groups, and democracy groups burgeoned across the country (Howell 2008: 172). However, the democracy movement and subsequent tragic events at Tiananmen Square on June 4, 1989 brought the rapid growth of independent organizations to a halt after the State Council introduced more stringent rules governing the registration of social organizations. During his tour in the south (*nanxun*) in 1992, Deng reiterated his determination to solve the emerging social problems by further pursuing the development of a market economy. Therefore, the market reforms continued to deepen while political tension after the events of 1989 started to ease. Moreover, in order to counter international condemnation of its handling of the June 4 tragedy, the Chinese government was keen to host the 1995 Fourth World Conference on Women, which subsequently created more political space for the growth of social organizations, including labor NGOs, coupled with more financial support from both the Chinese government and international donors and foundations (Spires 2007: 2–3; Howell 2008: 173).

The first labor NGOs appeared in Beijing in 1996: Home of Beijing Migrant Women (Beijing *dagongmei zhijia*) and Beijing Action for the Community Sisters (Beijing *shequ jiemeixing*). At approximately the same time, a labor NGO called the Chinese Working Women's Network (*nugong guanhuai*) was set up in Shenzhen in 1996 by anthropologist Pun Ngai together with other labor activists and academics. The Chinese Working Women's Network is often described as the first labor NGO in the PRD (Chan 2013: 10). In 1998, a migrant worker established the Migrant Workers' Document Handling Service (*dagongzu wenshu chuli fuwubu*) in Guangzhou to help migrant workers draft legal documents of their grievances.[4]

Since the late 1990s, the number of labor NGOs has continued to grow, and more importantly, this is related to a change in attitude toward migrant workers from the Chinese leadership. In 2002–2003, following a shift in political leadership with Hu Jintao and Wen Jiabao coming to power, the Chinese government's attitude toward migrant workers started to change. The government issued a number of important policies calling for the protection of migrant workers' legal rights (Howell 2008: 177). In 2004, just before the Chinese New Year, Hu and Wen stressed that giving migrant workers their basic overdue wages from 2003 was a priority task. In August 2003, the All-China Federation of Trade Unions (ACFTU), the only official trade union in the country, for the first time, made it a national priority and launched a nationwide campaign to urge migrant workers to join the trade unions (Froissart 2005: 3). While the ACFTU's campaign helped raise public awareness of the plight of migrant workers, it also highlighted its ineffective role as a trade union because it has been and still is hamstrung by its political subordination to the CCP.

Created in 1925, the ACFTU is the only legal representative of Chinese workers. The ACFTU is divided into 31 provincial trade union federations, 10 national industrial unions, and more than one million grassroots trade union organizations, both in enterprises and institutions, affiliated with the ACFTU. Other independent trade union organizations are strictly forbidden. The ACFTU's responsibilities include organizing an enterprise-level trade union, protecting and representing workers' legal rights and interests, negotiating contracts between workers and companies, and aiding workers during labor disputes; however, the union does not have the right to organize a strike or take action during work. As part of the mass organization apparatus of the CCP, the ACFTU was "intended to act as a 'transmission belt' relaying party edicts and government policies to workers, while conveying worker concerns and suggestions to the leadership. In practice, of course, the former function was fulfilled more effectively than the latter" (Gallagher 2004: 429, emphasis in original).

There have been strong efforts by local governments to sideline local trade unions due to competition to attract new investment. It is very common for private- and foreign-invested factories that dominate in the export industries not to have workplace trade unions. Even if setting up a union branch in these foreign-owned factories is permitted, the local union tries its best to be docile in exchange for its existence. Furthermore, local unions often go to the factory and handpick a couple of management staff members and ask them to serve as the union chair and deputy chair. Therefore, many union branches are so inactive that the workers either don't know about their existence or don't want to reach out to the union knowing that they would not be of much help. That the only legally recognized trade union in the country is ineffective has also made room for the development of labor NGOs.

The role of the ACFTU as the "transmission belt" between the Chinese Communist Party and Chinese workers was reiterated by Premier Li Keqiang when delivering his Report on the Economic Situation at the 17th National Congress of the ACFTU in October 2018. During the Congress, some amendments to the Constitution of the ACFTU were made including the addition of "sincerely serving the mass of workers" to the ACFTU's earlier mission of "protecting the legal rights of the workers" in response to the evolving contradictions in Chinese society according to the union officials ("The Chinese trade union," 2018). Another notable amendment was the incorporation of President Xi Jinping Thought as an essential part of the guiding ideology of the ACFTU (ibid.). After the Congress ended, Xi urged the ACFTU to reform the organization to better represent its members in light of self-proclaimed Marxist and Maoist student activists who have been staging labor rights protests since the summer of 2018 in at least five Chinese cities including Beijing, Shanghai, Guangzhou, Shenzhen, and Wuhan. Ironically, two weeks after Xi's call for putting workers first, crackdowns on these young labor activists were launched, leading to at least 16 of 22 activists missing (Lau 2018).

Under the rule of the CCP, the management of social organizations remains restrictive. Industrial relations and labor-related issues have always been strongly affected by the concurrent domestic political atmosphere in China and economic issues such as rising unemployment rates and labor disputes, which can easily be turned into political issues. An official notice issued by the Central Government General Office and State Council General Office in 1991 illustrates clearly the government's concern with the contentious nexus between the economic and the political. According to this notice, special groups such as retired soldiers, laid-off workers, and migrant workers are prohibited from organizing themselves or setting up their own organizations (Howell 2008: 176). Not only has this notice made it legally impossible for migrant workers to create their own organizations, but it has also led to a situation in which many labor-related social organizations are treated with more caution and have been pressed to operate informally by the government (Gallagher 2004: 436).

As mentioned previously, more stringent rules governing the registration of social organizations were introduced soon after the events of June 4, 1989. One significant change was the requirement of dual registration. Social organizations were required to be affiliated with a supervisory body (*yewu zhuguan danwei* or commonly called *guakao danwei*), usually a governmental institution or governmental nongovernmental organization (GONGO),[5] and to register as civil non-enterprise institutions (*minban feiqiye danwei* or *minfei* for short) with the Division of the Supervision of Social Organizations in the Ministry of Civil Affairs (Ma 2006: 64). A supervisory body was responsible for overseeing the day-to-day affairs of the social organization and would be held accountable should the social organization do something wrong. This was not a responsibility that many in the government were willing to take on. The requirement of dual registration made it very difficult for social organizations to register. The new rules created a mechanism whereby the government could shut down organizations deemed threatening, such as groups focused on advocacy, religion, labor, and policy, and encourage organizations viewed as safe. As a result, many social organizations were either unregistered or registered as private companies, which has been a common practice among the labor NGOs. For the labor NGOs in my study, to register as private companies is nothing but a pragmatic way to obtain some kind of legal and administrative status. They neither see themselves nor operate as for-profit business organizations. They consider themselves NGOs devoted to doing good for workers.

To have some kind of registered status usually makes it easier for them to receive foreign funds. In my conversations with foreign foundations, many of them understand the difficult process of registration in China and are willing to be accommodating. They did stress that they were more inclined to support NGOs that are registered, either as a social organization or a private company, as it can ensure a certain degree of accountability. The labor NGOs' pragmatic approach to their registration status also shows how the category of NGO is inherently ambiguous and thus can be utilized flexibly acquiring different meanings across different contexts (Fisher 1997; Schuller & Lewis 2014). Nevertheless, the ambiguity of the legal status of many labor NGOs—unregistered, or registered as private companies yet operating as a nonprofit organization—makes them an easy target of government harassment and crackdowns; because of this, many social organizations are careful to avoid challenging party rule (Howell 2003: 143–171; Ma 2006: 47–75).

Another important feature that characterizes the Chinese official policy on regulating social organizations is the "anti-competition" rule (Ma 2006: 67). The "anti-competition" rule forbids the establishment of any new organization if an organization of the same type already exists in the same administrative field and in the same region (ibid.). This rule was a direct response against the protest events in 1989 when many students and workers set up their own organizations. In 1992, the government also announced that China was considering establishing only one united federation of trade unions (ibid.). In addition to the "anti-competition" rule, another important regulation was put forth in the 1998 Regulations for Social Organizations, which prevents national organizations from having regional branches. This is to limit the opportunity for social organizations to grow and expand. As a result, branches of national organizations are required to become independent and register separately with their corresponding bureaus of civil affairs. The government's concern with the potential influence that social organizations can have is further illustrated by the establishment of the regulation that national and local organizations with a similar mission and/or in the same field can only engage in cooperation and exchange, not directional and organizational relations (Ma 2006: 67).

In 2012, the central government relaxed its regulations on the management of social organizations by abolishing the dual registration requirement. This means that social organizations can now directly apply for registration with the Ministry of Civil Affairs. As a typical bureaucratic documentary practice, this change in the regulation can arguably be viewed as the government's attempt to make society more "legible" (Scott 1998) and has prompted many social organizations to try to register. However, there are still some obstacles even in the relaxed policy environment. For example, there is a lack of specific procedural rules for implementing this revised regulation, which, in effect, has led to more confusion and uncertainty for the social organizations in relation to filling out the application forms and meeting the criteria, which are not specified publicly.

What this means is that it gives local administrative officials greater discretionary power in deciding whether a social organization can register successfully or not. The uncertainty caused by this changed policy and how it affects labor NGOs will be discussed in detail in the next chapter. In the section that follows, I will discuss further how the development of law in China has not only created some measure of operational space for labor NGOs but may have concomitantly strengthened the Chinese state's interest in and capacity for holding onto power (Gallagher 2007 [2005]: 101), which, paradoxically, constitutes a complicit relationship between the labor NGOs and the state.

The turn to the rule of law

There are two main reasons why China has turned to the rule of law, and both are closely related to the issue of securing legitimacy. First, after the tumultuous and devastating years of the Cultural Revolution, the CCP turned to legalization to restore its political legitimacy and reinstitute social order. Second, since the introduction of market reforms in 1978, the socialist ideology upon which the CCP was based has been weakened, creating an ideological uncertainty and thus leaving the Party to search for a new way to justify its rule. Although the CCP has found much of its justification in economic growth, the Party-state has also garnered increased legitimacy by developing more reliable institutions, both political and legal. These institutions are beneficial for sustaining an attractive environment for investors and for facilitating China's participation in international organizations.

The development of China's legal system and infrastructure has engendered extensive debate concerning the nature and role of law in China, the relevance and function of law in an authoritarian state, and the contribution that a more developed legal system would have toward a more democratic politics (Gallagher 2007 [2005]: 101). Many legal scholars hold a pessimistic view of the rule of law in China because of the CCP's tendency to prioritize its political power over submission to legal regulations as well as the formidable difficulties of implementing and enforcing the law in China (Michael 1988; Potter 1995; Lubman 1999; Turner et al. 2000). Although these concerns are well-grounded, they overlook the intricate relationship between the CCP's rule and the development of Chinese law. In effect, as several scholars have argued, the expansion and maturation of China's legal infrastructure may have enhanced the legitimacy of the CCP and thus strengthened its political power (Peerenboom 2002; Gallagher 2007 [2005]).

> The Party-state might gamble that rule through law and the added benefits of increased legitimacy both at home and abroad are worth the risk of activating social forces and enlarging space in which new interest groups make their voices heard.
>
> (Gallagher 2007 [2005]: 101)

As such, China's turn to the rule of law also facilitates the growth of social organizations. In the case of labor NGOs, the state-led process of formalization and legalization of labor relations has resulted in some space where market and social forces converge, leading to the possibility of law being instrumentalized for private gains as well as pragmatic activism.

Since the beginning of economic reforms in 1978, 350 national laws and 6,000 regulations related to labor relations have been passed (Peerenboom 2002: 239) including the Trade Union Law (1992, revised in 2001), National Labor Law (1994), the Labor Contract Law (2007), the Labor Dispute Mediation and Arbitration Law (2007), and the Social Insurance Law (2010). Labor laws and regulations, in particular the National Labor Law of 1994, were promulgated as a response to the increasing complexity of labor-management relations (Gallagher 2007 [2005]: 98). In 1993, the government issued its Regulations on Handling Labor Disputes in Enterprise. Together with the Labor Law enacted in 1994, the Regulations set out a four-stage framework of labor dispute resolution, which begins with an informal consultation between the two parties. If the consultation fails to resolve the dispute or is simply ignored, both parties can then pursue their case via the following stages: voluntary internal firm mediation, compulsory labor arbitration through committees overseen by local labor bureaus, and finally, civil court litigation in the event of an appeal of an arbitrated decision (Gallagher & Dong 2011: 42). This framework allows workers in non-state sectors to go directly to labor arbitration and gives them the opportunity to appeal the arbitration decision in court (ibid.).

During my fieldwork, many workers expressed a lack of faith in a fair internal firm mediation, as the mediators were too closely linked with the firm management (Pan 2017: 143). Hence, workers tended to go to the local labor arbitrators and civil court. However, the compulsory labor arbitration stage has been beleaguered by such problems as "weak institutional capacity, lack of professionalism and training, political interference from powerful local actors, lack of legitimacy due to the strong dependence of committees on local labor bureaus, and lack of finality given the court appeal option" (Gallagher & Dong 2011: 42). These problems have also increased the burden of the civil court system and undermined the authority of labor arbitration, as well as complicated and lengthened the process for workers (ibid.). This has also led to the trend that dispute resolution of labor conflict has become increasingly legalized since the early 2000s (Gallagher 2007 [2005]: 116), leading to the higher demand for legal services. Lawyers have been quick to tap into this market of law and are commonly seen to distribute their business cards outside labor authorities and inside hospitals where workers suffering from work-related injury are treated.

As mentioned in Chapter 1, there has been a significant increase in labor disputes since the mid-1990s.[6] The majority of labor disputes in China are collective by nature; grievances and claims are lodged by a group of employees against the employer. However, the labor dispute arbitration committees and the courts are often reluctant to take on collective cases. This is perhaps due to the concern that if not handled properly, collective cases may transform into "mass incidents" (*qunti shijian*) that may undermine the legitimacy of the CCP. "Mass incidents" is a press term coined by the Chinese government to describe public disturbances by a substantial number of people attempting to safeguard their interests and rights. In addition, the current labor dispute resolution system is, in essence, designed for individual labor disputes, so the authorities often try to break down collective cases into individual plaintiffs. This practice inevitably increases the time and expense for the workers concerned. Moreover, law firms that choose to handle a collective case involving three or more workers are required to report to the local chapter of the All China Lawyers Association. If a collective case involves more than 20 workers, the law firm is required to submit a written report to the Municipal Bureau of Justice. These requirements indicate the political sensitivity of collective cases and of labor NGOs that are involved with collective cases (Pan 2017: 143). In Chapter 6, I will discuss in detail how labor NGOs navigate through the sensitive terrain of assisting workers in their collective action.

Since the Ministry of Justice doesn't have enough human resources to provide legal aid to workers through official channels, labor NGOs fill the void. By helping the government to disseminate information and provide legal advice, labor NGOs have managed to carve out a space to operate, regardless of their legal status (Pan 2017: 144). As migrant workers with little or no education often find it daunting to prepare the required documents and talk with the authorities, some labor NGOs also help workers draft legal documentation of their grievances and represent workers in court. The reason why a labor NGO could represent workers in court has to do with China's civil procedure law. According to China's pre-2013 civil procedure law, a Chinese citizen who is not a professional law practitioner could represent and defend a person in a legal proceeding. Such a person was called *gongmin daili*, a citizen's legal agent. A citizen's legal agent could be a close relative, someone recommended by a registered social organization or the citizen's employer or work unit (*danwei*), or any Chinese citizen approved by the local people's court of law. Although the law stipulated that it was illegal for a citizen's legal agent to charge anything for his or her services, it was common that migrant workers were asked to pay for services offered by a citizen's legal agent (Pan 2017: 144).

These agents, who might charge their clients anything from a few hundred to a few thousand RMB, were sometimes called "black lawyers" because they were not licensed law practitioners. A licensed lawyer representing a worker before the arbitration tribunal would cost a worker between 4,000 RMB and 5,000 RMB.[7] If the worker wanted to bring the case to court, the litigation fee could rise to 7,000 RMB or 8,000 RMB, putting that option out of reach for many migrant workers. As such, the service offered by "black lawyers" was relatively affordable. In fact, it was not uncommon that some labor NGO activists had worked as fee-based citizens' legal agents before they transitioned to nonprofit organizations. Green Grass Workers' Service Center, one of my field sites, went through such a transition.

Green Grass was founded by a migrant worker named Liu Xiaowen[8] in 1998 (Pan 2017: 146). Liu Xiaowen came to Guangzhou from the province of Sichuan in 1993 and had worked as a security guard in several companies since his arrival. In 1996, a fellow townsman (*laoxiang*) was injured at work; one of his fingers was severed by a machine. The employer was only willing to pay a one-time sum of 6,000 RMB as compensation. Upset about the unjust treatment that his fellow townsman received, Liu Xiaowen decided to study the law so that he could use it to demand just and fair compensation for his fellow townsman. Liu Xiaowen negotiated with the employer and submitted the case to the labor authorities, where he succeeded in getting 12,000 RMB for his fellow townsman. A few weeks later, a similar incident happened to a female migrant worker who also lost a finger and came to Liu Xiaowen for assistance. Liu Xiaowen intervened and claimed 10,800 RMB in compensation for her. After these two incidents, Liu Xiaowen felt confident about using legal means to help migrant workers defend their rights, so he began to work as a citizen's legal agent representing migrant workers in court, charging fees ranging from thirty to a few hundred RMB for his service. Gradually, he set up Green Grass Workers' Service Center and invited two assistants to work with him: Chen Kemin, a lawyer from Hubei Province and Yang Haiqin, a law graduate from Guangdong Province. Green Grass was set up primarily to draft legal documents for migrant workers and help them bring their cases to court (Pan 2017: 146). While Green Grass was created at a time when increasing numbers of labor disputes were being reported, it was also a time when the Chinese state placed renewed emphasis on legal institutions and encouraged workers to "use the law as a weapon," which was a popular slogan from the official media in the 1990s reflecting "the increasingly contentious and even violent state of labor politics" (Gallagher 2007 [2005]: 98).

Working as a fee-based citizen's legal agent, Liu Xiaowen was treading on sensitive ground. With his increasing publicity as a defender of migrant workers' rights, Liu Xiaowen had attracted attention from many different directions: the local and national media, the local government, the labor authorities, the local Public Security Bureau (PSB), and employers. In several interviews with the media, Liu Xiaowen revealed that he frequently received malicious calls and threats from employers. According to some media reports, Liu Xiaowen was detained by the local PSB on three different occasions because he was accused of inciting social instability. A local newspaper in Guangzhou published a letter from a migrant worker who claimed Liu Xiaowen took money from him but failed to help him as promised. This letter triggered heated discussions among the migrant worker community and further exacerbated the ongoing controversy over Liu Xiaowen. One day, three months after Green Grass was registered as a private enterprise, Liu

Xiaowen disappeared. Rumor had it that Liu Xiaowen couldn't handle the pressure so he left without saying a word. It was under these circumstances that his assistant Yang Haiqin took over Green Grass and has been the director since.

The history of Green Grass is a typical example of how a labor NGO emerged and established itself in response to the unjust treatment that many migrant workers have encountered at their workplace, and how the wider socioeconomic transformations and legal institutional changes have opened up a space in which a labor NGO can operate through actively engaging with law. But this operational space was further restricted. In January 2013, the civil procedure law was amended to make it illegal for nonprofessional law practitioners to represent citizens in court. This new amendment has tightened the criteria for citizens' legal agents and made it illegal for nonprofessional practitioners of law to represent other citizens in court. According to the new amendment, a citizen can only be represented in court by the following people: (1) a lawyer, (2) a close relative or coworker, or (3) someone who is recommended by the citizen's residential community, workplace, or a legal social organization.[9] The 2013 law has significantly reduced the number of nonprofessionals working as citizen's legal agents, but it did not eradicate all of them. During my fieldwork in March 2013, I encountered two citizen's legal agents and was able to shadow one of them for a day to see how he continued to work as a citizen's legal agent. Since this Shenzhen-based citizen's legal agent has been operating since the early 2000s, he is a familiar figure in the local district court and the court continued to allow his presence at the time of my fieldwork. A few labor NGO directors expressed to me that this new amendment signifies the government's further efforts to diminish the operational space for labor NGOs so that they can no longer legally represent workers in court. Many labor NGOs continue to offer other services such as drafting legal documents and writing petitions for the workers, which are still within legal bounds dictated by the state.

The security state

While by engaging with the law, labor NGOs manage to carve out a space for their activism regardless how restricted that space is, their engagement, which is well-intentioned, can become complicit in sustaining the Chinese Communist regime's political agenda. As mentioned earlier, the 1990s saw a mushrooming of social organizations, which, paradoxically, occurred in tandem with the Chinese state's expansion of its security apparatus in the name of maintaining social stability. Against this backdrop, many social organizations including labor NGOs were woven into this control mechanism.

Since the 1990s, in the wake of the dramatic events of 1989, the Chinese Communist regime has deliberately adopted different governing strategies that distinctly departed from those of the 1980s (Lee & Zhang 2013; Wang & Minzner 2015). In the country's performance of "stability maintenance" (*weiwen*), there has been a clear shift of focus from the Mao-style campaigns of "strike hard" (*yanda*) policy which targeted criminals, vices, and cults in the 1980s and 1990s to the more recent notion of "social management," which suggests governing from a "people-centered" and "service-oriented" approach (Fewsmith 2012: 2; Lee & Zhang 2013: 1483). The term "social management" was first officially articulated in 2003, and its importance in China's policymaking was renewed by General Secretary Hu Jintao, who delivered a speech at the opening session of a Study and Discussion Session on the Special Theme of Social Management and Its Innovation for Principal Leading Cadres at the Provincial and Ministerial Level (Fewsmith 2012: 1). In this speech, Hu Jintao stressed that strengthening and making innovation in social management was key to maintaining social order and promoting social harmony (ibid.). The issue of social management was also highlighted in the "Outline of the 12th Five-Year Plan for Economic and Social Development," adopted by the Fourth Session of the 11th National People's Congress (ibid.: 2).

What is significant about the Chinese government's formulation of social management is its emphasis on the role of the local government, especially at the street office level (Fewsmith 2012: 4). In Chinese cities, a neighborhood is both a residential location in its geographic sense and a social organization managed by the street office. A street office is the grassroots branch of the Chinese government that manages residents of a neighborhood through the neighborhood committee, the lowest of the administrative hierarchy in China (Zhong 2009: 115). This clear downward transfer of responsibility for stability maintenance from the central government to the local government, which had already begun in the early 1990s soon after the student democracy protests in 1989 (Lee & Zhang 2013: 1483), opens up a space where social organizations, for example, can tap into and be allowed to exist as long as they share the load of maintaining social stability.

In 1991, the Central Party Committee and State Council issued a joint "Decision on Strengthening the Comprehensive Management of Public Security" which laid down the administrative principle of "jurisdictional management" (Lee & Zhang 2013: 1483). This Decision signaled the government's renewed commitment to social control and public security followed by a systematic process and codification of localizing the responsibility of maintaining social stability that continued into the 2000s. What is prominent about the jurisdictional management is that it gives Party leaders and municipal governments the power to evaluate, reward, or punish lower-level officials. In other words, the salary and career promotion prospects for local leaders are tied to how well they perform their job at maintaining social order (Lee & Zhang 2013: 1483; Wang & Minzner 2015: 346–347). To make things more complicated, if a social disturbance occurs in one jurisdiction, for example, the hierarchy of leaders responsible for that jurisdiction will all be subject to the "one veto rule" (*yipiao foujue*), which means "failure in one policy area will negate all other accomplishments by the government unit and deprive officials of bonuses, promotion, and the eligibility of the unit to compete for organizational honors" (Lee & Zhang 2013: 1483–1484; Wang & Minzner 2015: 350).

In response to Chinese leaders' policy shift, bureaucratic institutions have also expanded accordingly. Since the late 1990s, Party authorities have set up specialized *weiwen* offices to deal with and respond to social unrest; these offices are managed by local police chiefs. What this means is that the rise in bureaucratic rank of police chiefs is closely intertwined with their work on maintaining social stability. In 2003, the central state made the decision that Party standing committee members or deputy government heads should lead provincial, municipal, and county-level public security organs. This means that these different levels of security organs enjoy a higher rank than their local government and court counterparts, which has "led to the widespread 'securitization' of local governance in China," (Wang & Minzner 2015: 351; cf. Foucault 2008, 2009). Consequently, the bureaucratic pressure of maintaining social order and harmony falls most heavily on the local officials who have to juggle attaining social stability targets, seeking career promotions (thus financial rewards), and avoiding career sanctions for citizen petitioning. It is not uncommon that local authorities resort to the use of "hired thugs to intercept petitioners seeking to reach higher authorities, and the calculated application of pressure on their family and friends [...] to convince them to give up their petitioning efforts" (Wang & Minzner 2015: 352).

The shift to social management illustrates the Chinese leadership's concern about the increasing numbers of mass incidents and how they might undermine the legitimacy of the Communist Party. These mass incidents are concomitant effects of the drastic economic and social changes that have been taking place in the last 30 years. In order to solve social problems that might disturb the harmony and stability of society, the Chinese government has enlisted a broad range of government functions such as social services, workplace safety, dispute resolution, and the police as social management tools (Wang & Minzner 2015: 354). Zhou Yongkang, the Politburo Standing Committee member in charge of politics and law between 2007 and 2012, noted that it is necessary to recruit social organizations, including the various mass organizations under the party's control to take on the work of social management (Fewsmith 2012: 1–2). As such, the strengthening and implementation of social management and its innovation have led to the expansion of the *weiwen* apparatus as well as the securitization of local governance, which has securitized an increasing number of issues such as food safety, environmental accidents, pollution, labor disputes, and unemployment rates, among others.

The securitization of the Chinese state is an important context in which labor NGOs exist, develop, and operate. As mentioned earlier, local governments are crucial in carrying out the work of maintaining stability, as they are the ones who build connections with and manage the local populace

(Lee & Zhang 2013: 1484), including the grassroots labor NGOs. One labor NGO activist in Shenzhen said in an interview, "We [labor NGOs] are like a buffer between the government and the workers. The government needs us. We are helping them perform *weiwen*." Acknowledging the complicit role of the labor NGOs, this labor activist laughed dryly at the last part of his comment tinged with self-depreciation and sarcasm. As will be shown in the chapters that follow, the survival and development of the grassroots labor NGOs depend crucially on their relationships with the local authorities such as township and street officials, trade union officials, and the police. The work and role of the labor NGOs need to be placed against the expansion of stability/security apparatus.

Secrecy and surveillance

With the introduction of a market economy, the Chinese state's role in production and distribution may not be as large as it was before the 1970s, but it does not diminish the extent to which the state exerts control and surveillance over society. The expansion of the *weiwen* apparatus and the securitization of local governance clearly shows that the post-reform Chinese state exercises power by delegating, regulating, ordering, disciplining, and normalizing society in a way that resonates with what Foucault has described as "biopower" (Foucault 2008). Nevertheless, as discussed previously, economic reforms have created conditions under which new social forces are activated and interest groups like labor NGOs are formed. They can be viewed as ripple effects of the ideological uncertainty that ensued from the reform program and thus demonstrate how the power of uncertainty sometimes deflects totalizing state power in the Foucauldian sense.

Being part of the *weiwen* apparatus does not exonerate the labor NGOs from state surveillance. On the contrary, labor NGOs are a common target of government harassment and surveillance not only because labor is a politically sensitive issue in China but also because most labor NGOs walk in the legal gray area of being either not registered at all or registered as private companies. As the majority of labor NGOs predominantly rely on foreign funds for their operations, I want to discuss the surveillance of labor NGOs with particular reference to China's state secrets system.

On February 3, 2014, China's state news agency *Xinhua* published new rules that instruct officials not to cover up what should be publicly available information using the excuse of state secrets.[10] The nine-page order was issued by the State Council and signed by Premier Li Keqiang. The new rules were to come into force in March 2014. The state media praised it as a move toward greater government transparency. However, in this newly published order, the Chinese government didn't say what information ought to be public. It was reported that "the scope of secret items should be adjusted in a timely manner according to changes in the situation," which is in line with the common vagueness of China's definition and application of state secret laws.

The protection of state secrets has long been considered a priority by the CCP because it is part of the Chinese political culture of secrecy as well as an essential tool for exerting and maintaining political control (Pye 1985: 200–201). China has a comprehensive and non-transparent state secrets system that consists of laws and regulations governing state secrets that work in tandem with state security, criminal procedure, and criminal laws. Not only does the state secrets system control what constitutes state secrets, but it also criminalizes the possession or disclosure of state secrets. As a tool for maintaining political control, the state secrets system functions both as a shield by classifying a broad range of information and keeping it from the public view, and a sword by suppressing individuals or organizations that are critical of the government.

The legal framework of the state secrets system originated in the Provisional Regulation on Protecting State Secrets promulgated in June 1951, and it stipulated that both Party members and non-Party members were responsible for safeguarding state secrets. On May 1, 1989, the State Secrets Law was passed for the purpose of "protecting state secrets, safeguarding state security and national interests and ensuring the smooth progress of reform, of opening to the outside world, and of socialist construction" (HRIC 2007: 9). According to the State Secrets Law, state secrets are defined as "matters that are related to state security and national interest in economic, military, and diplomatic areas."[11] The State Secrets Law lists six types of matters considered state secrets plus a seventh provision that captures everything that is not included in the other six types. The following are the seven types of state secrets:

1   major policy decisions on state affairs;
2   construction of national defense and activities of the armed forces;
3   diplomatic activities, activities related to foreign countries, as well as commitments to foreign countries;
4   national economic and social development;
5   science and technology;
6   activities for safeguarding state security and investigation of criminal offenses; and
7   other matters that are classified as state secrets by the National State Secrets Bureau.[12]

These seven types of state secrets are very broadly defined and can be easily subject to arbitrary interpretation and politicized manipulation. The National State Secrets Bureau and other departments have issued some specific regulations under each of the broad categories listed above. However, specific information that is considered a state secret is also set forth in numerous other regulations. Such information includes, for example, information on news publishing, information about strikes, data on the number of people executed every year, the figures on pollution, and the unemployment rate. Not only is there an absence of a specific definition concerning what and how information is classified, but there also exists, to complicate the matter even more, a lack of state entities that have the authority to classify information.

In 2010, new amendments were made to the State Secrets Law. In addition to adding standards for identifying and handling classified information, the new amendments prohibit connecting computers that contain classified information to the Internet and other public information networks; the new revision to the State Secrets Law also stipulates that private communications may not mention state secrets and requires Internet service providers and other public network operators to cooperate with state secrets investigations. In March 2014, the National State Secrecy Bureau issued the Interim Provisions on Management of State Secrets Classification, or simply the Classification Provisions, as an attempt to clarify issues of definition and procedure, which were lacking in the 2010 State Secrets Law and 2014 State Secrets Law Implementation Regulations.[13] According to the Classification Provisions, aside from the Communist Party and state bureaucracies, the state organs that can classify information as state secrets include Supreme People's Court and Supreme People's Procuratorate, Academy of Sciences, Academy of Social Sciences, Chinese Red Cross, All China Federation of Trade Unions, China Council for the Promotion of International Trade (China Chamber of International Commerce), and several other semi-official organizations (Finder 2014). However, the Classification Provisions did not specify what information should be classified as secret, nor did it define which entities can classify information, which is a cause of concern because some state-owned enterprises as well as national academic institutions exercise this authority.

Most labor NGOs in South China are either not registered or registered as private companies and largely rely on funding from foreign foundations. Based on the state secrets system described above, these labor NGOs are the easy target of being labeled as having connections with foreign forces and prone to being viewed and treated with great suspicion. Besides, the rising number of labor protests in China has attracted attention from foreign media, international human rights and labor groups, and labor scholars. Consequently, labor NGOs have become important sites where information on current labor relations in China can be gathered. During the first six months of my fieldwork, I frequently ran into foreign scholars and research students (based in foreign academic institutions) visiting the labor NGOs. At a legal training workshop in Shenzhen where I was observing, three people from a French television station came to interview the director and film some parts of the workshop. Such attention is good publicity for the labor NGOs, but it also increases risks for more intensified surveillance. A labor NGO director was taken away by the police right before he was heading out to meet a foreign journalist. He ended up spending the night at the police station. These incidents are vivid illustrations that labor NGOs are closely monitored by the state. As such, labor NGOs are commonly targeted for state surveillance.

Two key state agents play an active role in surveilling social organizations in China. One is the Public Security Bureau (*gonganju*, or popularly referred to as *guobao* by my interlocutors).[14] They are the local police whose responsibility is to keep law and order in the community where they are based. The other one is the National Security Agency (*guojia anquan ju* or *guoan*, as it was commonly referred to by my interlocutors). The National Security Agency deals with issues that concern China's national security, so it operates vertically on municipal, provincial, and national levels. Both *guobao* and *guoan* pay visits to the labor NGOs. The labor NGOs use the euphemism of "drinking tea" to describe these police visits. Many labor NGO leaders describe such visits in friendly terms and see their meetings with the state security agents as "a routine," "very common," or "they are just doing their job." A Shenzhen-based labor NGO director described to me a typical encounter with these state security agents as such:

> Before the crackdown,[15] they usually came and visited us in the office once a month.[16] They asked questions about our work and what we have been doing recently. Just to follow up on what they learned from the previous visit. No big deal. They check if there are any new staff and visitors. They also ask to read some of our documents such as our monthly plan schedules and some work reports [which include] what workshops we have organized, how many people have participated in the workshops and what topics were talked about or discussed at the workshops. They would ask us to print these reports out and read them. They bring the copies with them when they leave. It's okay. There are no secrets or anything. There are no personal details of the workers who attend the workshops, so it is okay.[17]

When I inquired about the emotional stress that can be incurred by such meetings, one NGO director said, "It's not a big deal. Plus you get a free meal!" Another director indicated that "they don't use violence as much nowadays so it's okay." One labor NGO director said that these state security agents are particularly interested not only in knowing if the NGO recently had any new foreign visitors but also in finding out if any of their superiors (*lingdao*) had been there. "They want to know if there was any information that their *lingdao* had but they didn't. If so, it would be a problem for them as it would mean that they were not doing a good job collecting information," explained the NGO director. This is a clear illustration of the way in which the security state is embodied on and affecting the lowest level of the administrative hierarchy. The state security agents endure the increasing pressure to do their job well so much so that they sometimes rely on the labor NGOs for providing information in their work reports while they are ordered to monitor these organizations. This shows one of the unintended consequences of the social management formulated by the central government—a complicit codependence of the state security agents and the labor NGOs that hinges on negotiations of the constantly shifting boundaries of state-sanctioned action. This is made even clearer by the following statement of a labor NGO director based in Guangzhou.

> It is usually the same people that come to visit us in the office. Over the years, you kind of get to know them. Sometimes they even complain about their job to us and say that it can be pretty stressful. They were not looking to cause trouble for us. They were just doing their job. On the other hand, we create jobs for them too.[18]

This labor NGO director's comment is indicative of the intricate dynamics between the labor NGOs and the local police: Their regular interaction through state surveillance has led to an intimate and complicit coexistence. This paradox is further illustrated by China's expansion of its surveillance mechanism.

China now spends more money on police and domestic surveillance than on the military.[19] Commenting on the surveillance that his organization is subjected to, a labor activist from a Hong Kong labor NGO even jokingly described the U.S. nonprofit organization National Endowment for Democracy (NED) as a "Chinese job program." Receiving funding from the U.S. Congress, NED funds projects that promote the growth and strengthening of democratic institutions around the world and has long been viewed with caution by the Chinese government. The Hong Kong-based labor activist said,

> I joke in my own mind: every dollar NED spends on China, the Chinese government spends 100 dollars in counter measures. So NED is like a Chinese job program. They have so many [people], literally a whole team that focuses on one organization. Can you imagine how much they are paying each one of these people? 10,000 or 20,000 RMB a month. [They] give them housing and health care. If you compare their salaries to what an NGO worker earns, they are probably five times greater.

The labor NGOs' experiences with state surveillance described above show that China is far from being an authoritarian state that harasses, detains, and arrests individuals deemed to be threatening to its rule. The Chinese state exerts control over its population in a more subtle way; aggrieved groups and individuals are allowed some space to voice their discontent and interests while being channeled into legal procedures and away from mobilizing to challenge the CCP. The relaxed regulations on the registration of social organizations is an example of this. The vast numbers of state security agents employed by the Chinese government to infiltrate and surveil political activists, dissidents, and progressive groups demonstrate the government's heightened sensitivity to social unrest.

International community

Although the social, economic, political, legal, and institutional changes discussed above have created the conditions in which labor NGOs in China can carve out a space of existence, their emergence has been facilitated most crucially by the labor organizations in Hong Kong. The labor groups in Hong Kong play a key role in helping the development of the labor NGOs in mainland China. This has to do with Hong Kong's distinct political, social, economic, and geographical relationship to China. In 1997, Hong Kong was transferred to China by the British government after more than 150 years of British administration. Long before the handover of Hong Kong, the Beijing government was in discussions with the United Kingdom over the sovereignty of Hong Kong. It was agreed that Hong Kong was to be given the status of a Special Administrative Region (SAR) of the People's Republic of China. This allows the governance of Hong Kong to follow the principle of One China, Two Systems, which means that the Hong Kong SAR retains its economic and political systems including its own government, multiparty legislature, legal systems, police force, monetary system, and immigration policy.

The Hong Kong labor groups' engagement in labor issues in mainland China can be traced back to the 1980s, but a critical turning point was in 1993 when a fire broke out in a toy factory in Shenzhen (Pun 2005). Hong Kong labor groups and activists were actively involved in helping the victims claim compensation from the factory owner. Since this incident, Hong Kong labor groups have become even more active in the region, including helping to establish labor NGOs in South China. Hong Kong has long served as the bridge between China and the rest of the world, channeling trade and investment flows both ways. When it comes to the mainland Chinese labor NGOs, Hong Kong also helps connect them with foreign funds and expertise. Moreover, due to their fluency in English and administration, Hong Kong labor NGOs often play the role of administering and managing projects for Western donors. The majority of labor NGOs in China receive funding from members of the international community such as Oxfam (Hong Kong), the Ford Foundation, the Asia Foundation, the International Labor Organization, the European Union Human Rights Committee, development agencies attached to foreign embassies, and foreign Christian foundations. Some funding also comes from foreign trade unions.

It should be pointed out that some Chinese labor NGOs are financed by multiple sources of funding, including academic grants, crowdsourcing via social media, and donations by NGO staff members and executive committees. Confronted with the intensification of labor unrest, the official trade union ACFTU has been increasingly financing labor NGOs in the name of maintaining stability. As mentioned earlier, pressure has been placed on the ACFTU to reform and become more responsive to workers' demands. During my fieldwork, a few labor NGOs revealed to me that they were approached by the ACFTU to organize legal training workshops for migrant workers and were considering collaboration with the ACFTU. The predominant source of funding of the four grassroots labor NGOs where I conducted ethnographic fieldwork came from foreign foundations and trade unions, which covered the running costs of these NGOs, including the office rent, staff salaries, and other expenses of implementing projects such as organizing training workshops, visiting injured workers in hospitals, and coach meetings with migrant workers. As such, during my fieldwork, these labor NGOs were dependent on foreign funding for their day-to-day operation.[20]

The more active labor NGOs in Hong Kong include Labor Action China (LAC), Labor Education and Service Network (LESN), Worker Empowerment (WE), Workers Rights Consortium, Students and Scholars Against Corporate Misbehavior (SACOM), Globalization Monitor (GM), International Labor Organization (ILO) in Hong Kong, Asia Monitor Resource Center (AMRC), Hong Kong Christian Industrial Committee (HKCIC), and the Chinese Working Women Network (CWWN).[21] These Hong Kong organizations all came into existence in the late 1990s and early 2000s and with time some have helped set up labor NGOs in mainland China. These Hong Kong labor organizations have close connections with one another. The founders know each other and hold regular meetings every three months to exchange information about their work.

Take Asia Monitor Resource Center (AMRC) for example. AMRC has played a key role in fostering the development of labor NGOs in the Pearl River Delta. It functions mainly as an intermediary between the foreign donors and Chinese labor NGOs. Apo Leung, former director of AMRC, said to me during an interview that AMRC started to more actively connect Chinese grassroots labor NGOs with foreign donors in the early 2000s. The labor NGOs that AMRC was interested in helping were those led by migrant workers themselves. Many of these NGO leaders do not have any knowledge of English. The language barrier makes it impossible for them to interact directly with the foreign donors, including submitting funding proposals and reports in English. As such, the Hong Kong labor NGOs help the Chinese grassroots labor NGOs by writing project proposals and when funds are secured, the Hong Kong NGOs are responsible for managing, supervising, and documenting the project. "Back in the late 1990s and early 2000s, China was still fairly closed to the outside world and our donors didn't know much about these labor NGOs. So they asked us to be the babysitter [of these organizations]. So if anything goes wrong, we would be the ones accountable," said Apo Leung. By "babysitter," Apo meant that AMRC was asked to be the "trustee" of these labor NGOs in mainland China. As a trustee, AMRC was responsible for managing, supervising, and documenting the projects carried out by the labor NGOs in China. Most importantly, AMRC was also in charge of distributing funds and submitting financial reports to the donors. This is a common model for the working relationship between the Hong Kong labor groups and the grassroots labor NGOs in mainland China. As a trustee, it is AMRC that signs formal agreements with the donors on behalf of the labor NGOs in mainland China because "it is not always easy for the labor NGOs in the mainland to meet with donors," according to a program coordinator at AMRC. The program coordinator admits that the role of AMRC "in the execution of the project is actually very small. We mainly carry out the administrative tasks. We help our donors administer and monitor the projects. We make sure that the funds are used appropriately."

One Hong Kong labor NGO worker jokingly described the relationship between his organization, foreign funders, and Chinese labor NGOs this way:

> It's a bit like outsourcing. We apply for money from foreign countries and then allocate the money to our partners in the mainland. It's a bit like money laundering [*xi heiqian*]. If the NGO in the mainland gets money directly from abroad, the NGO can become sensitive and will be closely watched by the government. So if the money comes to Hong Kong first and to the mainland later, it is then de-sensitized.[22]

This Hong Kong labor NGO worker's comment indicates how the special administrative and economic arrangement between mainland China and Hong Kong has resulted in some level of flexibility whereby the translocal and transnational connections are crystallized and expressed vividly in such words as "outsourcing" and "money laundering," illustrating calculating and risk-taking behavior.

However, the notion of a "trustee" or "trusteeship" has its origins in the ways in which development was understood and constructed from the beginning of the Enlightenment period and the ways in which colonial humanitarianism was reinvented after the formal end of colonial and imperial rule (Power 2003: 130–131). Ingrained in the notion of "trusteeship" in colonial administration was the mission to "civilize others, to strengthen the weak, to give experience to the 'childlike' colonial peoples who required supervision" (ibid.: 131). With this reference, my intention is to highlight the power dynamics embedded in the relationship between the Chinese labor NGOs and their counterparts in Hong Kong. More than once during my fieldwork, I have heard the Chinese labor NGO staff call their partners in Hong Kong "boss." When the Hong Kong NGO was coming to the office of the Chinese labor NGO for a meeting, the staff would say, "The supervisor is coming [for an inspection] (*dudao laile*)." It is a remark indicative of a hierarchy in the relationships between the Chinese grassroots labor NGOs and the Hong Kong labor groups, which, nevertheless, are often described as partnerships by the Hong Kong intermediaries.

That my interlocutors sometimes experienced their relationships with the Hong Kong labor NGOs as hierarchical also reflects another socialist legacy where the country is governed through a vast nationwide bureaucracy with layers of administrative units ranked one above the other. Hence, the sense of hierarchy is a general characteristic of political life in China. From time to time, this unspoken feeling of being subordinate to the Hong Kong labor NGOs did put some strain on the collaborative efforts between these NGOs. During my fieldwork with the labor NGOs in the Pearl River Delta, I sometimes heard the NGO leaders complain about their relationship with the Hong Kong labor organizations. Blue Sky Social Work Service Center has been working with a Hong Kong labor organization for several years. With the help of this Hong Kong labor group, Blue Sky has been receiving funds from a German foundation. A few months before I started my fieldwork at Blue Sky, they had successfully registered as a social organization. Currently they have two sources of funding: one from a German foundation, the other from the government. Wei Peng, director of Blue Sky, has more than once complained about the lack of transparency in his relationship with the Hong Kong organization.

"Next time I see him [the program coordinator from Hong Kong], I want to ask him to sign an agreement with me. It is he who signs the agreement [with the German foundation]. We don't know what's in the agreement. I want to have a more formal partnership with him. I want to have things written down on a piece of paper and both parties sign on it. It's better this way," said Wei Peng. He continued,

> You know when you get money from the government, it's all clearly stated in the agreement that once the contract is signed, the government will issue 50% of the funding so the operation can start. Then they will conduct a mid-term evaluation. If the organization passes the evaluation, the government will then give 40% of the funding. Then there is the final evaluation. Once you pass the final evaluation, the government will give you the remaining 10% of the funding. It is all very clear in the agreement. I never have anything like this with the Hong Kong people.

Wei Peng's comment largely came from the fact that the Hong Kong labor NGO had not been transferring funds for the past few months and he had to use his own money to pay for the rent and office expenses. The only reason that the Hong Kong labor group gave Wei Peng was that the German foundation was going through some restructuring which was causing a delay in transferring the funds. Wei Peng didn't like the uncertainty and lack of control over his relationship with his funding agency.

> In the last few years, I sent all the receipts to them [the Hong Kong labor NGO] and let them do all the financial reporting. Now I have got some funds from the government and I have to hire an accountant to do the bookkeeping for me. You can't mess with the government. They want all original receipts. Sometimes I feel it is more transparent with the government. I have a contract with them, and I know when the money is coming.[23]

Wei Peng's words clearly show the tensions and micropolitics that can arise in the collaboration between the Chinese grassroots labor NGOs and their Hong Kong intermediaries (Fisher 1997), which are made more complicated when these labor groups, both in mainland China and Hong Kong, have to operate against pervasive state surveillance. Under such circumstances, how these organizations cultivate trust in their relationships and carry out activism together becomes an important question, a subject that will be addressed in the following chapters.

Conclusion

China's economic reforms have resulted in unprecedented prosperity in contemporary China and unleashed social forces that have created a new social landscape with its own aspirations and demands. It is a China that is significantly different from Mao's China not only in degree but also in kind (Gries & Rosen 2004: 1). The economic, social, and legal changes discussed in this chapter are both the conditions for and part of the newly emerging social landscape which is still intricately and contentiously embedded in the rigid political system of authoritarianism. The presence of labor NGOs is situated in such a contested terrain of embeddedness, which becomes more complicated when the Chinese state has expanded its security apparatus and exerted state control through increasingly subtle channels such as social management. Against the expansion of the security apparatus, the role and development of labor NGOs become even more ambiguous and contested. In the following chapters, I will discuss how labor NGOs strategize to negotiate this ambiguity while trying to seek legitimacy and stability for their organizations.

With the example of Green Grass, I historicized the development of a grassroots labor NGO and described what kind of work it could do under the restrictive political environment in China. Against the transformation of China's legal system and infrastructure, Green Grass illustrates how a labor NGO can carve out a space of existence. I also discussed the role played by the labor NGOs in Hong Kong and the sense of hierarchy and micropolitics in the partnerships between these organizations. In the chapters that follow, I will go further to demonstrate ethnographically how the micropolitics between these NGOs and their foreign donors is dictated by their perception and imagination of the state as well as uncertainty about the boundaries of permissible activism. Moreover, I will show how the contested existence of labor NGOs has resulted in certain forms of existence, subjectivity, and practices that have emerged from the domain of uncertainty and are employed to navigate uncertain political terrains while shaping state-society relationships in contemporary China.

Notes

1 For example, a provision was put in place in the 1990s that allowed rural residents to purchase temporary urban residency permits so that they could work

and live legally in the cities. Since the 2000s, the hukou system has been further weakened. In 2003, migrant worker Sun Zhigang was taken to a detention center after being unable to produce his temporary residency permit and identity card when he was stopped by the police. Sun Zhigang suffered physical abuse while being detained and died of the severe injuries from the beatings in the detention center. His death sparked wide protests across the country and led to the government's repeal of the laws regarding the arrest and repatriation of migrant workers found illegally living and working in the cities (Liang 2011: 83–102).

2 The word *henhei* literally means very black. In this context, it refers to the underhanded tactics of the village committee.

3 This interview was conducted in May 2013.

4 The names of the labor NGOs mentioned here are all authentic.

5 GONGOs are government-sponsored NGOs that may resemble an NGO. GONGOs are usually created for the purpose of promoting issues that the government wants to bring attention to. GONGOs can also be created in order to qualify for outside aid or to mitigate specific issues related to certain aspects of domestic affairs or international relations.

6 Mary Gallagher has noted that although the national statistics showed there was a rapid increase in labor disputes in the mid-1990s, it is not entirely clear what this increase signifies. She suggests the rise in labor disputes could result from the lack of legal regulation of labor prior to the reform era so the rate of increase is from an extremely low base point (2007 [2005]: 116).

7 The exchange the rate was 6.66 RMB per dollar during the time of my fieldwork.

8 The story of Liu Xiaowen, which is a pseudonym, was gathered from the blog of Green Grass and my interviews with labor NGO activists. For reasons of confidentiality, I will not provide the link to the blog.

9 More information on the new amendment is available at http://baike.baidu.com/view/703598.htm accessed August 27, 2019.

10 From: www.gov.cn/zwgk/2014-02/03/content_2579949.htm accessed August 27, 2019

11 From: www.gov.cn/flfg/2010-04/30/content_1596420.htm accessed August 27, 2019.

12 Information on the different types of state secrets is available at www.gov.cn/flfg/2010-04/30/content_1596420.htm, accessed August 27, 2019.

13 Finder, Susan. 2014. How China classifies state secrets. *The Diplomat*, December 23. Available at: http://thediplomat.com/2014/12/how-china-classifies-state-secrets/ accessed March 9, 2015.

14 *Guobao* is a shorthand for the Domestic Security Department of the Public Security Bureau. It is a branch of the police force within the Ministry of Public Security, which is responsible for and specializes in collecting intelligence and infiltrating and dealing with political dissidents, human rights activists, petitioners, religious groups, and others engaged in "subversive" activities.

15 He was referring to the crackdown in 2012, which will be discussed in detail in the next chapter.

16 The frequency of the visits by the state security agents seems to vary, and it is not easy to infer whether such factors as the location of the NGO and the services provided by the NGO determine the frequency of these visits. For example, some labor NGOs in Guangzhou City have visits almost once a week or every other week.

17 This interview was conducted in January 2013.

18 This interview was conducted in Februray 2013.

19 Buckley, Chris. 2011. China Internal Security Spending Jumps Past Army Budget. *Reuters*, March 5. Available at: www.reuters.com/article/us-china-unrest-idUSTRE7222RA20110305 accessed October 30, 2014.

20 My discussion on the funding received by the Chinese labor NGOs can also be read in my chapter titled "Thinking like a state: doing labor activism in South China" in *Handbook of protest and resistance in China*, edited by Teresa Wright (2019: 151–165).
21 The names of the NGOs in Hong Kong are all authentic.
22 The interview with the Hong Kong NGO worker was conducted in May 2013. The word "sensitive" here is used to refer to something that is politically sensitive and risky. In Chapter 5, I will discuss this issue in more detail.
23 This interview was conducted in June 2013.

Bibliography

Bach, Jonathan. 2010. "They come in peasants and leave citizens": urban villages and the making of Shenzhen, China. *Cultural Anthropology* 25 (3): 421–458.

Chan, Anita. 2001 *China's workers under assault: the exploitation of labor in a globalizing economy*. New York: M.E. Sharpe.

Chan, Chris King-chi. 2013. Community-based organizations for migrant workers' rights: the emergence of labor NGOs in China. *Community Development Journal* 48 (1): 6–22.

Dillon, Nara. 2011. "Governing civil society: adapting revolutionary methods to serve post-communist goals." In *Mao's invisible hand: the political foundations of adaptive governance in China*, edited by Sebastian Heilmann and Elizabeth J. Perry. Cambridge, MA: Harvard University Asia Center, pp. 138–164.

Fewsmith, Joseph. 2012. "Social management" as a way of coping with heightened social tension. *China Leadership Monitor* 36: 1–8.

Finder, Susan. 2014. How China classifies state secrets. *The Diplomat*, December 23. Available at: http://thediplomat.com/2014/12/how-china-classifies-state-secrets/ accessed March 9, 2015.

Fisher, William F. 1997. Doing good? The politics and anti-politics of NGO practices. *Annual Review of Anthropology* 26: 439–464.

Foucault, Michel. 2009. *Security, territory, population: lectures at the collége de France 1977–1978*. Translated by Graham Burchell. New York: Picador.

——— 2008. *The birth of biopolitics: lectures at the collége de France 1978–1979*. Edited by Michel Senellart. New York: Palgrave-Macmillan.

Franceschini, Ivan. 2014. Labor NGOs in China: a real force for political change? *The China Quarterly* 218: 474–492.

Froissart, Chloé. 2005 The rise of social movements among migrant workers: uncertain strivings for autonomy. *China Perspectives* 61: 1–15.

Gallagher, Mary E. 2007 [2005]. *Contagious capitalism: globalization and the politics of labor in China*. Princeton, NJ and Oxford: Princeton University Press.

——— 2004. "China: the limits of civil society in a late Leninist state." In *Civil society and political change in Asia: expanding and contracting democratic space*, edited by Muthiah Alagappa. Stanford: Stanford University Press.

Gallagher, Mary E., and Baohua Dong. 2011. "Legislating harmony: labor law reform in contemporary China." In *From iron rice bowl to informalization: markets, workers, and the state in a changing China*, edited by Sarosh Kuruvilla, Ching Kwan Lee, and Mary E. Gallagher. Ithaca, NY and London: Cornell University Press.

Gries, Peter Hays, and Stanley Rosen. 2004. "Introduction: popular protest and state legitimation in 21st century China." In *State and society in 21st century*

China: crisis, contention, and legitimation, edited by Peter Hays Gries and Stanley Rosen. New York and London: Routledge.

Howell, Jude. 2008. "Civil society and migrants," In *Labor migration and social development in contemporary China,* edited by Rachel Murphy. London: Routledge.

——— 2003. "New directions in civil society: organizing around marginalized interests," in *Governance in China,* edited by Jude Howell. Oxford: Rowman & Littlefield Publishers.

Human Rights in China (HRIC). 2007. *State secrets: China's legal labyrinth.* New York: HRIC. Available at: www.hrichina.org/sites/default/files/publication_pdfs/hric_statesecrets-report.pdf accessed March 9, 2015.

Huang, Shumin. 1998. *The spiral road: change in a Chinese village through the eyes of a communist party leader.* Boulder, CO: Westview Press.

Lau, Mimi. 2018. Chinese campus crackdown on young Marxist activists expands in major cities. *The South China Morning Post.* Available at: www.scmp.com/news/china/politics/article/2173090/chinese-campus-crackdown-young-marxist-activists-expands-major accessed August 23, 2019.

Lee, Ching Kwan, and Yonghong Zhang. 2013. The power of instability: unraveling the microfoundations of bargained authoritarianism in China. *American Journal of Sociology* 118 (6): 1475–1508.

Liang, Zhiping. 2011. "The death of a detainee: the predicament of status politics in contemporary China and the way out." In *Governance of life in Chinese moral experience,* edited by Everett Zhang, Arthur Kleinman, and Tu Weiming. London: Routledge.

Lin, George C. S. 1997. *Red capitalism in South China.* Vancouver: University of British Colombia Press.

Lubman, Stanley. 1999. *Bird in a cage: legal reform in China after Mao.* Stanford: Stanford University Press.

Ma, Quisha. 2006. *Non-governmental organizations in contemporary China: paving the way to civil society?* London and New York: Routledge.

Michael, Franz. 1988. "Law: a tool of power." In *Human rights in the People's Republic of China,* edited by Yuan-li Wu, Franz Michael, John F. Copper, Ta-Ling Le, Maria Hsia Chang, and A. James Gregor. Boulder, CO: Westview Press.

Oi, Jean C. 1995. The role of the local state in China's transitional economy. *The China Quarterly* 144: 1132–1149.

Pan, Darcy. 2019. "Thinking like a state: doing labor activism in South China." In *Handbook of protest and resistance,* edited by Teresa Wright. Cheltenham, UK: Edward Elgar Publishing, pp. 151–165.

——— 2017. "Agents of change or status quo? Labor NGOs in South China." In *Uncertain times: anthropological approaches to labor in a neoliberal world,* edited by E. Paul Durrenberger. Boulder: University Press of Colorado, pp. 135–160.

Peerenboom, Randall. 2002. *China's long march toward the rule of law.* New York: Cambridge University Press.

Potter, Pitman. 1995. Foreign investment law in the People's Republic of China: dilemmas of state control. *The China Quarterly* 141: 155–185.

Power, Marcus. 2003. *Rethinking development geographies.* London: Routledge.

Pun, Ngai. 2009. "The making of a global dormitory labor regime: labor protection and labor organizing of migrant women in South China." In *Labor migration and social development in contemporary China,* edited by Rachel Murphy. London: Routledge.

――― 2005. *Made in China: women factory workers in a global workplace.* Durham, NC and London: Duke University Press.

Pye, Lucian W. 1985. *Asian power and politics: the cultural dimensions of authority.* Cambridge, MA: Harvard University Press.

SACOM. 2005. Looking for Mickey Mouse's conscience: a survey on working conditions of Disney supplier factories in China. Available at: http://sacom.hk/wp-content/uploads/2008/07/disney.pdf accessed September 15, 2015.

Schuller, Mark, and David Lewis. 2014. Anthropology of NGOs. Oxford Bibliographies. doi:10.1093/obo/9780199766567-0090 accessed March 16, 2016.

Scott, James C. 1998. *Seeing like a state: how certain schemes to improve the human condition have failed.* New Haven, CT: Yale University Press.

Siu, Helen F. 2007. Grounding displacement: uncivil urban spaces in postreform South China. *American Ethnologist* 34 (2): 329–350.

Solinger, Dorothy J. 1999. *Contesting citizenship in urban China: peasant migrants, the state, and the logic of the market.* Berkeley: University of California Press.

Spires, Anthony. 2007. *China's unofficial civil society: the development of grassroots NGOs in an authoritarian state.* PhD dissertation, Yale University.

"The Chinese trade union holds its national congress." *Made in China* (2018, October 26). Available at: https://madeinchinajournal.com/2018/10/26/the-chinese-trade-union-holds-its-national-congress/ accessed August 23, 2019.

Turner, Karen G., James V. Feinerman, and R. Kent Guy. 2000. *The limits of the rule of law in China.* Seattle: University of Washington Press.

Unger, Jonathan. 1996. "Bridges": private business, the Chinese government and the rise of new associations. *The China Quarterly* 147: 795–819.

Wang, Ya Ping, Yanglin Wang, and Jiansheng Wu. 2009. Urbanization and informal development in China: urban villages in Shenzhen. *International Journal of Urban and Regional Research* 33 (4): 957–973.

Wang, Yuhua, and Carl Minzner. 2015. The rise of the Chinese security state. *The China Quarterly* 222: 339–359.

Wank, David. 1995. Private business, bureaucracy, and political alliance in a Chinese city. *The Australian Journal of Chinese Affairs* 33: 55–71.

Zhang, Li. 2001. *Strangers in the city: reconfigurations of space, power, and social networks within China's floating population.* Stanford: Stanford University Press.

Zhong, Lena Y. 2009. *Communities, crime and social capital in contemporary China.* Cullompton, UK: Willan Publishing.

3   Uncertainty at work

How does uncertainty work and manifest itself in the labor community in South China? How can uncertainty be problematized as "emergent problem spaces" (Samimian-Darash & Rabinow 2015: 1) where labor NGOs try to pinpoint a less risky point of engagement on the shifting boundaries of state tolerance while being accountable to the Western donors' demands. These questions are the main concern of this chapter in which I illustrate and discuss how uncertainty is perceived, played out, managed, and dealt with in the labor NGO community by drawing on two ethnographic examples: a large-scale crackdown in 2012 and the revised and relatively relaxed policy concerning social organizations introduced in the same year. In the previous chapter, I have described the kind of work done and services provided by the labor NGOs of my study. Nevertheless, in the years leading to 2012, some labor NGOs in the Pearl River Delta region have progressively shifted the focus of their work toward assisting workers in collective action, a subject to be discussed in finer detail in Chapter 6. A number of reasons can account for this shift in attitude and modus operandi, and they include the increasing numbers of strikes as a result of workers' demand for more pay; compensation related to work injury and the relocations of factories; and social insurance payments, and the local government's implicit tolerance of such labor NGOs (Chen & Yang 2017).

Some also point out that the Honda strike in 2010 has played a crucial role in catalyzing a wave of strikes across the country and, more significantly, changing the nature of labor struggles in China (Chen & Yang 2017; Zhang 2019).[1] Indeed, the shift toward more active involvement in workers' collective action in the years following the Honda strike marks a new development in labor NGO activism in China. This new dynamic also helps put into perspective the government's large-scale crackdown on labor NGOs in the PRD region in 2012, as well as the even more severe crackdown of 2015, when several NGO leaders were detained, an incident I will return to in the final chapter.

The two inherently contradicting events that occurred in 2012—the crackdown on the labor NGOs in Shenzhen and the relaxation of policy on social organizations—are two telling examples whereby I illustrate and discuss the ambiguous terrain that the labor NGOs have to navigate. With these two examples, I consider how uncertainty constitutes and is constitutive of the relationship between the NGOs and the state.[2] I treat uncertainty as a productive notion through which an emergent problem space of beliefs and acts of self-censorship and forms of activism can be explored and understood. It is in such a space that the existence and the work of the labor NGOs and their relationships with the Chinese state as well as with one another become imaginable. Such a space is a fertile ground on which the workings of state power through shaping modes of governing and subjectivity can be examined.

The examples to be discussed in this chapter show how uncertainty about state tolerance of labor activism becomes instrumental in fostering a kind of complicity and collusion that sustains the political order distinctive of paradoxes, indeterminacy, and contingency. With the examples, I discuss how the uncertainty of the parameters of state control is constitutive of the existence and development of the labor NGOs, which, in turn, is productively conducive to maintaining the existing political order of things. To navigate through these different epistemological levels requires an understanding of what the hidden rules are—a type of intimate knowledge—and how one can avail themselves of these rules. In other words, one needs to work at acquiring and accumulating this sort of intimate knowledge, which is often circulated through informal channels. As such, this emergent problem space is also a space of intimacy and complicity in which uncertainty is experienced and managed. The intimate knowledge required to navigate through the uncertainty about the limits of state-sanctioned activism is an exercise of complicity which concerns the "engagement between the official state and the sometimes disruptive popular practices whose existence it often denies, but whose vitality is the ironic condition of its own continuation" (Herzfeld 2016: 9). Viewed as such, the uncertainty that permeates through the different epistemological levels is also a consequence of the process of state formation that has increased the "objective power of the state" (Cohen 1998: 8).

The crackdown

When I started my fieldwork in the Pearl River Delta region in the summer of 2012, the labor NGOs were just reeling from the shock of the rare and large-scale suppression by the authorities of Guangdong Province. A dozen labor NGOs in Shenzhen, a city predominantly populated by migrant workers, were harassed by the local authorities and police, and eventually evicted by their landlords. Li Hua, a labor NGO director based in Shenzhen, described to me his experience of the crackdown.

When it [the harassment] first started, they would come every day or every other day. At its worst, four different departments came in one afternoon. There was the fire department, the *guobao* [Public Security

Bureau, PSB], the *guoan* [National Security Bureau, NSB], the labor bureau and even the administration for industry and commerce came too! Basically, everyone that could come came. They took turns visiting you and harassing you so that you couldn't work. At last, the landlord came too. When they came, they came to do a check (*jiancha*). For example, when the labor bureau came, they wanted you to show the employment contracts of all the staff; they wanted you to photocopy the pay slips and identification documents of every employee. Then they wanted you to put a stamp on every photocopy. The exact same thing happened when the administration for industry and commerce came. So each department [that came to visit] wanted you to show and photocopy these things. They were giving you such a hard time that you couldn't work. You ended up making photocopies every day. Then they asked you if you had violated any law. In the end, they told us that our office didn't meet the fire safety regulations so we couldn't work here. We were told to move. The entire floor [of the building] was rented out for office use but we were the only ones that didn't pass the inspection. We were the only one that had to move.[3]

The interview quoted above illustrates the kind of harassment that some Shenzhen-based labor NGOs had to face in 2012; for some NGOs, the harassment lasted for a few months, after which they were asked to move by their landlords. Some Hong Kong labor organizations revealed that many landlords were pressured by the local police and authorities to ask their NGO tenants to relocate.[4] The crackdown is an illustration of how the Chinese government exerts control through state-endorsed repression, sometimes through routine regulation, in order to maintain political order.

Sitting at his desk in his new office on the sixth floor of an office building in a district center in Shenzhen, Li Hua told me that the local authorities began to harass his organization in April in 2012. "After a month and a half, we decided to give in and move. But it didn't just end there. It (the harassment) continued. We have moved four times since May (in 2012). No one wanted to rent to us. The most extreme one was that we were asked to move one day after we just signed the rental contract! We have been closely followed," noted Li Hua. It showed that Li Hua had only just moved to this new office not long ago, as some boxes were still sealed and stacked against the wall in his office. There was one other room adjacent to his office. On my way into Li Hua's office, I caught a glimpse of this other room and saw two people sitting at a long table working on their computers. The long table and a few chairs were the only furniture in the room. He told me that he had to throw away some furniture during the move and some furniture was damaged. Li Hua noted that no one had come here yet so maybe things had quieted down. The continuous harassment from the local authorities and moving between places had forced Li Hua to discontinue the operation of his NGO. But even months after settling into the new office, he still decided to keep a low profile and hold off on resuming the operation of the organization for fear of any further harassment.

Hong Kong labor groups pointed out that the government harassment had started in February 2012, but many targeted labor NGOs were too scared to speak up. Largely thanks to these groups in Hong Kong, the news of the government crackdown on the labor NGOs was widely posted on the websites of many of these groups.[5] The Hong Kong labor organizations were particularly active, initiating a petition and issuing press releases denouncing the crackdown.[6] In August 2012, one of the targeted Chinese labor NGOs, Little Grass (*Xiao Cao*) Workers' Home (hereafter Little Grass), posted a video online which vividly showed the government crackdown and reached the wider public and international media.[7]

This video shows a group of thugs smashing windows and breaking down the front door of the labor organization's office in front of the local police and some other bystanders.[8] Little Grass had been pressured and visited by the town authorities as well as various government departments since June 2012. The landlord of Little Grass's rented office also came to ask the staff to move out of the location despite having two more years on the rental contract. On August 30, 2012, a dozen unknown men showed up and forced themselves into the office of Little Grass.[9] Without revealing their identity, these men completely ignored the staff's protest and started moving the furniture, books, and folders from the office, and threw them to the street. Before they left, they welded the iron door so that no one could get in. One of the staff had called the police, but they didn't arrive until these men had left. The police insisted that this episode of violence was nothing but a disagreement between the landlord and Little Grass. The police didn't take any written statement on what happened and told Little Grass to resolve the issue with the landlord privately. Soon after this incident, Little Grass, like the other harassed labor NGOs, succumbed to the pressure and moved to a different area.

In early September 2012, three suppressed labor NGOs joined together to send letters and pay visits (*xinfang*) to the local authorities and demand an explanation. These three labor NGOs all had partnerships with Hong Kong labor organizations. Their petitions were all disregarded by the authorities, who simply dismissed their petition as an issue they had with their respective landlords so there was nothing they could do. After a few unsuccessful attempts to try to meet with the authorities on why they were forced to relocate, these three labor NGOs decided to make a joint statement on the government harassment. On September 19, 2012, each of the NGOs brought with them six red-colored pennants. Each of the pennants was filled with texts from the workers lauding and supporting the provincial authorities' dedication to a more liberal policy on social organizations. With these pennants and their recommendations for the regulations governing social organizations in their hands, the three labor NGOs slowly walked to the

Shenzhen Municipal Bureau of Letters and Calls. One of the participating NGO directors told me that when the NGOs arrived, a staff member from the bureau came out from behind his window and told them to "just insert the pennants through one of the windows." The NGOs were still waiting and hoping to have a meeting with some of the staff members' superiors. The NGO director continued, "A few minutes later, the same staff member who came to meet with us came out again, declined the pennants and said, 'We do not need your pennants.'" In the end, the NGOs returned to the reception office located at the entrance of the bureau and left the pennants and recommendations with the security guard hoping that the security guard would deliver these to the people in charge. Unsurprisingly, the request was met with silence.

When asked why the crackdown occurred, Li Hua shook his head and said that he had no idea. "You know, I was the second NGO harassed. Zhang Zhi [leader of another labor NGO] was the first one.[10] I even helped him move! But he didn't tell me why he was moving. He just asked me to help so I did. I wish he could have told me that he was being harassed, then I could have been better prepared. I was pretty upset after I found out," explained Li Hua, who has known Zhang Zhi for many years and said they are good friends. However, Li Hua's comment tellingly exhibits the limited interaction, lack of trust, and caution that have marked their friendship. In effect, when I later talked to Zhang Zhi, he jokingly remarked, "If it were not for the crackdown, would you have known what labor NGOs there are in Shenzhen? Would you have known that at least there are a dozen labor NGOs in operation in Shenzhen?" When commenting on the targeted labor NGOs in this crackdown, one labor activist in Hong Kong said, "If a labor NGO came out and said they were harassed by the government, how would you know they were telling the truth?" These comments revealingly describe the atmospheric secrecy and opacity of the environment in which the labor NGOs operate. They show that not only do the labor NGOs have limited interaction with one another, but they are also rather guarded with one another. The comments indicate that the labor NGOs operate in an environment fraught with uncertainty, which is also rife with suspicion and distrust, rumor, and gossip, as will be shown in the ensuing chapters. In the next section, I will discuss the labor NGOs' responses to and speculations about the crackdown and suggest that stories circulated via informal speech acts such as gossip and storytelling are a self-designed coping mechanism whereby the labor NGOs try to make sense of the incomprehensible and glean some degree of certainty out of the uncertainty.

Theorizing the crackdown[11]

The large-scale crackdown in 2012 caused great anxiety among the labor NGOs, many of which responded by engaging in self-censorship by either scaling back services or discontinuing operations. A common and rather obvious explanation for how the seemingly random crackdown and its atmospheric uncertainty can lead to self-censorship is fear. The function of political fear is "not to quell one individual, but to make an example of her, to send a message to everyone else that they should be careful, or they might be next" (Robin 2004: 179). However, to focus on the fear engendered by coercion does not get us very far if we want to understand how "the message" is perceived, speculated on, and interpreted by the people concerned. "The key point is that speculation surrounding a warning or punishment generates a set of imagined rules designed to prevent future clashes with authority" (Stern & Hassid 2012: 1241). To learn how activists understand and interpret political events can shed light on how they navigate the gray zone between the forbidden and tolerated, and more importantly, how they form beliefs about the limits of political tolerance, which, in turn, shapes their practices of activism.

The uncertainty accentuated by the 2012 crackdown on the labor NGOs in Shenzhen arises not only from the absence of clear signals from the top leaders but also from the paradoxical timing of its occurrence. The crackdown occurred at a time when the Guangdong Provincial Government announced its plan to implement what seemed to be rather liberal policies. These policies included stricter enforcement of labor law, raising the minimum wage, encouraging direct representation for factory workers, and permitting social organizations to register independently without having a government sponsor. But why suppress labor groups when the Guangdong authorities seemed to be relaxing their labor policies? This question was on everyone's mind in the labor community both inside and outside mainland China, but no one seemed to have a definite answer. In the absence of the real motives behind the crackdown, what emerged and circulated in the labor NGO community both in Guangdong and Hong Kong were stories, interpretations, and commentaries on the government suppression, similar to Stern and Hassid's notion of "control parable."

Control parables are "*a type of* didactic story that invents or recapitulates an understanding of why certain types of action are dangerous or even impossible" (Stern & Hassid 2012: 1240, emphasis in original). Sometimes the moral of the parable can be so open-ended that different people glean different lessons from the same event (ibid.: 1241). The kind of control parables that Stern and Hassid focus on is those that deal with one particular type of uncertainty: "ambiguity about which actions political authorities consider off-limits" (ibid.: 1242). Control parables born of fear and uncertainty about political events illustrate that "small acts of education among the victims are central to the economy of fear. They minimize the amount of actual coercion perpetrators must apply, and they maximize the effect" (Robin 2004: 181). As such, control parables dispel political possibilities from below without the direct involvement or knowledge of the state (Stern & Hassid 2012: 1241).

During my fieldwork I heard and overheard conversations from labor NGO staff, academics, and lawyers speculating about the motives behind the 2012 crackdown. These stories were often told and discussed informally in settings such as during conference breaks or over meals, and also in confidential circumstances for the most part (cf. Humphrey 2003: 177). These conversations were an attempt to unravel the mystery of the crackdown by, for example, comparing it to the previous crackdowns and looking for what these targeted NGOs have in common or how they differ from other labor NGOs. Those targeted included both rights-based and service-oriented NGOs, and they had all received foreign funding with or without the mediation of Hong Kong NGOs. Therefore, the common assumption that rights-based NGOs were the easiest target was almost immediately disregarded. But why did the crackdown take place and why did it only target labor NGOs in Shenzhen?

Personal power politics

During a capacity building workshop in Shenzhen in the spring of 2013, some labor NGO leaders and staff members gathered to share their experience with promoting workers' awareness of their employment rights. I went with one of the labor NGO directors as a staff member of his organization. In the wake of the crackdown, a feeling of watchfulness and demoralization was palpable at the workshop. On arrival at the workshop, some labor NGO workers were bantering with one another for having the courage to come to the workshop. One labor NGO director made a self-deprecating and sarcastic comment and said, "they may as well come and take me away so I don't have to use my own savings to pay the rent for the office." At lunch, I was sitting next to the labor NGO director that I worked with. We were at a table with eight people from Guangzhou, Shenzhen, and Hong Kong. A labor NGO leader based in Guangzhou was having a conversation with my NGO director, but his voice was high enough for everyone around the table to hear it if they wanted to. Reflecting on the crackdown, he said,

> There was an issue between Wang Yang and the Shenzhen Party Secretary. It was some personal power politics [*geren zhenzhi douzheng*], I heard. The Shenzhen Party Secretary was trying to make Wang Yang look bad at the 18th Party Congress.

Stories about the power struggle between Wang Yang and Wang Rong were reported in the media, so it was known to the public.[12] Wang Yang has served as one of the four vice premiers of China since January 2013. Before that, he served as the communist party secretary of Guangdong Province. In the 18th National Congress of the Chinese Communist Party in 2012, Wang Yang was officially given a seat on the Politburo of the Communist Party of China. Wang Yang has been viewed as one of the

leading reformers in China's leadership. During his time as the party secretary of Guangdong Province, Wang Yang had laid emphasis on private
enterprise, economic growth, and a greater role for civil society in establishing a stable society, which is widely known as the Guangdong model
of development. "Wang Yang's political career was going very well and it
made Wang Rong [Shenzhen party secretary] jealous. He wanted to cause
some trouble to make the Guangdong model not look as good," explained
the NGO leader. A project manager of a labor NGO in Hong Kong was
sitting next to me. I had met her once so I was not a complete stranger to
her and she was aware of my project and what I wanted to study. She didn't
think that personal power politics lies behind the crackdown. Instead of
openly disagreeing to the Guangzhou-based labor NGO director, she explained to me quietly,

> The crackdown lasted for ten months. To launch such a crackdown,
> they need to collect information on the targeted NGOs and then set up
> a timetable on when is the best time to attack which NGO. I have dif-
> ficulty believing that this was just some political struggle between two
> politicians. It requires detailed planning.

It is not clear to me why she chose to only express her viewpoint to me at the
time. But my speculation is that she wanted to avoid any open discussion
about such a sensitive topic in a restaurant, even though it was with a group
of labor NGOs that her organization had been working with.

Carrot and stick

Later during a tea break after a session of discussing leadership and team
work, another theory on the motive behind the crackdown was revealed to
me. One Shenzhen-based labor NGO director said, "I heard that the government has chosen Shenzhen and Guangzhou as two 'experimental points'
(*shidian*) (Heilmann 2011: 62–101). Shenzhen is the stick while Guangzhou is
the carrot." By that, this NGO director meant that the labor NGOs in Shenzhen were being punished for being "too aggressive" (*guoji*) and "there were
too many [labor NGOs]" whereas those in Guangzhou were spared from the
crackdown and allowed to continue operating because they knew how to
keep a low profile. He continued,

> The experiment is not over yet. They [the authorities] need to do an eval-
> uation of the test. There are two purposes of this test. One is to decrease
> [the labor NGOs'] capacity for resistance, and the other is to make them
> change, transform so they will function more as social service provid-
> ers. They want to cut off [the labor NGOs'] overseas connections so they
> must get funding from the government. If their funding all comes from
> the government, it will be easier to control [them].

The NGO director I was working with came to join the conversation. He didn't dismiss this theory and seemed to believe that there is no future for labor NGOs because he said,

> They [the government] really just want to eliminate [the labor NGOs]. They have invested so much money in creating those social work service centers. Two million RMB per street![13] But it is not easy to apply for government money. You have to register first!

Both of them were critical of the newly relaxed registration policy because it just created more red tape. These two NGOs have tried to apply for a legal registration of their organizations but failed. For them, even if the NGO follows through the red tape process, there is still no guarantee that the organization will be granted a legal permit. I will discuss the issue of registration in more detail later.

The Shenzhen-based labor NGO leader shook his head to indicate that it was really a tough time to run a labor NGO. Sneering at the difficult situation, he told that he also heard from his friends working in the media in Beijing that the government simply wanted to see how much support the labor NGOs have actually gained from the workers after all these years. "Not much, as you can see. Little Grass got 100 signatures from their workers. Did you see any workers coming out to support the NGOs? No," said the NGO leader with a measure of cynicism.

All China Federation of Trade Union losing face

A few months later after the workshop in Shenzhen, I went to Hong Kong to interview some NGOs there. As it turned out, the carrot and stick theory was also discussed in Hong Kong, but the focus was shifted to the official trade union: the All China Federation of Trade Union (ACFTU). In Hong Kong, the crackdown was particularly alarming for the labor groups that have partnerships with the labor NGOs in mainland China. One Hong Kong labor organization believed that this crackdown was a result of long-standing tensions between the ACFTU and the labor NGOs. "The Shenzhen ACFTU was really looking bad because of all the work these labor NGOs had started doing [and] because they are competitors to some extent. When they work to protect workers, it makes the local ACFTU look bad. Locally, the ACFTU is part of the *weiwen* committee and someone from that committee was in charge of the crackdown. You know, they [the ACFTU in Guangdong] announced the Federation of Social Service Organizations for Guangdong Workers within the same week or month [as the crackdown happened], I am not sure.[14] So they were saying that they were trying to get some groups closer to the fold and close down others. Basically, it is a carrot and stick approach. It is possible but the only issue is that action was taken by the ACFTU of Guangdong and I have never seen evidence that the ACFTU of Guangdong was involved in the crackdown in Shenzhen. It's different people," said the project coordinator of a Hong Kong-based NGO. By "evidence," this project coordinator was referring to the media reports and the information he acquired from his partner NGO in Shenzhen, which was one of the targeted NGOs.

He noted, "You know, Chen Weiguang and Liu Xiaogang are in Guangzhou. As far as I know they are not aware of the day-to-day details of the crackdown on Shenzhen groups."[15] Chen Weiguang was the chairman of the ACFTU Guangzhou Municipal Trade Union from 1993 to 2013, while Liu Xiaogang was the vice chairman of the ACFTU Guangzhou Municipal Trade Union from 2007 to 2013. The project coordinator continued,

> In either case, it sounds fairly reasonable to me. But we don't know any of this for sure. That's the honest answer. All we have is a few competing theories. I was once in a room with a representative from a foreign trade union and their partners, which were practically all of the Hong Kong labor groups. They were there to talk about their experiences with the crackdown. It was clear that it was a coordinated attack, not a random personal attack. So we know that, but we don't know what caused it.

Among the labor activists, both in mainland China and Hong Kong, the most common theories about the motive behind the 2012 crackdown go from personal power politics, carrot and stick, to ACFTU losing face. No one knows for sure what caused the crackdown, but many people certainly have an opinion about it. While trying to decipher the motives behind the crackdown, these labor activists were also telling stories about how they understood the crackdown. There is usually an "evaluative component" in a story, which indicates why the story is important to tell (Labov & Waletzky 1966: 33–39). The evaluative component "reveals the attitude of the narrator towards the narrative" (ibid.: 37). Storytellers rarely say explicitly to their audience what the moral of the story they are telling is; "[r]ather, the story's larger meaning seems to arise from the events themselves" (Polletta 2006: 10). This is because "it is through the structure of a story that we tame time, map space, and understand character and motive" (Khalili 2007: 226). Viewed as such, storytelling is an instrument of contention whereby we make excuses, give explanations, mobilize, and are moved to take action or not take action (ibid.). The different theories about the motive of the 2012 crackdown in Shenzhen described above are all plausible explanations, but the more interesting point is how these labor activists try to draw meaning from this political event. A significant point is that none of the explanations criticized the political system, which, according to Stern and Hassid, is one of the most notable political consequences of control parables: They shift the blame away from the existing political system (Stern & Hassid 2012: 1243). Research on NGOs in China has shown that activists who rarely run into trouble with the authorities tend to see those who do as having done something wrong to upset the authorities (Hildebrandt 2013: 5).

During one of my conversations about the 2012 crackdown, one labor NGO director criticized the behavior of Little Grass as "putting on a show" when they refused to move. "They want you to move so you move. Why cause trouble and make it difficult for all of us?" he said. The failure to blame the Chinese leadership indicates both a sense of powerlessness and general acceptance of the status quo by the labor community, which poses challenges for imagining and bringing about radical change. A project manager in a Hong Kong labor NGO, which has partnerships with a few labor NGOs in South China, noted that there is a deep sense of uncertainty and insecurity experienced by the NGOs operating in mainland China; however,

> having to continuously deal with the political uncertainty has also made the circumstances fairly stable for the NGOs. We still continue to do our work and we have been allowed to do it for a long time. So ironically, our work has been quite stable—outreach, legal consultation, etc. So workwise, there has not been much of a sense of crisis. The worst-case scenario is that the government comes to ask you to move. Then you move to a new place and resume your work. This has been the case, including the recent crackdown.

Her words keenly point out a poignant paradox where the uncertainty about state tolerance has induced the labor NGOs to create a coping mechanism largely based on their own lived experiences in order to manage such uncertainty. Paradoxically, this long-term uncertainty becomes predictable and even reproductive in inducing compliance and maintaining order. As an illustration of self-censorship, being attentive to what is said and not said or who is blamed or not blamed in the commentaries and explanations of the crackdown in 2012 sheds light on the degree to which the powerful have "successfully inserted themselves and their interests into the processes by which the weak understand themselves, their goals, their possibilities, and their constraints" (Stokes 1991: 270).

The registration

As mentioned earlier, the 2012 crackdown took place at a time when the Guangdong Provincial Government introduced more liberal and labor-friendly policies. In this section, I want to show how the unclear implementation of the policies, especially the one concerning the registration of social organizations, has mobilized the labor NGOs to employ *guanxi* practices to navigate through the opaque bureaucratic procedures of registration and devise survival tactics to negotiate the uncertain political climate.

Two important policies related to social organizations include reducing restrictions on registration and social service outsourcing,[16] both of which were actively pursued by Wang Yang, Guangdong's Communist Party Chief at the time, and had support from the Ministry of Civil Affairs. One significant change with regard to the issue of registration is the abolition of the dual registration requirement for social organizations, which allows social organizations to register without having a government sponsor. The range of organizations that are able to avail themselves of the new rules include industry associations, chambers of commerce with cross-border affiliates in Hong Kong and Macau, organizations performing public service or charitable and community services, and organizations in the fields of economics, science and technology, sports, and culture.[17] This new registration policy had, in fact, already been encouraged by the Guangzhou city government from the beginning of 2012 and was later extended to the whole of Guangdong Province from July 1, 2012, when the labor community was still shaken by the crackdown on labor NGOs in Shenzhen. On the one hand, many labor NGOs chose to distance themselves from the state by laying low in the wake of the crackdown; on the other hand, some labor NGOs tried to engage with the state by attempting to avail themselves of the new registration rules in hopes that once registered, they would be spared from government harassment. The new registration policy has removed government sponsorship, one of the biggest obstacles to registering for social organizations, but its implementation on the ground still generates a lot of ambiguity, frustration, and confusion among the labor NGOs.

Chen Yanhua is the director of Shenzhen-based labor NGO Heart to Heart Workers' Center (hereafter Heart to Heart). Heart to Heart was one of the labor NGOs that fell victim to the government crackdown in 2012. Since the crackdown, Chen Yanhua had been very busy finding a new office location. When I met with her early in March 2013, we were sitting at a local McDonald's in Shenzhen. Chen Yanhua told me that Heart to Heart had been trying to register but it wasn't going well. "There is always a problem when we submit our application," said Chen Yanhua.

> In the beginning, they [the Bureau of Civil Affairs] disapproved of our name so we were rejected right from the onset. Recently they have started to look really carefully into what kind of services we want to provide. They keep talking about the level of professionalism of our staff. They said we need to have professionals with the corresponding expertise as our supervisors. I asked them who I should look for. They said they don't specify nor designate. It's up to us. They keep emphasizing that the qualifications of our staff have to show that they are capable of providing the kind of services we want to provide.

Heart to Heart wants to provide free legal consultation, promote occupational safety, provide reproductive health education for female workers, and provide psychological support for workers with work-related injuries.

According to the Bureau of Civil Affairs, Heart to Heart had to have qualified experts in each of the fields. Chen Yanhua explained,

> We asked them what kind of experts but they didn't respond to our questions and just said it's up to us to decide. We tried to make changes according to their comments. We ended up taking away those specific descriptions of what we do. We even looked at the mission statements of some of the registered social work centers and tried to learn their language but it is very general and broad. They write things like "to help migrant workers better integrate into the city" but don't say exactly how they will do it. So we revised our description and made it less specific and more general and submitted the application again. But they criticized us for being too vague, not specific enough, and unable to prove if it's feasible. I don't know what to do. It feels that they were just making it difficult for us. If we were to follow their requirements, we may as well just disband the organization because none of us have the specialized qualifications required by the authorities and we do not have the money to hire lawyers and doctors.[18]

Chen Yanhua's frustration was shared by another Shenzhen-based labor NGO that tried to register. While participating in an outreach activity, the NGO's director told me that the Bureau of Civil Affairs insisted that "we find people with legal expertise to support the quality of the services we intend to provide. Then they gave us a pile of documents and asked us to go home and study them carefully." The documents contained the general guidelines on how to apply for registration. Soon after the new registration policy came into effect in July 2012, the All China Women's Federation organized a workshop in which several labor NGOs and officials from the Bureau of Civil Affairs in Guangzhou were brought together to share and ask questions about the registration rules and specific procedures. One official from the Bureau of Civil Affairs said bluntly to the director of the labor NGO where I was doing fieldwork at the time, "You don't have to try to register. You won't succeed because you help workers defend their rights (*yinwei ni zuo weiquan*). That's just not possible now." After the workshop, the director of the labor NGO was demoralized and said to me, "[The policy change] makes no difference for us really. It looks like the government has relaxed its control of social organizations but there are still hidden rules (*qianguize*) and it is those that really matter."

The mentioning of hidden rules reveals that for an authoritarian state, deployments of legibility such as legal regulations and strictures often signify a move away from overt repression. Although the new registration rules are more relaxed and seem to facilitate more operational space for labor NGOs, they may have concomitantly strengthened the Chinese state's interest in and capacity for holding onto power (Gallagher 2007 [2005]: 101). These labor NGOs' experiences show that even though the wider policy environment seems to have relaxed, the administrative authorities can still exert discretionary power over the process and procedures of registration, which can make it very difficult for these NGOs to register in practice. This also leads to some sense of confusion and uncertainty about the real intention and direction of government policy. Nevertheless, a few labor NGOs did succeed in registering. In the text that follows, using the example of a labor NGO where I conducted fieldwork, I will discuss how one of the key hidden rules of registering successfully is to have the right connections or *guanxi* acquired and mobilized at the right time, which also illustrates a temporal embodiment of state control. I treat *guanxi* as a practice that emerges from the domain of uncertainty and that is employed to navigate through the uncertainty of state limits of permitted activism. I will also discuss how the legally ambiguous status of an unregistered labor NGO has led to some creative tactics through which a collusion of the labor NGO and the state is crystallized.

Blue Sky Social Work Service Center

Located on the ninth floor of a commercial building in central Anhui District, Wuhua City in Guangdong Province, Blue Sky Social Work Service Center (hereafter Blue Sky) started out as a branch office of Green Grass Workers' Service Center between 2007 and 2012. Blue Sky left Green Grass and became an independent labor NGO in the spring of 2012. The main focus of Blue Sky's work is to help injured workers to defend their rights and claim financial compensation from their employers. As noted, it is through hospital visits that Blue Sky comes into contact with injured workers and distributes copies of their own legal booklet. This booklet contains a brief introduction of the organization and information on labor laws, labor contract law, social security law, and the procedures for claiming financial compensation when work-related injuries occur. According to Blue Sky, since 2007 the organization has visited a total of 19 hospitals in Wuhua and has helped 10,000 injured migrant workers to successfully claim financial compensation from their employers.

In addition to the hospital visits, Blue Sky also organizes legal training workshops once a month in which migrant workers can come to share their experiences and consult with legal experts free of charge. This training workshop also offers an opportunity for Blue Sky to recruit potential volunteers, which play an essential role in the day-to-day operation of the organization considering the limited financial resources of the NGO. Since 2007, Blue Sky has collaborated with the Department of Law at Sun Yat-sen University[19] in Guangzhou, which runs a legal clinic offering free services to migrant workers. Every weekend, law students go to the office in Anhui District and write legal documents for the migrant workers. The collaboration with educational institutions is desired by many labor NGOs, as it can lead to more human resources and sometimes funding opportunities through working with researchers. In addition to providing legal help, Blue Sky also uses theater as a means to empower migrant workers and raise awareness of their plight. With the assistance of the university, Blue Sky puts on a theater performance every year where injured migrant workers tell and act out their own stories in front of students at the university.

On entering the office of Blue Sky in Anhui District, one is immediately greeted on the left by a wall full of red banners trimmed in gold. These banners contain words of gratitude from the migrant workers who have received help from Blue Sky. Underneath the red banners are some newspaper clippings showing how Blue Sky has assisted the workers in their long battle of claiming what they are legally entitled to. The wall next to the front door is covered with group pictures of the outdoor activities that Blue Sky has organized for the workers. Right under these pictures are numerous sticky notes indicating the time of the next meeting, workshop, and hospital visits. Next to these reminders hangs a folder containing tables documenting the number of visitors to the organization and phone calls as well as the number of media reports in the last month. Underneath the wall lies two long rows of paper boxes filled with copies of the booklet about the organization and the law.

In the back of the office, there are two bookshelves with glass doors, which store different kinds of documents such as the records of the workers that have visited the organization, legal documents of court cases, and journals of volunteers. In addition to these documents, there are three rows of books, most of which are stories about the difficult lives of migrant workers living in cities. Above these bookshelves is a framed registration certificate that shows that Blue Sky has been officially registered as a civil non-enterprise institution since April 2012. When I asked Wei Peng, director of Blue Sky, about how he succeeded in applying for registration, he shook his head and said laughingly,

> I have no idea. I guess I was just lucky. It is through the help of many people that I got to register successfully. But there are two people that I am most indebted to: Professor Liu in the Department of Law at Sun Yat-sen University and social worker Li Jun.

Mobilizing relationships at the right time

Li Jun is a social worker and the deputy head of the government-supported NGO Incubator Center (*fuhua zhongxin*) in the Hengbao District of Wuhua City. Through Professor Liu, who helps Wei Peng run the legal clinic, she came to learn about Blue Sky at a performance by and about migrant workers at Sun Yat-sen University in 2011. As it turned out, Professor Liu and Li Jun have known each other for decades. After the performance, Professor Liu introduced Li Jun to Wei Peng making a joke about broadening Wei Peng's professional network. When recounting his first meeting with Li Jun, Wei Peng told me that he never enjoyed meeting people from the government and he did his best to avoid them if he could. But he was pleasantly surprised by how accessible and sincere Li Jun was.

> She [Li Jun] told me that she was really impressed with the performance and deeply sympathetic to the difficulty that many migrant workers face. She said that she admires people who are on the front line providing services for this vulnerable group.

Later over a dinner hosted by Professor Liu, Li Jun revealed to Wei Peng that there was a funding opportunity from the local government in Hengbao District, as the government was looking for an experienced organization to design and carry out a migrant worker-oriented project.

This was one of the government-funded projects in which the government relied on non-state organizations to deliver services, a practice that is generally associated with global processes of neoliberalization and has become more and more common in recent years in China. As mentioned earlier, another important policy change concerning social organizations introduced by the Guangdong Provincial Government is social service outsourcing. Some labor activists point out that this policy has become a governing tool whereby the government wants to control and manage the increasing numbers of social organizations in China.[20] The Beijing government has made improving social management innovation a focal point of its 12th Five Year Plan (2011–2015). By social management innovation, it refers to the Party-state's as well as the local governments' ability to manage and coordinate with a range of civil society organizations and other non-state actors in addressing the country's many pressing social problems. As such, the central government calls for collaboration between the state and civil society organizations to address common goals. The NGO Incubator Center in Wuhua's Hengbao District is an example of such a collaboration. Hengbao, an area that is largely inhabited by migrant workers, has been given a great amount of money to help establish social organizations, especially in the form of social work centers that cater to the social needs of migrant workers.

Wei Peng admitted that he was not as enthusiastic as Professor Liu and Li Jin when they encouraged him to apply for the government-funded project. He explained, "I didn't think I would have a chance as my organization was registered as a private company. If you want government-funded projects, you need to be registered as a *minfei* (civil non-enterprise institution)." Nevertheless, Li Jun was very persistent and asked Wei Peng to write a project proposal that targeted the community of migrant workers, the kind of work that Wei Peng has been doing in the last six years. What Wei Peng didn't realize at the time was that Li Jun was pulling a lot of strings for him so the NGO Incubator Center had already decided to give him the project even before his organization became legal.

As soon as Wei Peng got the government-funded project, he proceeded to prepare for registration. He explained that the government funds only go to a bank account that belongs to a legally registered *minfei* so he had to register as one to receive the funding. When he went to the Bureau of Civil Affairs to inquire about how to register, a woman told him that he should try to register as a social work center because "it has the best chance of success now. So I did," said Wei Peng. He explained to me that to register as a social work center, at least one-third of the organization's staff has to be licensed social workers, one of whom has to be on the organization's board. Li Jun agreed to put her name on the list and helped Wei Peng to get a presentable list of staff to make the application look good. "The Bureau of Civil Affairs knew at the time that I had already gotten the government project so it wasn't just that it increased my chance [of registering successfully], it's that they would almost have to let me register—otherwise there would be problems between these departments," explained Wei Peng. Since April 2012, Blue Sky has become a legally registered civil non-enterprise organization.

Reflecting on his experience of registration, Wei Peng saw it as a combination of luck, personal relations, and good timing, and stressed that

> having the right *guanxi* and meeting the right person at the right time is so important. If it were not for Professor Liu, I would not have met Li Jun; if it were not for Li Jun who was well-connected with the local authorities, I would not have succeeded in registering because I know it is impossible for any rights-based organization to register.

Later, when I got a chance to talk with Li Jun, she shook her head and said, "You have no idea how many meals I had [with the people at the NGO Incubator Center in Hengbao District] before Wei Peng got the project." But Li Jun also emphasized that she had to repeatedly remind Wei Peng not to associate the government project with any work on rights defense. With "good timing," Wei Peng referred to the broader political environment in which there is a concerted effort from the government to encourage social organizations to take over some services. In other words, Wei Peng's organization succeeded in registering because it fits the interests of the local government (Hildebrandt 2011: 981). The successful registration of Wei Peng's organization illustrates the other side of uncertainty that labor NGOs have to negotiate, that is, the uncertain parameters of state policy and how they change, which sometimes leads to ad hoc implementation of policies and make inroads into rational-legal objective domination (Yang 2002: 471). With the creation of incubator centers, the state improvises opportunistically in its policy making and production of institutions. More pertinently, it also shows how the interest of the state colludes with the NGO's interest and need to survive.

For Wei Peng, the government funds couldn't have come at a better timing when he was the crossroads pondering which way to take next largely because of financial difficulties in and political risk of running the NGO. In my conversations with Wei Peng, he had repeatedly told me how grateful he was to Professor Liu, whom he has known for years and who has been a great support for his organization. Wei Peng often said that he was indebted to Professor Liu, or owed Professor Liu *renqing* (human sentiments, feelings) while he talked about his work with Li Jun as cultivating *guanxi* with the government. In common usage, *guanxi*, broadly understood as a cultural institution of reciprocity and trust, refers to webs of social relations through which an individual can achieve various ends (Jacobs 1979; Walder 1986; Oi 1989; Yang 1994; Yan 1996; Kipnis 1997; Osburg 2013). In earlier Western scholarly accounts, *guanxi* is often defined and characterized by instrumentality and individual manipulation, and thus carries a negative connotation (Gold 1985). More recent studies have challenged this view, pointing out that *guanxi* consists of relationships with a mixture of interest, feelings (*renqing*), and morality (Yang 1994; Kipnis 1997; Osburg 2013). *Renqing*, a word used by Wei Peng to describe his relationship with Professor Liu, is a particularly multifaceted term that its literal meaning can be translated as human sentiments, but, in practice, it can refer both to "affective relationships between kin, friends, and colleagues and 'the norms and values that regulate interpersonal relationships' (Yan 2009: xxxiv)" (Osburg 2013: 23).

While the instrumental, affective, and moral dimensions of *guanxi* and their interrelations have received increasing attention from social scientists, the normative discussion of the logic of *guanxi*, often understood as a traditional form of gift economy, tends to call into question the compatibility between *guanxi* and market economy as well as the rule of law. Such a perspective situates *guanxi* practices in the questionable divide between the traditional/rural, where *renqing* and sentiments play a larger role in *guanxi*, and the modern/urban, where *guanxi* is more prominently characterized by individual and instrumental calculations (Osburg 2013: 24). Mayfair Mei Hui Yang has challenged this divide by adopting the perspective of *guanxixue* (关系学)—the art of social relations—to argue that *guanxi*, understood as "dyadic relationships that are based implicitly (rather than explicitly) on mutual interest and benefit" (1994: 1) entailing both instrumental benefit and personalistic obligation, forms the rhizomatic warp and woof of Chinese social life (Yang 1994: 308) where webs of personal relationships crisscross and overlie one another.

Focusing on the network of affective ties, Yang holds that *guanxi* practices, which can be employed to negotiate through a maze of bureaucratic obstacles, constitute a realm that is subversive to the normative hegemony of the socialist state. Yang's work shifts the focus from discussions of civil society, which are often dominated by the clear distinction between state and society, toward social relations and takes into account the blurry interpenetration of the state and society in the Chinese context. She shows how a social realm, long realized in social practice, is manifesting in a more institutional form under changing social and economic conditions. In a similar vein, in her study of the consequences of how neoliberal development projects try to offer ordinary people the tools of enterprise as the way to a good life and empowerment, Julia Elyachar argues that projects to empower women via finance were not predominantly about changing women's lives but that "specific outcomes of women's social practices were empowered" (Elyachar 2010: 453). According to Elyachar, the development project of financial empowerment has made certain existing practices of sociality such as gossip and visiting and chatting with neighbors visible as "a social infrastructure on which other projects oriented around the pursuit of profit could be constructed" (ibid.).

Nevertheless, Yang's and Elyachar's focus on affective relationships fails to illuminate the specific nature and processes in which institutions have come into existence and interact with the state. Not only does Wei Peng's registration process illustrate the explanatory insufficiency of such a focus, but it also shows how different kinds of relationship practices converge and are viewed differently. Not all relationships are considered *guanxi*, but one can basically cultivate *guanxi* in any social interaction. Wei Peng viewed his work with Li Jun as building *guanxi* with the local government, an aspect of his social network that he found particularly weak. Both Professor Liu and Li Jun, according to Wei Peng, were a critical node in this new relationship-building. When it comes to his relationship to Professor Liu, however, Wei Peng used *renqing* instead of *guanxi* mainly because of the affective element in their relationship which includes their shared values. As Wei Peng explained himself,

> I have known Professor Liu for a long time. I respect his expertise and advice. He has been very supportive of the NGO and our work so it feels we are in the same community all along. He has mobilized his connections and resources to help us in many ways over the years and only wanted us to do good for the workers. I don't have to worry about giving him something in return when I accept his help or support. All I need to do is to keep doing what I am already doing [serving the labor community].

As for the relationship with Li Jun and her incubator center, Wei Peng clearly sees it as an instrument to establish *guanxi* with the authorities. Li Jun becomes a sort of "lubricant" for the bureaucracy's operation, as Wei Peng described it. For Li Jun, Wei Peng's NGO is a "partner" to the state: "We [the government] need partners like this to better serve the community. It is a collaboration," noted Li Jun when asked to comment on her relationship with Wei Peng's NGO. Through the government-funded project, her relationship with Wei Peng's NGO is very much characterized by a patron and client relationship that is contractual. Both get something out this arrangement. As much as Li Jun described her role in Wei Peng's registration process as "helping" and "collaborating with" the organization, it is undeniable that Li Jun was very much acting on her own initiative in establishing her own credentials as head of a new institution that manages state-labor NGO relations. As described in Chapter 2, one consequence of the shift to social management policy with the principle of jurisdictional management is that local bureaucrats are evaluated by how well they perform their job to maintain social order. Li Jun mobilized her *guanxi* (Professor Liu and work colleagues) to do well on her job.

The story of Wei Peng's registration process shows that *guanxi* practices have adapted to new conditions where the Chinese developmental state exercises power by strategically utilizing and mapping itself onto global capitalist neoliberal orders and discourses legitimated through an explicit appeal to a vibrant civil society marked by the rule of law, transparency, and good governance. The successful registration of Wei Peng's NGO complicates the neat division between the state and civil society, and demonstrates how different relationship practices play an even more important role in China's transformation from a planned economy to a more market-based one, as well as its importance in China's pursuit of legal reforms. It illustrates an ongoing state-formation process in which state-like practices and "state effects" are embodied and manifested in a labor NGO (Trouillot 2003: 91). Nevertheless, having obtained legal status as a *minfei* does not assuage the uncertainty that Wei Peng feels about his work with migrant workers. In the text that follows, I will discuss how he tried to ascertain the limits of state-permitted activism and manage his partnership with the Hong Kong labor NGO and foreign donors while moving between projects involving social service provision and rights defense.

One bank account, two offices

With the government-funded project, Wei Peng set up another office in Hengbao devoted to providing social services for migrant workers. Situated in one of the urban village enclaves, this government-funded office is on the ground floor of a five-floor residential building. Wei Peng told me that it is important that this office is on the ground floor so that "the workers can see from the outside what we are doing. They will be less afraid or skeptical of coming in." Services offered in the Hengbao-based office include distributing information on occupational hazards, reproductive health, and employment opportunities; visiting disadvantaged families in the community; and organizing cultural and social activities, as well as organizing art classes and activities for the children of migrant workers. This project has a special focus on catering to the needs of the children of migrant workers. As such, half of the office is converted into a library and a playroom. The idea is that the children living in the neighborhood can come and spend time there while their parents are at work. This office is usually referred to as "the library" by the Blue Sky staff. There are no red banners from the workers, nor are there media reports about how Blue Sky helped the workers defend their rights. The office is decorated with bright colors like yellow, blue, and green to make it more appealing to children. At the reception, there are some booklets with information on how to live in the city and leaflets about how to look for employment. The booklets on labor contract law are nowhere to be seen.

Wei Peng makes a clear distinction between the two offices. The office in Hengbao District or "the library" is almost always talked about as the place where he "deals with the government" (*yu zhengfu dajiaodao*), whereas the office in Anhui District is described as the place where he "does the real work for workers" (*zuo gongren de gongzuo*). In contrast to the office in Hengbao District, the office based in Anhui District deals with "more sensitive (*mingan*) things," noted Wei Peng. The notion of *mingan* will be addressed in detail in Chapter 4. By "*mingan* things," Wei Peng was referring to the legal education and aid that his organization provides. "We do rights defense here. We help injured workers bring their cases to court so they can get financial compensation from their employers. We encourage the workers to bring their disputes to court instead of settling in private. By going through the legal procedures, not only do the workers learn about the law but also about how to deal with the authorities. We assist the workers but we do not do all the work for them," explained Wei Peng when we were sitting in the Anhui-based office. The office in Anhui District is funded by a German foundation with a Hong Kong labor NGO as an intermediary that administers the funds and oversees the implementation of the project.

During my fieldwork, one constant topic of discussion with my interlocutors was their relationship with the government. If an NGO was closed down, one of the typical explanations and interpretations that other labor activists gave was that this NGO "offended" or "displeased" (*dezui*) someone in the government and "ruined *guanxi*" (*gao huai guanxi*) with the government. If an NGO was spared from a crackdown, common speculation from other labor NGOs would be that this NGO had a good relationship or *guanxi* with the government (*gen zhengfu guanxi bucuo*) (ibid.). These comments indicate that managing the relationship with the government is not only necessary but also an intricate balancing act. Many labor NGOs do not want to be viewed as having too good of a relationship with the government, as they may run the risk of being seen as being coopted and thus jeopardize their relationships with other labor NGOs, especially those in Hong Kong and their opportunities to receive foreign funding. Nevertheless, having a good relationship with the government is often crucial to the survival and operation of labor NGOs, especially when the boundaries of permitted labor activism are unclear. That Wei Peng deliberately differentiates his two offices is his way of negotiating the complex political and economic conditions under which labor NGOs operate. Moreover, having described one of his offices as the place where he does the real work for workers, Wei Peng suggests that dealing with the government is not the same as doing real work for workers. With this distinction, he implicitly criticizes the government for its lack of concern and efforts to address the real needs of workers, which are often regarded as "*mingan* things" by the government. Wei Peng's tactical differentiation of the two offices can also be viewed as an act of complicity and collusion: He grudgingly accedes to the government's inaction and takes matters into his own hands, which, in turn, carves out a space for his NGO to operate.

Wei Peng told me that the office in Anhui District was registered as a private company, but he canceled the registration as soon as he successfully registered as Blue Sky. He explained,

> The tax [for private enterprises] is too high. Besides, since the registration, I have started to use two different titles when I am dealing with the outside world [*gen waijie dajiaodao*]. One is Blue Sky, the other is Wei Peng's Workshop [*gongzuoshi*]. If it's about something positive, I will ask the media to use the name of Blue Sky. If it's about something *mingan*, like rights defense, I will ask the media to use Wei Peng's Workshop instead. I think it's better this way. Take a look at the media reports [he pointed at the media reports on the wall]. If it is about rights defense, they rarely use the name of Blue Sky. I have communicated with the reporters. They all know about it.[21]

The reason why he makes such a distinction is that he hopes that the local government will not make trouble for him. It also shows that he took Li Jun's advice and distanced his rights-based work, "the real work for workers," from the government-funded project. "So far so good, they have not caused me any trouble," said Wei Peng. When I asked Wei Peng why he keeps the framed registration certificate in the Anhui-based office, he replied,

> To protect the office, I guess. The *lingdao* [superiors] change their policy whenever they want to. A different *lingdao* may have a new idea. Who knows if he will make trouble for you? They haven't made trouble for me but who knows if they will [make trouble for me] later? If something happens, I will take it down.

Not only do Wei Peng's words indicate his lack of trust in the government, but they also demonstrate his concern that the funding is not necessarily more certain and may be easily withdrawn at the whim of officials. Displaying the registration certificate at his unregistered office, Wei Peng uses the certificate as a talisman to mitigate the uncertain and ambiguous status of the Anhui-based office in hopes that he can continue doing the more *mingan* work funded by the German foundation without too much harassment from the local government. Wei Peng's concern about the uncertainty of the government funding is further illustrated by his effort to get the registration fee back.

Looking at the registration certificate, Wei Peng said to me,

> Do you know how much that certificate cost me? Thirty thousand RMB. I paid for it out of my own pocket! The people in Hong Kong wouldn't help me with it either. I couldn't get the money back even if I closed the library [the Hengbao-based office]. But I am trying to get it back from the government fund. I am doing their work anyway. Do you want to hear something funny? The local labor authorities refer the workers

to us. They should help and answer questions for the workers but they don't. They send the workers to our office. Isn't that ridiculous?[22]

Wei Peng said he knew that the workers were referred by the labor authorities because the workers told him adding jokingly that the labor authorities were giving him free publicity. Then Wei Peng paused for a few seconds and said to me in a lower voice,

> If you have any receipts, please give them to us. It's very difficult with the government money. They need receipts for everything. But it's getting more and more difficult to get receipts. Many shops don't like to give receipts because they don't want to pay taxes.

With the mentioning of receipts, I realized how Wei Peng was trying to get the registration fee back from the government funding, which is akin to hidden-transcript practices such as poaching, pilfering, clandestine tax evasion, tampering with land titles, or shabby work for landlords described by James Scott (1990: 14). Wei Peng's effort not only illustrates an example of survival tactics but also gives a glimpse of the moral universe of the NGO, which is often diverse and refracted, ranging from the common perception of NGOs doing good to the association with opportunism and corruption.

Before Blue Sky was registered as a *minfei*, the funds from the German foundation were wired by the Hong Kong intermediary to Wei Peng's personal bank account. This is a fairly common practice among the unregistered NGOs and NGOs registered as private companies. With the successful registration of Blue Sky as a *minfei*, Wei Peng's NGO now has an official bank account to receive the funding from the government. Wei Peng decided to have the funds from the German foundation wired to this official bank account as well in order to save on administrative costs. Wei Peng told me that since the registration, he has hired an accountant to do the bookkeeping for the government-funded project because "they [the government officials] are very picky. You need to make sure that the bookkeeping meets their requirements and they will not make trouble for us." Besides, he continued to complain about the extra cost of bookkeeping and said,

> The accountant charges by how many books they keep, so one unit of bookkeeping is 300 RMB per month. In order to save money, I have asked one of our volunteers to separate the funds first and give the accountant the receipts for the government project.

As for the German funding, Wei Peng said, "It's easy. It's always the people in Hong Kong that do the bookkeeping. I just give them the receipts."

Wei Peng's discussion of the registration and financial arrangement of his NGO exhibits the financial woes that many labor NGOs have to contend with and how they do their best to cut down on expenses just to make ends meet. Confronted with such financial difficulties, any opportunity to acquire funding is almost always welcome, even if the funding comes from the government. Wei Peng's deliberate distinction between the two offices, his tacit agreement with the media, the way he manages the organization's bank account, and his tampering with receipts are tactics of complicity that both elude and facilitate collusion with state power. These tactics illustrate how uncertainty constitutes and facilitates a way of thinking about and dealing with the state, which is characterized by a palpable sense of distrust and precarity. These tactics show how self-censorship is conceptualized and performed, and thus how the appropriate distance from the state is measured by the activists.

Conclusion

In this chapter, I discussed how uncertainty is played out and manifested in the daily work of the labor NGOs and their relationships with the Chinese state as well as their partners in Hong Kong. I used two examples to discuss how uncertainty is conducive to certain tactics that foster a mode of complicity in the labor community, which is in accordance with the Chinese state and thus sustains the political order of things. Instead of merely focusing on the NGOs' visceral experiences of suppression, I focused my analysis on their efforts to make sense of this particular incident of state violence in order to show how uncertainty regarding the state is productive to sustaining the existing political structure. By juxtaposing competing theories about the 2012 crackdown, I drew attention to the significance of storytelling and showed how the uncertainty about the motives behind the crackdown sheds some light on the ways in which the labor NGOs perceive and navigate through the unclear limits of state tolerance while largely accepting the status quo.

With the newly revised registration rule, I used the example of Heart to Heart to discuss the opaque implementation of the revised policy, which has generated confusion as well as frustration in the labor community. The NGOs' frustration about the revised registration rule is further highlighted by one labor NGO director's comment that the explicitly stated policy does not matter as much as the hidden rules, which can only be understood through hands-on experience. Drawing on the example of Blue Sky, I discussed how this legally registered NGO devised tactics to maneuver through the unclear boundaries of permissible activism while treading over the sensitive terrain of rights defense. Wei Peng's tactics illustrate how he tried to gauge an appropriate distance from the state by trying to move fluently between the different epistemological levels of engaging with and distancing himself from the state. In the next two chapters I further break down how such power works and explore the forms and practices of engagement that have taken place in the domain of uncertainty.

Notes

1 The strike started on May 17, 2010 when workers and interns at the Nanhai Honda Auto Parts Manufacturing Company in Foshan, Guangdong province, staged a walkout demanding a significant wage increase. Gradually, the strike had spread

to other Honda plants in the country and had paralyzed production of four plants in China. The strike lasted 19 days, and 1900 workers were estimated to have participated in the strike. The workers obtained the wage rise they demanded and were promised that they would be able to elect their own trade union committee.

2 My discussion and analysis of the crackdown in 2012 was published in my chapter "Thinking like a state: doing labor activism in South China." In *Handbook of protest and resistance* (2019), edited by Teresa Wright. Cheltenham, UK: Edward Elgar Publishing, pp. 151–165.

3 The names of the individuals mentioned in the discussion of the 2012 crackdown are all pseudonyms. When citing news reports as well as public support campaigns about the suppressed NGOs, I do not change the names of these NGOs and use the names as they appear in these public documents. This interview was conducted in January 2013.

4 Standaert, Michael. 2012. Labor NGOs face tough times in Guangdong; group alleges child labor, corruption in factory audits. *Bloomberg BNA*, August 16. Available at: www.workerempowerment.org/en/media-coverage/46 accessed on May 20, 2014.

5 From: www.workerempowerment.org/en/updates/36 accessed on April 24, 2015.

6 Unnamed author. 2012. Support Chinese Labor NGOs (聲援中國勞工維權組織). *Inmediahk*, December 12. Available at: www.inmediahk.net/node/1014958 accessed on April 23, 2015; unnamed author. 2012. Stop the crackdown on labor NGOs in China. *Talking Union*, October 17. Available at: https://talkingunion. wordpress.com/2012/10/17/stop-the-crackdown-on-labour-ngos-in-china/ accessed on April 24, 2015; unnamed author. 2012. China: stop the crackdown on labor NGOs. *Good electronics*, October 15. Available at: http://goodelectronics.org/ news-en/china-stop-the-crackdown-on-labour-ngos accessed on May 22, 2014.

7 Since this is an event that has been reported on in the media and circulated on Chinese social media, I use the real name of the labor NGO, shown in parenthesis, and provide an English translation. The story of how this labor NGO was unjustly and violently treated by the authorities was widely reported and circulated. See www.rfa.org/cantonese/news/ngo-08312012092248.html accessed April 20, 2013.

8 Unnamed author. 2012. Government crackdown on labor groups worsens in South China. *Public Radio International*, September 2. Available at: www. globalpost.com/dispatch/news/regions/asia-pacific/china/120831/south-china-labor-crackdown accessed on May 20, 2013. The video is no longer available on the Internet.

9 Little Grass posted a lot of information on their blog and website about how they were suppressed by the local authorities. http://bbs.tianya.cn/post-838-33197-1. shtml accessed on April 23, 2013.

10 In fact, the crackdown started in late 2011 but was not reported in the media until 2012. Dagongzhe Migrant Workers' Center is believed to be the first victim of the crackdown. The labor NGO posted a chronology of the government harassment on their blog (http://blog.sina.com.cn/s/blog_6b0ef6fc01013mlp.html accessed on May 22, 2014.) But the entry has been deleted later and is no longer available.

11 The discussion of how the labor NGOs and activists develop different theories about the crackdown was published in my chapter "Thinking like a state: doing labor activism in South China." In *Handbook of protest and resistance* (2019), edited by Teresa Wright. Cheltenham, UK: Edward Elgar Publishing, pp. 151–165.

12 Unnamed author. 2012. Shenzhen Party Secretary Wang Rong supports Jiang Party platform and attracts enmity from Wang Yang (深圳市委书记王荣为江派站台与汪洋结怨). *Epoch Times*, June 16. Available at: www.epochtimes.com/ gb/12/6/16/n3613795.htm accessed on June 25, 2014.

13 Guangdong has invested a lot of resources into its project to enhance the role of social organizations in building a harmonious society. One of the policy

objectives is to establish as many social service centers as possible. In Guangzhou, the goal is that each street will have one social service center with a budget of two million RMB to provide their services.

14 The Federation of Social Service Organizations for Guangdong Workers was announced and created on May 16, 2012 in Guangzhou. This Federation was initiated and is led by the ACFTU of Guangdong Province. It encourages worker-oriented individuals, research institutes, and social service organizations to join. According to the website of the ACFTU of Guangdong Province, the Federation currently consists of 34 organizations and 55 individual members. More information is available at www.gov.cn/gzdt/2012-05/17/content_2139311.htm accessed on June 3, 2014.

15 As I found out later, the director of this Hong Kong labor NGO had regular meetings with the officials from the Guangdong ACFTU.

16 From the Department of Civil Affairs of Guangdong Province. www.gdnpo.gov.cn/home/index/newsview/m8le3144483 accessed on February 28, 2016.

17 The regulation on social organizations has been updated since it was implemented in 2012. The link here is the updated version from 2015: www.gd.gov.cn/zwgk/zcfgk/content/post_2531906.html accessed on February 28, 2016.

18 This interview was conducted in April 2013.

19 The name of the university is authentic.

20 Unnamed author. 2012. Guangdong uses new policy to suppress dissident social organizations (广东借新政策打压异见社会组织). *Radio Free Asia*, August 20. Available at: www.rfa.org/cantonese/features/hottopic/feature_ngo-08202012120313.html accessed on February 28, 2016.

21 The interview was conducted in May 2013.

22 The interview was conducted in May 2013.

Bibliography

Chen, Feng, and Xuehui Yang. 2017. Movement-oriented labor NGOs in South China: exit with voice and displaced unionism. *China Information* 32 (2): 155–175.

Cohen, Benjamin. 1998. *The geography of money*. Ithaca, NY: Cornell University Press.

Elyachar, Julia. 2010. Phatic labor, infrastructure, and the question of empowerment in Cairo. *American Ethnologist* 37 (3): 452–464.

Gallagher, Mary E. 2007 [2005]. *Contagious capitalism: globalization and the politics of labor in China*. Princeton, NJ and Oxford: Princeton University Press.

Gold, Thomas B. 1985. After comradeship: personal relations in China since the Cultural Revolution. *The China Quarterly* 104: 657–675.

Heilmann, Sebastian. 2011. "Policy-making through experimentation: the formation of a distinctive policy process." In *Mao's invisible hand: the political foundations of adaptive governance in China*, edited by Sebastian Heilmann and Elizabeth J. Perry. Cambridge, MA: Harvard University Asia Center, pp. 62–101.

Herzfeld, Michael. 2016. *Cultural intimacy: social poetics and the real life of states, societies, and institutions*. New York: Routledge.

Hildebrandt, Timothy. 2013. *Social organizations and the authoritarian state in China*. Cambridge: Cambridge University Press.

——— 2011. The political economy of social organization registration in China. *The China Quarterly* 208: 970–989.

Humphrey, Caroline. 2003. "Stalin and the blue elephant: paranoia and complicity in post-communist metahistories." In *Transparency and conspiracy: ethnographies of suspicion in the new world order*, edited by Harry G. West and Todd Sanders. Durham, NC and London: Duke University Press.

Jacobs, Bruce J. 1979. A preliminary mode of particularistic ties in Chinese political alliances: kan-ch'ing and kuan-hsi in a rural Taiwanese township. *The China Quarterly* 78: 237–273.

Khalili, Laleh. 2007. *Heroes and martyrs of Palestine: the politics of national commemoration*. Cambridge: Cambridge University Press.

Kipnis, Andrew B. 1997. *Producing guanxi: sentiment, self, and subculture in a North China village*. Durham, NC and London: Duke University Press.

Labov, William, and Joshua Waletzky. 1966. "Narrative analysis: oral versions of personal experience." In *Essays on the verbal and visual arts: proceedings of the 1966 annual spring meeting of the American Ethnological Society*, edited by June Helm. Seattle, WA: American Ethnological Society.

Oi, Jean C. 1989. *State and peasant in contemporary China: the political economy of village government*. Berkeley: University of California Press.

Osburg, John. 2013. *Anxious wealth: money and morality among China's new rich*. Stanford: Stanford University Press.

Pan, Darcy. 2019. "Thinking like a state: doing labor activism in South China." In *Handbook of protest and resistance*, edited by Teresa Wright. Cheltenham, UK: Edward Elgar Publishing.

Polletta, Francesca. 2006. *It was like a fever: storytelling in protest and politics*. Chicago: University of Chicago Press.

Robin, Corey. 2004. *Fear: the history of a political idea*. Oxford: Oxford University Press.

Samimian-Darash, Limor, and Paul Rabinow. 2015. "Introduction." In *Modes of uncertainty: anthropological cases*, edited by Limor Samimian-Darash and Paul Rabinow. Chicago: University of Chicago Press.

Scott, James C. 1990. *Domination and the arts of resistance: hidden transcripts*. New Haven, CT: Yale University Press.

Stern, Rachel E., and Jonathan Hassid. 2012. Amplifying silence: uncertainty and control parables in contemporary China. *Comparative Political Studies* 45 (10): 1230–1254.

Stokes, Susan C. 1991. Hegemony, consciousness and political change in Peru. *Politics & Society* 19 (3): 265–290.

Trouillot, Michel-Rolph. 2003. *Global Transformations: anthropology and the modern world*. New York: Palgrave Macmillan.

Walder, Andrew G. 1986. *Communist neo-traditionalism: work and authority in Chinese industry*. Berkeley: University of California Press.

Yan, Yunxiang. 2009. *The individualization of Chinese society*. New York: Berg.

——— 1996. *The flow of gifts: reciprocity and social networks in a Chinese village*. Stanford: Stanford University Press.

Yang, Mayfair Mei-hui. 2002. The resilience of guanxi and its new deployments: a critique of some new guanxi scholarship. *The China Quarterly* 170: 459–476.

——— 1994. *Favors and banquets: the art of social relationships in China*. Ithaca, NY: Cornell University Press.

Zhang, Lu. 2019. "Worker protests and state response in present-day China: trends, characteristics, and new developments." In *Handbook of protest and resistance*, edited by Teresa Wright. Cheltenham, UK: Edward Elgar Publishing, pp. 119–136.

4   The politics of *mingan*

Mingan (敏感) is a term that permeated my fieldwork experience in China. During my interactions with members of the labor community—NGOs, funding agencies, trade union officials, and labor academics—they often mentioned *mingan* when talking about their work. In Chinese dictionaries and translation tools, the word *mingan* is often translated as "sensitive" or "susceptible" in English.[1] The Oxford Dictionary of English offers the following definition of "sensitive":

   Adjective:

1   quick to detect or respond to slight changes, signals, or influences;
2   having or displaying a quick and delicate appreciation of others' feelings;
3   kept secret or with restrictions on disclosure to avoid endangering security.

(Stevenson 2010: 1621)

In the context of my fieldwork *mingan* is invariably used, related to, and talked about in relation to the Chinese state and thus is often associated with issues such as security, surveillance, and censorship. *Mingan* is sometimes employed to describe a person who is sensitive enough to quickly pick up and respond to changes or signals which may be suggestive of political risks. It corresponds to the first meaning of the English word "sensitive." Another sense of *mingan* describes that which is so politically sensitive that it may entail risks and thus must be handled with caution and discretion. It can describe a person, an organization, an activity, a subject, a national identity (e.g., a foreign national as opposed to a Chinese national), a place, and timing. This sense of *mingan* is close to the third meaning of the English word "sensitive," a subject to be discussed in the next chapter where I specifically address the role of secrecy in the day-to-day work of the labor NGOs. As discussed in the previous chapter, central to the domain of uncertainty is the ambiguity of the limits of state tolerance toward labor activism. At the core of this ambiguity are the situational interpretations, applications, and sometimes seemingly arbitrary workings of the emic notion of *mingan*, which plays a key role for labor activists in gauging a less risky distance from the state.

In this chapter, I will show and discuss the ways in which the relationships and interactions between the labor NGOs, donors, and the Chinese state are enacted and structured around the idea of *mingan*. As such, in the domain of uncertainty *mingan* opens up a site of intimacy in which the relationships between the NGOs, the state, and donors are mediated through discursive and performative practices of self-presentation in relation to the larger systems of representation where certain ideal types of NGOs and activists have strong purchase in international development.

Situating *mingan*

After having spent nine months doing fieldwork in Guangdong Province, I moved to Hong Kong in the summer of 2013 to study the partnership between the Chinese labor NGOs and Hong Kong-based labor NGO Chinese Workers' Front (CWF). I continued to maintain contact with some of the labor NGO leaders in mainland China via mobile phone and social media. Chen Tong was one of them. One day I was talking to Chen Tong on the social networking website QQ while I was doing fieldwork in the office of CWF. He was telling me about recent developments in his organization, including his plans to start a new project in an industrial area. He mentioned that a program officer from a foreign foundation was going to visit a labor NGO in X District in a neighboring city and that he was also going to meet with the program officer to inquire about funding opportunities.

I am familiar with X District, having spent three months doing fieldwork with a labor NGO there. On hearing this, I asked Chen Tong whom the program officer was going to visit. Here is our conversation[2]:

ME: Who is he going to see?
CHEN: Who do you think he is going to visit?
ME: Yang Bo [I suggested a name].
CHEN: Female
ME: Oh?
CHEN: You are?
ME: I know who you mean [I was responding to his hint that it was a female labor NGO leader that the program officer was going to visit. I took Chen Tong's cue not to reveal too much information on QQ].
ME: So have you made an appointment with him [the program officer]?
CHEN: He gave me a call.
ME: Oh? That's good. So are you going to do your project in Y District or somewhere else?
CHEN: What? What project?

At this point, Chen Tong suddenly requested a video chat. Caught off guard, I didn't accept the request as I was sitting in the office of CWF and it was not appropriate for me to talk. I responded with a text message.

ME: I am in the office of CWF. I can't really talk right now!
CHEN: I know. But it just doesn't feel like you.
ME: Hehe
CHEN: Tell me the truth.

It was at this point that I realized that Chen Tong suspected that I was someone else and he was serious about it. In order to reassure him and regain his trust, I immediately asked him to call again.

ME: Okay. Why don't you call me again so you can see that it is really me.
But I won't make a sound as I need to be quiet here.

Chen Tong called again and saw that it was me.

CHEN: Okay. I see you now. Hehe. Sorry. I am a bit mingan.

Then he hung up and we resumed our online conversation via text.

This conversation succinctly brings the different senses of *mingan* into view. It shows how a labor NGO worker is constantly vigilant and becomes suspicious when he or she is unsure about certain information. It was not readily clear to me at that time why Chen Tong would question my identity. It was only after our conversation when I went back and read the chat history that I could see where his suspicion came from. It has to do with two pieces of information, or misinformation, I gave during our conversation. The first was my wrong guess of the person that the program officer from the foreign foundation was going to visit. There are a few labor NGOs in the city where X District is located. Chen Tong and I talked about this program officer at length when I was doing fieldwork in his office. He was telling me about his idea to do a project in an industrial area inhabited predominantly by migrant workers and to apply for funding from this foreign foundation. Chen Tong talked about how this program officer showed a specific preference for this X District-based labor NGO led by a female migrant worker, a fairly well-known figure in the labor community in South China. The fact that this female worker's name didn't come to my mind first gave Chen Tong a reason to doubt whom he was talking to on QQ. The second "blunder" I made was that I named the wrong site for Chen Tong's new project. It was a slip of the tongue. The place I mentioned is where Chen Tong's other project was located. But this innocent slip, together with the first one, was enough to make Chen Tong express his concern about my true identity and request a video chat. It was clear from this conversation that Chen Tong was sensitive to everything I said and used it as a way to verify my identity as we were talking online.

It is also necessary to situate my "blunders" against the backdrop of doing fieldwork in the office of CWF, a politically sensitive organization that was believed to be closely monitored by the Chinese government. Therefore, in the conversation with me, Chen Tong also demonstrated a highly indexical suspicion which was both an expression of "state paranoia" and a consequence of an institutionalized form of distrust (Glaeser 2004: 244). In his study on practices of belonging and the production of state paranoia in the former German Democratic Republic (GDR), Andreas Glaeser notes that one crucial characteristic of state paranoia and pervasive distrust in the GDR was the practice and fear of "synecdochical mischief," which refers to "someone's readiness to discredit a whole by virtue of discrediting any of its parts" (Glaeser 2000: 261, 2004: 246). Similarly, based on my two careless mistakes in the conversation, Chen Tong was ready to discredit and expose my true identity by requesting a video chat. It shows that the domain of uncertainty is also a domain of suspicion where these labor activists have to constantly watch their backs and worry about any potential infiltration. It also illustrates how the political environment is conducive to cultivating a specific kind of subjectivity that is more sensitive to certain signals and information. As a result, my "blunders" become a tool for revealing this suspicious environment and the constant negotiation of the boundary between insider and outsider (Merton 1972). My oversight lays bare the fragility of social relationships in general and more particularly, my uncertain position in the field where, as discussed previously during my process of learning to gossip, I was sometimes given permission to participate in the NGOs' activities and thus had to continuously negotiate trust with my research participants.

For those doing research in China, *mingan* is a familiar term. Most scholars tend to deal with the issue of *mingan* in two ways. One is through the ways censorship and self-censorship—what is *mingan* and what is not—affect the behavior of different social groups and what spaces there are for these groups to voice their criticism of the government (Hassid 2008, 2010; King et al. 2013). This kind of research has gained significance after the emergence of the Internet in China in the 1990s (Yang 2008, 2009). The other way of talking about *mingan* is to offer methodological strategies on how to carry out research on politically sensitive topics in politically restrictive contexts (Spires 2007; Tsai 2010). Lily Tsai points out that in an authoritarian or transitional system, all sorts of topics may be considered politically sensitive and the researcher does not always know which ones are included. Moreover, "[w]hat is considered politically sensitive may also vary across regions and over time" (Tsai 2010: 250). As such, Tsai suggests a "socially embedded" approach which attends to the social relationships in the field and can help alleviate problems of political sensitivity (Tsai 2010: 246).

Against the background of the literature that touches upon the issue of *mingan*, I want not only to illustrate how the labor NGOs perceive the idea of *mingan* but also what they do with it. To an extent, I am also interested in showing how *mingan* affects the behavior of my interlocutors, but a significant difference between my analysis and the existing research is that I foreground and demonstrate how the idea of *mingan* can be invoked, employed, and applied in different settings as an organizing affect, notion, and rule dictating behavior, practices, and relationships that travel across different analytical categories such as organizations, topics, time, and space. As such, the idea of *mingan*, like uncertainty, is treated both as an analytical tool and an ethnographic emergent of this interactive and crisscrossing process, unfolding the zone of political and cultural intimacy in which activists try to determine the boundaries of permissible activism and articulate their identities.

That *mingan* seems to be so fluid, ambiguous, and able to move in these different realms suggests that it is polyvalent and raises the questions: What does *mingan* mean? What do people do with *mingan*? How do people perceive, use, experience, and respond to *mingan*? These questions directly address the politics of *mingan* and can shed some light on the interpretation and self-generation of, and adherence to the guidelines for acceptable behavior and speech as well as parameters for transgressions. Hence, inherent in the politics of *mingan* is the dynamics of the interaction and relationships between labor NGOs, donors, and the state. All too often, such interaction and relationships entail essentializing strategies that depict the state and activists themselves in stereotypical ways in order to be meaningful and effective. While the politics of *mingan* enacts discursive and performative practices to estimate the appropriate distance between labor NGOs and the state, it is also imbued with the potential for forming new relationships, for example, with foreign donors. In other words, the politics of *mingan* also provides a different logic whereby a specific nature and process of *guanxi* practices can be understood.

Having described the analysis of strategic or tactical deployment of ideal types as "social poetics," Herzfeld reminds us that cultural intimacy should be understood as a,

> complex process rather than as a static type of insiderhood characterized by one institutional framework (such as the nation-state, especially), one idiom of representation (in which embarrassment is the only mode of response to revelations of its content), and one orientation (specifically to 'the West').
>
> (Herzfeld 2016: 51)

As such, to tease out the politics of *mingan* is also to explore the social and political poetics in the labor community (see also Brandtstädter 2016: 122–137). More specifically, with the politics of *mingan*, this chapter discusses how the politics of engagement—junctures and disjunctures—is played out when discourses and practices of international development and local empowerment converge.

Common understanding

In the labor community, *mingan* was a term widely used by my interlocutors when they talked about their work and relationships with the state as well as their foreign collaborators. They often talked about *mingan* as a governing principle that helped them determine the scope, scale, type, place, timing, and the method of their work so as to, they hope, reduce political risks. When I asked about the meaning of *mingan*, the definition appeared messier.

> So how do you explain *mingan*? There are no standards (for what is considered *mingan*) in China. It could be that someone in the government doesn't like you because there is some kind of power struggle within the government. Nobody knows. It depends on personal feelings [*ping geren gangjue*]. If [the government] feels that you are not easy to deal with [*bu hao dajiaodao*], or feels that you are dangerous, you are *mingan*. But if you adjust your work strategy at a certain moment, you may stop being *mingan*. But if it is not that you adjust your strategy but that the [government's] understanding of you changes, then you may also stop being *mingan*. It's up to the leadership to decide that they have a different opinion of you. For example, in this district, say a certain cadre doesn't like me and thinks I am *mingan*. One day, he quits and leaves. Another cadre comes. Then I may not be *mingan* anymore. So I haven't changed and I still don't do any dangerous things. Sometimes it can be that a person is *mingan* for the entire system. For example, Li Jie. It is not only that he is a *mingan* person to me but also to the entire government. Then that is troublesome.[3]

The above passage was an excerpt from a conversation I had with Wu Xiangjun, director of a Shenzhen-based labor NGO. Having described *mingan* as something that "depends on personal feelings," Wu Xiangjun points to the ambiguity of *mingan* in that it is prone to subjective interpretations and can be person-, context-, topic-, and time-specific, which, in turn, affects the individual's behavior and decision-making. However, the ways in which a person, an organization, context or time qualifies as being *mingan* are difficult to pin down, which further reveals the fluidity of the term. Wu Xiangjun's words also suggest that having a good relationship with the local government may be useful to mitigate political risks linked with certain politically sensitive activities or individuals. Furthermore, Wu Xiangjun mentioned Li Jie, who is the director of CWF. Because of his connection with the student protests in 1989, Li Jie is not only a well-known labor activist around the world but is also viewed as a sensitive person by the Chinese government in the sense that any association with him may easily be construed as having the potential to threaten or damage the Chinese Communist Party's regime. Having described Li Jie as a *mingan* person to "the entire system," and thus "troublesome," Wu Xiangjun also noted the scale of Li Jie as a *mingan* person who needs to be treated with caution. Li Jie has not been allowed to return to China since he went into exile in the 1990s.

Regardless of the ambiguity of the term, when I was working with the labor NGOs in South China, there seemed to be a common understanding (*gongshi*) regarding what constitutes *mingan* issues and activities that are prone to being considered politically risky. It was generally agreed upon that it is *mingan* "to organize or mobilize workers," noted one labor NGO leader, because "it is *mingan* to get involved in mass incidents." There is no shortage of stories about labor NGO staff being taken away by the police because they were suspected of mobilizing workers. Zhang Guoqi, a senior staff member at Green Grass Workers' Service Center, related to me how an NGO staff member had to spend a week at the police station because this person shared the news of a group of protesting workers on QQ. "He was accused of inciting workers to protest," said Zhang Guoqi. One recent and well-known example is that two NGO staff members, one of whom was the director, were taken away in April 2014 during what was described as the biggest strike in the history of contemporary China; 40,000 workers walked off the job at a shoe factory in Dongguan, Guangdong.[4] The two NGO staff members had met with some of the workers' representatives after the strike had already occurred, and the police believed them to be involved with mobilizing the workers. Later when they were released and returned home, the NGO director revealed that he was taken to a hotel resort and he described it jokingly as "being asked to go on a vacation" (*bei dujia*).

Owing to the politically sensitive nature of organizing and mobilizing workers, many labor NGOs tend to focus on social service provisions, including free legal consultation, and the dissemination of, for example, the Labor Contract Law and Social Security Law, and organizing social and cultural activities for workers such as an outing to the mountain, a barbecue in the park, or a singing contest. As mentioned in Chapter 3, some labor NGOs do help migrant workers bring their grievances to the court and these are mainly dealt with on an individual basis. Most of the grievances have to do with delayed wages and workplace injuries. The latter is a particularly sensitive issue as it can have a negative impact on the local government's ability to attract investors. Such NGOs are often viewed by the local authorities as a rights defense NGO (*zuo weiquan de*) and thus are more politically sensitive in the sense that they make the local government look bad or may engender social instability by highlighting workers' grievances and bringing their cases to court. Hence, these NGOs usually do not openly describe themselves as rights defense NGOs.

The donors have mixed views on funding rights-related projects. David, a political counselor at a European embassy, said that he is very interested in supporting rights-based projects and NGOs because "it's more meaningful." David thinks it is important to educate people about their rights as it is "the first step towards the empowerment of workers." However, Judy, head of the political section of a North American embassy in Beijing, is a lot more reserved. Judy stressed that she is very careful with the rights-related projects she chooses to support, which are usually the kinds that are accepted by the local government because she doesn't want to get anybody "in trouble." For Judy, to determine whether a project proposal is too sensitive to fund is always a difficult judgment call to make. She explained that when evaluating different proposals and organizations, she usually considers whether or not a certain project or organization will attract too much attention that will ultimately be negative. She noted that many of these organizations want to do similar things, one of which is to bring a number of NGOs that do the same thing together.

> But alliance building and networking, which, theoretically, is not welcome in this country. But if we think it is useful, we will find ways to support it. But if there is going to be a lot of publicity and reports that say we [the embassy] are building an alliance here and the purpose of the alliance is to be critical and claim that we [the NGOs] have international support for the criticism, that's not necessarily going to do them good [...] so if it's going to be really sensitive like that, it may not be a useful project.[5]

Here, Judy points out one crucial dilemma for both domestic and foreign organizations that want to be involved with any kind of organizational work to enhance awareness, solidarity, and rights of disadvantaged groups in China. It is considered to be political risky to try publicly to provide platforms or funding whereby individuals or organizations can meet, connect, network, or collaborate. Judy described such an endeavor as "politically sensitive" and stressed that if a project was so politically sensitive that it might generate unwanted political attention, risks, and consequences, she would not fund it.

It is also generally understood that any connection with the issues of Taiwanese independence, Tibet, and Falun Gong is politically sensitive, so the labor NGOs and funding agencies do their best to avoid being associated with any of them (Stern & Hassid 2012: 1236). Another sensitive issue concerns money. It was not until the end of my fieldwork that I was able to discuss the issue of funding with a few labor NGO leaders. A senior labor NGO worker in Hong Kong explained to me that money is a sensitive issue because there are very limited resources for labor NGOs and the competition for funding is very intense. "The NGOs themselves don't like to talk about who funds their organizations because they are concerned that you might compete with them," said the NGO worker. In addition, another perhaps more important reason is that some donors are more politically sensitive and risky than others. There is an unspoken understanding within the labor NGOs that receiving funding from the United States is more sensitive than receiving it from Europe; within the United States, some foundations are more sensitive than others. For example, the National Endowment for

Democracy and Open Society Foundations are widely viewed as highly sensitive donors (Stern & Hassid 2012: 1243). In order to protect themselves, NGOs are hesitant to receive money from them.

Another labor NGO worker in Hong Kong went further to stress that sometimes the donors would ask their partners not to reveal where they receive their funds from so as to "avoid political pressure from the Chinese government." However, a relationship with a sensitive funding agency or intermediary organization like CWF can also be utilized by some labor NGOs to evade supervision and management from their collaborators. A project manager at CWF revealed to me that sometimes their partners would ask her not to visit because they had been asked to drink tea and needed to lay low for a while.

> There is no way for me to verify whether they were indeed asked to drink tea. We are a sensitive organization so when our partners ask us not to come to visit, we usually agree not to. But it's tricky since it is my job to visit our partners and oversee our projects.

Although these general guidelines were talked about in such a way that they seem to be useful for the labor community to estimate the approximate parameters within which they can carry out their projects, they often fall short when it comes to the specifics of implementing a project, which, as discussed earlier, is complicated by such factors as timing, location, or relationships with the local authorities. This is where the ambiguity and dynamics of the idea of *mingan* lies. Such ambiguity entails the need to seek more nuanced and specific knowledge of the bounds of state tolerance and cultivate more refined skills to deal with the state. In Chapter 6, I will discuss in more detail how the labor NGOs collect information and apply skills when carrying out a development program. As shown in the words of the NGO leader Wu Xiangjun, regardless of the general guidelines, it is difficult to specifically determine what is *mingan*, and it depends on other things such as personal feelings and the relationship with the local authorities.

Mingan is thus suggestive of a type of tacit knowledge (Polanyi 1958, 1966) that is not explicitly written down but is obtained by "feeling our way" through (Polanyi 1958: 62). Polanyi writes about how the blind man eventually finds what he is looking for by bumping and touching to illustrate how the discovery of knowledge is a product of the integration of conscious knowing and unconscious knowing. Viewed in the context of the labor community in China, *mingan* almost always has to be learned and acquired from the individual's hands-on experience with the state or/and gathered indirectly from informal interaction such as shared meals, offhand remarks, gossip, and rumor among the NGO activists, donors, trade union officials, academics, and journalists. In other words, it is a type of knowledge that is predominantly captured in action and often related and circulated as a currency of trust and solidarity among a small group of people.

While the general guidelines are useful for the activists to picture and cal-culate the *"mingan* contour" of their activism, they also illustrate the ways in which the state as a fickle being is imagined and perceived by these so-cial actors. As much as the specific content of what is *mingan* is difficult to pin down, the general guidelines also show a certain degree of the fixity of state logic, which makes it possible for activists to try to gauge what the state can see and predict how the state might think and react. This suggests that the ambiguity of the notion of *mingan* is predicated on certain essentialized ideas and stereotypes of the state. Such a seemingly ironic discrepancy shows that social life is "much more complex than a simple binary model of op-pressor and subaltern would suggest" (Herzfeld 2016: 33). The term *mingan* is not only an expression of uncertainty and contingency but also opens up an entry point to everyday interpretations and sociopolitical uses of stereo-types. When navigating uncertain political terrains, labor activists often find themselves relying on essentialized ideas of the state in order to strategize for political empowerment. It is both an ironic maneuver and a dialectical practice characterizing political life which consists of processes of reification and essentialism as well as challenges to these processes (Herzfeld 2016: 32).

Following Herzfeld, rather than distrusting essentialism and making as-sumptions about the structure of human cognition, treating the politics of *mingan* as a zone of intimacy, I ask questions about "where people find the binary oppositions that they actually deploy and [examine] how they use them in their negotiations of power" (ibid.). With a focus on both perception and action (including inaction), the politics of *mingan* moves away from what James Scott discusses as "seeing like a state" (1998) and goes on to explore the domain of "instigating like a state" from the perspective of the labor activists. It is an ambiguous space where activists try to gauge what the state can sense and what is likely to be instigated if the state senses something.

In the section that follows, I will draw on a training workshop I attended in Beijing to illustrate the ways in which the idea of *mingan* is managed, em-ployed, and invoked in order to form as well as disrupt relationships among different actors against the discourse of international development with special regard to democracy and human rights advocacy. The alliance and disruption of these relationships indicate strategic representations of and by different actors drawing on their specific imaginings of the state. It is in this space, among the intention, discourse, and use of certain imaginings and stereotypes of the state, that the politics of *mingan* is played out.

Managing *mingan* through time and space

In March 2013, I attended a four-day workshop that took place in Beijing organized by Beijing-based labor NGO Big Ocean, which has branch offices in two other Chinese cities. Titled "Capacity Building for Labor NGOs in China" (*laogong* NGO *nengli jianshe gongzuo fang*), this workshop was en-tirely funded by the International Labor Organization. According to Big

Ocean, a total of 33 labor-related organizations across China (Guangdong, Hubei, Tianjin, and Shanxi) were invited to attend the workshop. The venue of the workshop was in a hot spring resort located in the suburbs of Beijing. The first two days were devoted to a series of coaching seminars focused on developing the skills of fundraising and establishing and maintaining good relationships with the local authorities, as well as using the media for advocacy. Experts and experienced NGOs were invited to share their knowledge and experiences. Some coaching sessions were followed by mock exercises wherein, for example, a case scenario was given and the participants were assigned roles to act out the scenario by putting into practice what they learned from the coaching.

I learned about this workshop while I was doing fieldwork at Blue Sky Social Work Service Center, which was discussed in Chapter 3. Wei Peng, director of Blue Sky, agreed to let me join him in attending the workshop. The date for the workshop went through a number of changes. Initially, it was set for mid-December in 2012 but was later changed to April, June, and finally to March 2013. Commenting on the changing dates, Wei Peng said, "they [Big Ocean] are probably having trouble with the *lingdao* [superiors]." After we had arrived at the venue for the workshop, I had a chance to talk to May Lin, a staff member at Big Ocean and coordinator of this workshop. I complimented her on pulling off the workshop and having brought together so many labor NGOs across the country, which was essentially a politically sensitive activity. She smiled and said, "We have communicated [with the local government]." I asked her about the changing dates for the workshop and she said, "Originally, we wanted to have the workshop in December (2012) but we didn't get permission [from the local government]. It was too close to the National Congress so we couldn't." May Lin was referring to the 18th National Congress of the Communist Party of China, which was held on November 8, 2012.[6] "We continued communicating [with the local government] and finally they agreed to let us hold the workshop in March," explained May Lin while rolling her eyes to indicate a sense of frustration as well as annoyance.

The changing dates for the Beijing workshop is an example of following the calendar of activism. As a type of tacit knowledge, the calendar of activism refers to "a collective understanding of the best and worst times to criticize the state, [and] can strike out entire months or even years [...] for action" (Stern & Hassid 2012: 1246). In the labor community, there is a general understanding that NGOs should lay low and be inactive during certain periods of time, such as during major events taking place during the meeting of the National Congress or in the run-up to the Olympic Games in 2008. As one Hong Kong labor NGO activist put it,

> You know the Chinese government tries to control the country through campaigns. So they organize a big campaign and increase security around National Day or some other major political event. Then a few

months before that PSB [Public Security Bureau] will be ordered to interrogate everyone. But the week that is over, they take time off; they
are on vacation. We have always recognized the campaign nature of it
and most likely things will go back to normal so there is no reason to
overreact. So we take a little bit of a low profile approach and wait until
it passes.[7]

To follow the calendar of activism is a tactic whereby the NGOs weigh, wait,
and try to avoid *mingan* timing when carrying out certain activities or projects. It is a way of operating and,

> a calculated action determined by the absence of a proper locus [...].
> The space of a tactic is the space of the other. Thus, it must play on
> and with a terrain imposed on it and organized by the law of a foreign
> power.
>
> (de Certeau 1984: 37)

The calendar of activism provides the parameters within which the labor
NGOs plan what they can or cannot do at certain periods of time. In other
words, the labor NGOs conduct self-censorship by keeping time with the
state. Marked by major national events, the calendar of activism illustrates
how the idea of *mingan* becomes a temporal mode of social organization
that dictates and censors the work of the labor NGOs. It is a calendric response that takes the form of quiescence that marks the state-society relationship as well as state power through inaction. The date for the 18th
National Congress of the Communist Party of China was not revealed until
October 2012. Although many labor NGOs were aware of avoiding sensitive activities when major political events occurred or were about to take
place in the country, the delayed announcement of the exact date of the 18th
National Congress of the Communist Party of China prolonged the period
of uncertainty and made it even more difficult for the labor NGOs to plan
their work and activities. Being attentive to the calendar of activism shows
the temporal dimension of power. As Bourdieu points out, "waiting implies
submission: the interested aiming at something greatly desired durably—
that is to say, for the whole duration of the expectancy—modifies the behavior of the person who 'hangs,' as we say, on the awaited decision" (Bourdieu
2000: 228, emphasis in original).

There is also the spatial dimension to gauging the distance from the state.
May Lin said that it took them a while to find a place that was "far enough"
from the political center. The hot spring resort chosen as the venue for the
three-day workshop was located just outside the sixth ring road of the mu-
nicipality of Beijing, which currently consists of seven ring roads. At the
time of the labor NGO workshop, the seventh ring road was still under construction. It takes approximately two hours by subway to travel from the
city center of Beijing to the sixth ring road area. De Certeau writes that

"[a] place is the order (of whatever kind) in accord with which elements are distributed in relationships of coexistence. It thus excludes the possibility of two things being in the same location (place)" (1984: 117). The venue of the workshop, which is a place for recreation, creates a "discreteness" (ibid.: 98) and signifies a deliberate decision to conform to the political order of things in which politically sensitive activities should not be conducted anywhere too close to the political center.

The hot spring resort is thus a place of "an instantaneous configuration of positions [that] implies an indication of stability" (ibid.: 117). Nevertheless, having gathered and interacted at the workshop at the hot spring resort, the labor NGOs and donors also temporarily transformed the hotel into a space that was useful for them (ibid.). Contrary to place, de Certeau notes that "space is composed of intersections of mobile elements. It is in a sense actuated by the ensemble of movements deployed within it" (ibid.). Although the hotel is designed as a place for recreation, that is not always what occurs on the premises. To distinguish between place and space directs the attention to the relationship between space, power, and social relations and captures the dynamic and relational nature of space. While being far away from the political center, the hot spring resort becomes a space that temporarily embodies the specific relations between the labor NGOs, the donors, and the Chinese state and opens up opportunities for collaboration.

The second day of the workshop I was sitting at a table with a dozen labor NGO workers and leaders, most of whom were from South China. We were gathering for lunch after having attended a seminar on how to manage and cultivate relationships with the government where several more seasoned labor NGO leaders shared their experiences. Over lunch, Xiao Yu, an NGO worker from a Zhejiang-based labor NGO, was complaining that he had not received his salary for four months and that his organization was in desperate need of funds. There were only two full-time staff members at Xiao Yu's NGO: himself and the NGO leader. Xiao Yu mentioned that they had recently applied for funding from the National Endowment for Democracy (NED). "But our email was locked and we couldn't open it," said Xiao Yu. It was an e-mail from NED. No one commented on Xiao Yu's words except for one labor NGO leader who simply said, "NED is more mingan [bijiao mingan; more sensitive than other foundations]." The rest of the people merely nodded their heads a little and went on to talk about something else. Their avoidance of discussing funding in such a public setting shows the sensitive nature of this topic. After lunch, I stayed and asked Xiao Yu more about it. He told me that in addition to the desperate need for funds, his NGO also sent in an application to NED because "we want to test the local government's bottom line. We want to know how far we can go and how much space (for development) our organization can possibly have."

Xiao Yu went further to say that he was in the middle of organizing a workshop to bring together the labor NGOs in the Yangtze River Delta, which includes Shanghai, Jiangsu, and Zhejiang. The workshop was going to discuss the transitioning role of labor NGOs in helping individual rights defense (*geren weiquan*) to engaging in collective rights defense (*jiti weiquan*). "It (the subject of collective rights defense) is a little *mingan*," said Xiao Yu, letting out a rueful laugh. "Unlike the Pearl River Delta region, there are very few labor NGOs in the Yangtze River Delta," noted Xiao Yu, adding that he was not sure whether it was possible to discuss this subject in the Yangtze River Delta, so officially he only said that the workshop was for labor NGOs to share and exchange experiences.

Xiao Yu's words express some of the ways in which the term *mingan* is used: to describe an organization (NED) and a subject (collective rights defense) that were considered to be sensitive enough that they might entail certain political risks for individuals and organizations that are believed or known to be associated with them. Moreover, Xiao Yu's words also show that geography (the Yangtze River Delta), that is, space, and timing can play a role in determining whether a subject is sensitive or not. The subject of collective rights defense, according to Xiao Yu, could be too sensitive to be discussed in the Yangtze River Delta in comparison to the Pearl River Delta region where the number of labor NGOs is much greater and the political climate is believed to be relatively liberal. Most important of all, Xiao Yu's words also illustrate that he is a sensitive person and that he pays attention to, detects, or responds to whatever signals, responses, or changes that occur in his surroundings. That his e-mail was blocked was viewed as a signal for him to consider and evaluate the political space that his NGO could have. As he stated himself, one of the purposes of the application to NED was to test the bottom line of the local government. As another labor NGO director said, "There is no bottom line in China. You keep pushing it until you are told to stop. Then you know where the limits are." It clearly shows that the criteria for what is considered *mingan* is not stable, which, in turn, creates opportunities to play with it and use it to negotiate boundaries. It is the "corollary to recognizing the strategic character of essentialism" (Herzfeld 2016: 32). Phrased differently, Xiao Yu can also be described as both having a degree of and trying to cultivate more political sensitivity as he learned to be attuned to as well as to figure out the limits of the tolerance of the local government. He was attempting to estimate how much space there was for his NGO to continue operating in the city as well as to engage in collective action.

Acting out *mingan*

The idea of *mingan* provides an entry point for teasing out the workings and boundaries of state control. It is revealed, as discussed earlier, by the ways in which labor NGOs perceive the idea of *mingan* and accordingly desensitize their behavior by, for example, following the calendar of activism. The idea of *mingan*, which often seems arbitrary and unstable, induces the tacit and self-assigned script for the labor NGOs to conduct themselves.

The ambiguity of the idea of *mingan* shows that "the rules for daily behavior" are not singly created by and handed down from the state but are jointly produced and reproduced by the labor activists and their government over-seers (Midgal 2001: 11).

In this section, I focus on a different engagement with the notion of *mingan*; I want to show how, instead of desensitizing, the labor NGOs actively sensitize themselves and mobilize around the idealized role of a labor activist. I use the meeting between the labor NGOs and donors during the workshop to illustrate the strategic representations and rhetorical practices of labor activists by utilizing certain *mingan* issues, comments, and images of the state. It enacts a network which consists not only people but also systems of representations in which support and legitimacy can be sought, mobilized, and maintained. The key trope here is the identity and role of a labor activist. Focusing on the self-representations of the labor NGOs to the donors, I draw on two labor NGOs to demonstrate how they address this particular audience while engaging with and embodying the popular idea of labor activists as empowered, progressive, and assertive advocates for work-ers' rights, both of which are considered politically *mingan* characteristics and conduct by the Chinese state. In the text that follows, I discuss how the labor NGOs display their politically *mingan* traits and adopt representation strategies and practices through the use of persuasion, irony, and humor when addressing a group of funding agencies.

Persuasion

The last day of the workshop was the "climax," in the words of some of the participants in the workshop, wherein the labor NGOs would meet with potential donors. The venue for the meeting was an assembly hall inside a two-story building adjacent to the hotel where the NGO participants were staying. At the front of the hall, there was a stage with a big red banner run-ning across the entire back of the stage. Printed on the banner was the title of the workshop in black Chinese characters. A podium was placed slightly to the left of the stage. In the middle of the hall were some tables arranged in a U-shape and two long tables placed in the middle, which were reserved for the international foundations and embassies as indicated by a sign placed on each of the two tables, "a display of hierarchy" (Riles 2001: 51). We were instructed by Big Ocean's staff to sit along the tables on the outside. As soon as everyone was seated, Liu Xiang, director of Big Ocean, went up to the stage and began, "Today is an important day because our friends from the international foundations and foreign embassies will come and listen to you. This is a great opportunity for you to introduce yourselves to our international friends."

Liu Xiang continued to talk about the schedule for the day and gave the participating labor NGOs instructions on how to prepare their presentations for the international organizations. Each labor NGO was given 10–15 minutes.

"This is a good opportunity to challenge yourself and see if you can introduce your own organization within 15 minutes. And I hope you all have enough business cards with you," said Liu Xiang with a smile on his face. I was sitting next to Blue Sky's director Wei Peng. I looked around and saw that some NGOs were well-prepared. Some had brought with them large-size posters with pictures and text describing their organizations. Some had PowerPoint presentations that had already been loaded onto the laptop on the stage. Some had the booklets and pamphlets that they distributed to migrant workers. Some NGOs had prepared T-shirts, CDs, and pins that had the logos of their organizations they could give to the international guests. But there were also other NGOs that did not bring anything with them. No posters, no leaflets. I talked to one of the poorly prepared NGOs and the director said to me, "We don't have any funding. I run my organization out of my own pocket. I don't have money to print posters or leaflets." In fact, the business card he gave me was a piece of white paper with his name and contact number handwritten on it. The NGOs' preparation for the meeting with the donors illustrates clearly how they learn to take up a specific form of engagement in order to facilitate their social action.

They were preparing to enter a global stage that depends on an audience whose opinion is assumed to have importance (Shryock 2004: 11). When successfully in place, global stages foster structures and sentiments and under such circumstances "cultural materials that cannot be easily displayed in public formats [...] take on exaggerated significance in situations of pervasive multicultural contact: distinctive models of time and space, ways of holding the body, [...] styles of talking [...]" (Shryock 2004: 14). It reveals how the control of cultural forms gives one license to play with cultural content. In the labor community, the idea of *mingan* and its often unspoken, uncertain, and context-specific content constitute the cultural materials, which, when displayed accordingly, can be productive of strengthening existing ties and sociality as well as generative of new relationships.

At 10 o'clock, the first international guests from the American and French embassies arrived. Before they got a chance to sit down, some NGO directors were quick enough to step forward and give them their business cards. One NGO director sitting close to me asked me, "Do they speak Mandarin?" I said, "They should be able to." Apparently, he was worried that he wouldn't be able to communicate with them. This was his first time participating in such an event. Later some representatives from a number of international foundations also arrived. The European Union representatives came last. A total of nine organizations with eleven people, including representatives from the embassies and the EU, came to this meeting.

At 10:30 a.m., Liu Xiang, the moderator, opened the meeting. There was no arrangement in the order of the presentations, so Liu Xiang stood on the stage and asked if there was any NGO that wanted to go first. The question drew laughter from the NGOs. Everybody was looking at one another. Then Zhu Ren, director of a Shenzhen-based labor NGO raised his hand and volunteered to be the first one. So began the presentations. Zhu Ren was one of only a few participants who wore a suit and tie to the workshop. As he got up, he took off his jacket and left it on the back of his chair, making his way to the stage. I noticed that Zhu Ren had lost half of his left arm as the sleeve of his white shirt was pushed up to his elbow. Once on the stage, Zhu Ren adjusted the microphone on the podium and began his presentation with his own personal transformation from a migrant worker to a labor activist.

Zhu Ren described how he was injured while working in a factory in Shenzhen six years ago. "When I was in the hospital, I realized that I was not the only person who got injured at work. There were many other workers who were in the same situation as I was," Zhu Ren said, stressing that it was during his treatment in the hospital that he decided to do something to help other workers. In order to obtain financial compensation from his employer, Zhu Ren went through a cumbersome process in which the labor authorities were passing the buck to each other. "At first, my boss simply said that it was my own fault that I got injured and refused to have anything to do with my injury," explained Zhu Ren. It was with the assistance of a labor NGO in Guangzhou that Zhu Ren was able to continue his battle with the labor authorities and initiate negotiations with his employer. It took him nearly two years to receive 20,000 RMB in compensation from his employer. On hearing this, Wei Peng said in a low voice, "No way! That was too little [for the kind of injury he had]!" His quick comment shows the unspoken yet intense competition among the labor NGOs when it comes to providing services for the workers and seeking funding from foundations. It also reflects the tendency to evaluate the capability and success of a labor NGO in material terms, a subject to be further discussed in Chapter 6.

Zhu Ren's presentation accompanied by his visibly injured body directly spoke to the international audience. His personal story of transforming from a migrant worker to an NGO worker appeals to the popular notion circulated in the international aid community in which examples of direct empowerment of the local community are measured against the efficiency of development aid. Touching upon the sensitive issue of workplace safety, Zhu Ren's presentation illustrated how the existing state of affairs in many workplaces poses a serious concern to the safety of workers without directly criticizing the government and its enforcement of the law.

William, a representative from the American embassy at the workshop, told me, "When I meet with an NGO, I am always curious about their motivation and oftentimes they don't have a good story." "What is a good story?" I asked. He said, "Someone who was injured, tried to claim compensation, and became an activist." As noted earlier, the workshop embodies a global stage that cultivates forms and feelings; it is a stage where actors are brought together to circulate the truths of the plight of migrant workers and the crisis of labor rights in China. Zhu Ren's presentation, a testimonial to the suffering of Chinese workers, is a typical representation of victimization that evokes sympathy and alarm intended to incite intervention to improve the situation many Chinese workers face (cf. Fassin & Rechtman 2009; James 2010). It makes for "a good story," in the words of William, and reaffirms the long-held hope that development projects are a vehicle for egalitarian values and distributive justice in the world regardless of the fact that many of the views of the rich/poor and democratic/undemocratic world, and solutions adopted by international development are so simple and optimistic that they have deflated many of its great hopes while, ironically enough, large investments of time and resources have continued to pour into the world of development projects (Fernandez & Huber 2001: 87–88).

Irony, humor, and complicity

After two presentations, Wei Peng asked me when he should give his presentation. I thought for a second and said, "As early as possible. They (the international guests) may get tired after a few presentations and lose concentration or interest." Taking my advice, Wei Peng raised his hand and gave his presentation after the third NGO was finished.

Wei Peng began by introducing himself and talking about how his organization tried to help migrant workers. He told the audience that the main thing his organization does is to visit injured workers in hospitals and to help them to defend their rights. Wei Peng explained that his organization informs the workers of their legal rights with regard to compensation so that they become more knowledgeable about the law and can defend their rights. In addition to the legal help, his organization also provides social and emotional support for injured workers. Wei Peng emphasized that his organization is largely run by workers who were injured in the past. "I myself am an injured worker," said Wei Peng, who paused and showed the audience his left hand which only has two fingers left: the ring and the little fingers, and he continued,

> Because of this, we know very well the psychological stress that injured workers go through and work hard to provide emotional support for these workers. Workers can come in for a chat if they need one. They can come to participate in any activities we organize. And they are more than welcome to become volunteers. Regarding the legal help we offer, we work closely with a number of academic institutions in Guangdong such as Sun Yat-sen University and South China Normal University. The teachers and students from the law department have been collaborating with us for many years.

After the brief introductory and generally appropriate remarks in a public gathering like this, Wei Peng stopped, looked around the audience, cleared his throat a bit, and resumed his presentation.

> Many NGOs are here today. We are all doing very similar work trying to help workers. One thing I really want to talk about on this particular

occasion concerns the recent reports that some international foundations have withdrawn their resources because they believe that China
today is wealthy enough to do philanthropic work for its own society. I
have heard that more and more foundations are thinking of doing the
same. I would like to take this opportunity and stress that if you really understand the true colors of the Chinese government, you will not
leave China. In fact, today you have even more reasons to stay.

Wei Peng was referring to the fact that a few major international organizations had announced plans to reduce or terminate support in China. Since
2008, some bilateral and multilateral international development agencies
have begun to reduce or terminate their aid to projects in China. Between
2010 and 2011, the Global Fund, the world's largest financier of AIDS, tu-
berculosis, and malaria programs, started phasing out support for China;
in 2012, the Bill & Melinda Gates Foundation also announced plans to
terminate direct funding support for projects in China.[8] However, some
foreign organizations are leaving not only because of China's burgeoning
wealth as a country but also because of the increasingly stringent legal environment. On April 28, 2016, China's National People's Congress passed
the third draft of Foreign NGO Management Law. Like domestic NGOs,
many foreign NGOs in China have operated in a legal gray zone. The new
law requires the foreign NGOs to register formally to carry out projects and
conduct activities. Moreover, this new law puts the foreign NGOs under the
supervision of the public security departments of the State Council. Many
believe that this new law will make it even more difficult for foreign NGOs
to stay and will have a major impact on a variety of organizations and activities, both domestic and foreign.

Wei Peng paused here, turned to Liu Xiang, and asked, "Can I say this?
There are no *lingdao* [superiors] here today, right?" This question made the
audience laugh. Liu Xiang was laughing too and nodded his head saying
"*keyi*," which means "ok." Wei Peng continued,

> Our government loves to save face [*mianzi*]. They are afraid to lose face.
> So when they say they work to help the people, they really do it for the
> sake of looking good, for face. They are not doing the real work for the
> workers. Just take the number of injured workers, for example. The offi-
> cial number of workers injured at work in X City in 2011 is 17,000. Hav-
> ing worked with the migrant worker community for six years, I know
> full well that this number cannot be true. From my experience on the
> ground, there are at least 100 workers who are injured at work every day
> and I am not exaggerating.

After this comment, Wei Peng apologized and said that he had a bad habit
of "saying inappropriate things at inappropriate occasions." After having deviated from his script for a few minutes, Wei Peng went back to his

PowerPoint presentation and continued to talk about what his organization has achieved with regard to policy advocacy in the last few years. Toward the end of his presentation, Wei Peng stressed that labor NGOs in China need to have more interaction and work together to survive in the future. In his concluding remarks, Wei Peng acknowledged that the government has realized the importance of providing services for migrant workers, and that the government has invested a lot of resources in setting up social work service centers in many big cities. But he also noted that how good their services are is debatable, but "they surely have the money and resources." Wei Peng appealed to the labor NGOs at present and said, "We can't always rely on the foundations. We NGOs need to work together and help one another so we can continue to survive and help our workers."

Wei Peng's presentation was given a big round of applause. He took a bow, stepped down from the stage, walked back to his seat, and sat down. As soon as Wei Peng was back at his seat, the officials from the American and French embassies, and a representative from an American foundation came to exchange business cards with him. It was obvious that Wei Peng had made an impression on them. After the exchange of business cards, he leaned toward me and asked in a low voice, "How was I? Was it ok?" I replied, smiling, "You did more than just ok, Wei Peng."

Similar to Zhu Ren, Wei Peng embodies a successful story of personal empowerment in the face of adversity. Like Zhu Ren, Wei Peng talks about the same topic but adopts a different representational strategy that actively engages with the idea of *mingan* and temporarily lays bare the intimate space where the image of an omnipresent state is evoked, ridiculed, criticized, and yet sustained. Wei Peng's presentation is politically sensitive in a number of ways. First, he openly appealed to the donors to stay in China and not to be blinded by the wealth that China has rapidly accumulated within a short period of time and which is concentrated in a small group of people. Second, he talked about the number of workers injured at work and openly refuted the official number. Third, he openly criticized the government for being interested in saving face rather than truly improving working conditions. After having made all of these critical comments, Wei Peng asked Liu Xiang whether he could express his opinion, and immediately followed up this question by asking if there were any *lingdao* present.

The laughter that followed is a vivid illustration of the shared intimate knowledge about government surveillance and possible infiltration among the participants. Wei Peng's question as well as the audience's laughter was a sheepish admission to, an uncomfortable self-recognition of, and a tacit protest against the restrictive political environment in which they have to operate. The laughter indicated a sense of acknowledgment and embarrassment while in that very brief moment, it also created sociality and solidarity in which everyone in the room got the joke and was in the same boat. It was a space of intimacy on display: "a zone of constant struggle between the dominant and subordinate" (Scott 1990: 14) where the line between the public and hidden transcript is persistently contested. Such is a zone of intimacy laid bare by strategic representational practices. It is an engagement in self-aware and other-conscious manipulation of the "process of mobilizing certain differences and linking them to group identity" (Appadurai 1996: 14). As such, aimed toward an audience that is in the know, intimacy is inevitably met by a corresponding publicness (Berlant 1998: 281), while the relationship between the speakers and the audience is structured around the politics of *mingan,* which, in turn, makes visible the zone of intimacy where the struggle to define the terms of showing and viewing takes place (Shryock 2004: 14).

Against the unclear limits of state-sanctioned activism, Wei Peng's presentation is a telling example of the extension of the idea of cultural intimacy coined by Herzfeld (2016) in that it is both an attempt to gauge an appropriate distance from the state and to manipulate and capitalize on the politics of *mingan* in front of the potential donors. He negotiates the balancing act by simultaneously presenting himself as an empowered migrant worker, a labor rights defender, a struggling labor activist, and a critic of the state. Embodying these different images, Wei Peng's performance leads the audience into an intimate space where variegated feelings such as pride, compassion, sociality, solidarity, frustration, vindication, and resentment are shared. And, it is in that space that a sense of a community of complicity is reproduced (Steinmüller 2013). The sense of complicity is specifically exemplified by the question raised by Wei Peng in his presentation as it directly speaks to the political conditions under which labor NGOs and donors have to operate. Part of the common and tacit understanding of state control, these conditions foster spaces of intimacy where knowledge and information are shared, and can be viewed as the ways in which the idea of *mingan* is perceived and put to use by the labor community in China. However, rather than being a source of embarrassment as suggested by Herzfeld's "cultural intimacy" (2016), what is enabled and mobilized by the idea of *mingan* in both Wei Peng's and Zhu Ren's presentations is a sense of sociality and solidarity predicated on the NGOs' as well as the donors' imagination of the omnipresent and omnipotent Chinese state. This is tellingly mediated by Wei Peng's joking performance.

Moreover, the joking performance is a practice that embodies the kind of duality described by Pitkin (1972: 261). It is dual because the audience can see what Wei Peng was doing and, more importantly, understand and sympathize with what he was doing. By inquiring about the presence of any *lingdao* at the workshop, Wei Peng temporarily stepped outside of and paid lip service to the permissible bounds of state tolerance. Moreover, the question is highly rhetorical in the sense that Wei Peng had already made several sensitive comments before he raised that question, which also suggests that he was not expecting to receive a truthful answer from the organizer either. In other words, at that very moment, the presence of any *lingdao* did not seem to matter much. The laughter which ensued from Wei Peng's question is an acknowledgment and endorsement of that; it subtly transmutes private sentiments into a public act of subversion. Humor, according to Mary Douglas, "is a play upon form [that] affords opportunity for realizing that an accepted pattern has no necessity" (Douglas 1975: 96). It is a deforming practice that both perpetuates an imagining as well as reification of the state and encourages the day-to-day subversion of norms (Herzfeld 2016: 27–28). Public stages of identity display need to be constructed with reference to zones of cultural intimacy; however, the public nature of these representational contexts often conceals such references and understandings (Shryock 2004: 18).

By posing the question in a joking and ironic way, Wei Peng plays with the normative form of conducting oneself in public events in China and makes the hidden references and understandings explicit.

> Whatever the joke, however remote its subject, the telling of it is potentially subversive. Since its form consists of a victorious tilting of uncontrol against control, it is an image of the leveling of hierarchy, the triumph of intimacy over formality, of unofficial values over official ones.
>
> (Douglas 1975: 98)

Inherently complicit, the transgression between the private and the public is key to the dynamics of cultural intimacy; and the laughter incited by Wei Peng's inquiry does exactly that: It transmutes private sentiments into public acts. Inherent in the potential subversiveness of Wei Peng's words is also a sense of irony which intentionally questions the accepted forms and established categories. Irony arises and depends on indirection, which, in turn, creates situations of contingency permissible for communication to continue (Fernandez & Huber 2001: 5; Steinmüller 2016: 5). "By stating one thing but suggesting more or less its opposite, ironists point to an alternative reading of a situation, while evading the challenge of direct dissent and protecting themselves from censorious response" (Fernandez & Huber 2001: 5). Wei Peng's question about the presence of any *lingdao* is rhetorical and ironic as he had already said a few things that he wanted to say and would have continued even if he had not posed the question. However, having voiced the question explicitly makes a distinct difference in that it skillfully employs humor and irony to evade the direct challenge of censorious responses while having managed to present himself as an outspoken and fearless labor activist. "[I]rony can afford political expression in circumstances where direct dissent is hard to formulate, risky, or unwise" (Fernandez & Huber 2001: 5).

However, the popular notion of a forward-looking and progressive labor activist is not always appreciated by the donors. Wang Lishi is a project manager at a foreign foundation that has an office in Beijing. Having worked with many labor NGOs in China, Wang Lishi shared with me his view on the politics of *mingan*:

> Most of the projects we fund are really not as *mingan* as you think. It is not that it [a project] is so *mingan* that we can't support it. But sometimes they [the labor NGOs] like to describe themselves as really progressive [*tai lihai* 太厉害].[9] It's the words and terms they use. Sometimes, they unnecessarily increase the risk for themselves. Imagine that I am the *guobao* and am reading whatever is exchanged via e-mail, such as conference and project reports. As a matter of fact, they sometimes increase their own risk by accident when the risk is in effect not so high. For example, they like to talk about themselves as being part of the workers' movement. Well, whether or not they are part of the workers' movement is another issue that can be further discussed. Personally, I think they overestimate their work. But they don't have to say it out loud [...] Another thing is that they might be describing themselves as very progressive [*tai lihai*] but the truth of the matter is they are not very threatening [to the state]. The government knows that you need to get projects so you have to describe yourself as if you are really progressive [*tai lihai*] but the fact is that you are not very critical. So, if you have communicated this to the government they know then there is nothing to worry about.[10]

Wang Lishi's words clearly show pragmatic and strategic thinking and the situated interest and effect of the politics of *mingan* enacted by certain popular notions and stereotypes of labor NGOs. As long as the labor NGOs have communicated clearly with the government that when they portray themselves as progressive; that is, *mingan*, they do so only in a rhetorical sense. This phrasing points to another intimate and implicit understanding that feeds on the ambiguity of the politics of *mingan*. Such ambiguity is productive in facilitating the labor NGOs' conducting themselves in complicit ways that manage their relationships both with the state and the donors, and optimize their interests. However, Wang Lishi's account of how some labor NGOs unnecessarily and sometimes falsely describe their work as "very progressive" and being part of the workers' movement is also imbued with irony and complicity; it reflects a jaded professionalism and an acceptance of the repressive regime by playing the official game in accordance with the official yet tacit rules determined by the formal political system. By using the word "unnecessarily," Wang Lishi's viewpoint is couched in terms of pragmatism, irony, and complicity, and distinctly illustrates how structures of power remain unchallenged and are reproduced in the power structures and interests of the governing regime (Ferguson 1994; Hirschman 1995). "This is the irony of a project, the Development Project, ostensibly and explicitly apolitical, having as a consequence significant political results in terms of the reproduction, indeed development, of a political apparatus" (Fernandez & Huber 2001: 92).

Gauging the state

A few days after the workshop was over, I went to meet with William, the representative from the American embassy. We talked about the workshop and William said that he was not very impressed with it, as most NGOs were pretty similar, so "there was nothing new, really." However, he noted, "Wei Peng is an interesting guy. I have told my colleague to get in touch with him." We continued to talk about that one constant worry of many labor NGOs, which is whether they will continue to receive funding from their donors. William responded,

> Yes, there is always a risk that the money will be pulled. But what is interesting is why the money is pulled. Is the money pulled because you are not performing [according to the demands of the donors] or you are performing too well [according to the expectations of the state]? Or are you not meeting the goals set by the government?

Imbued with irony, William's comment clearly conveys not only the difficulty of determining the boundaries of state tolerance of activism but also the challenge of maintaining relationships with actors of varied geopolitical interests.

The NGOs' presentations as well as their interaction with the donors show a contrast to the preparations prior to the meeting in which the organizers carefully "desensitized" the workshop by rescheduling the event several times and finding a remote enough location. During meetings between labor NGOs and donors, NGO leaders do and say sensitive things to make an impression on the donors. Given the current climate of economic and political neoliberalism within which NGOs are necessarily embedded, NGOs are popularly accorded a central role in strengthening civil society and facilitating the process of democratization in the dominant development discourse (Fisher 1997; Mercer 2002; Fernandez 2004). Inherent in such a role is the normative idea that NGOs are nonstate organizations independent from for-profit businesses working in international development, humanitarian action, human rights, labor rights, or environmental issues (Schuller & Lewis 2014). This normative idea of NGOs plays a crucial role in the larger discursive universe in which the Western notion of civil society and more flexible forms of good governance have long been promoted by international development agencies and practitioners. In the world of development, "[a]ctors assume identities in relation to their strategies of interaction, and political representations inform the negotiations that take place between these actors" (Lewis & Mosse 2006: 14). The labor NGOs at the workshop engaged with this normative discourse about NGOs. Their presentations to the funding agencies clearly show how this idealized notion of NGOs defines practices, and facilitates and encourages NGOs defined as appropriate (Fisher 1997: 442). More importantly, the labor NGOs' interaction with the donors illustrates different sets of relationships among variously positioned actors: the NGOs, the funding agencies, and the state are crystalized in a specific locale and at a specific time. My focus on the interaction and relationships disengages the universalizing models and discourses about NGOs and brings to the fore the local, national, and global processes and connections whereby the flows of funding, ideas, and people move through different levels and sites (Appadurai 1991; Lash & Urry 1994; Fisher 1997: 449).

Mobilized by the notion of *mingan*, the representational strategies such as the enactment of the image of a victim-turned-activist, and rhetorical practices such as irony and humor described in the workshop in Beijing is similar to a kind of "phatic labor" (Elyachar 2010) which produces communicative channels whereby certain kinds of semiotic meanings and economic value can be transmitted and connected with the normative discourse of development. In the case of Wei Peng, his presentation did lead to a substantial outcome. A few months after the workshop, Wei Peng received new funds from a European funding agency that was present at the meeting in Beijing. In conjunction with the representational strategies and rhetorical practices, the idea of *mingan* works as a boundary setter which demarcates the insiders from the outsiders in such a way that it both conforms to and defies the power of the state while at the same time enacting and connecting relationships, a kind of *guanxi* practice. Viewed as such, the common notion that *guanxi* is an institution of trust and reciprocity and that trust is the ontological basis of social relationships is subverted. Against the politics of *mingan*, trust arises from the point when representational practices are successfully employed and thus where relationships are enacted.

In his discussion of the processes in which stereotypes of national characters are employed and converted to present a supposedly objective description of reality, Herzfeld brings to the fore the ways in which the immediacies of social interaction on the ground reproduce and reshape the stereotypes produced at the top of bureaucracies (1992: 71). Herzfeld argues that as much as many of the features attributed to bureaucrats of particular nations are quite real, it is not because

> the French, the Germans, or the British have the innate characteristics attributed to them, but because people everywhere adopt rhetorical strategies on the basis of a presumed 'national character.' Their efficacy lies not in their recognition of some unchanging reality, but in their appeal to the conventions of collective self-representation.
>
> (1992: 72)

What people do with stereotypes, following Herzfeld, resonates with what the labor community does with the idea of *mingan*. As much as the Chinese state appears to be capricious and elusive, the labor community does their best to adhere to the general guidelines of what constitutes *mingan* while trying to carve out a space for their activism. As such, what consists of *mingan,* regardless of its ambiguous and unstable content, becomes a ground on which the state is imagined and perceived in a certain and sometimes static way (Abrams 1988 [1977]; Taussig 1992, 1997).

The politics of *mingan* shows the endeavors of navigating the uncertainty of state tolerance and how they need to be anchored to certain fixed notions of the state in order to be pursued further. Fully aware that the Chinese state can be very unpredictable, elusive, and sometimes erratic, labor activists still have to hold on to their stereotypical understanding of the state while drawing on their previous hands-on experiences. They do not always know if their action and its consequences will be within bounds, but with the stereotypes of the Chinese state as an omnipresent and omniscient oppressor, they can at least obtain a degree of certainty that roughly delimits the parameters of their action. This is what stereotypes do: They are simplistic, unambiguous, and prejudiced portrayals; they are not necessarily true or factual, but they provide a sense of certainty and therefore stability. Thus, the politics of *mingan* is also about understanding, negotiating, manipulating, and putting to use the stereotypes of the Chinese state, labor NGOs, and Western funding agencies so as to locate some degree of certainty in the midst of uncertainty. "Stereotypes are one of the currencies of social life" (Herzfeld 1992: 72). That several international representatives wasted no time in giving their business cards to Wei Peng clearly shows that Wei Peng had succeeded in using the currency of *mingan* and gaining support. He successfully played the role of an outspoken labor activist who publicly defies the Chinese state.

Conclusion

In this chapter, I discussed the understanding and usage of the term *mingan* and the politics it entails in the labor community. With the example of my online conversation with Chen Tong, I demonstrated how *mingan* is embodied through the lived experience of labor activists. I illustrated how the domain of uncertainty is also a domain of suspicion where labor activists are always on the alert for government surveillance. My "blunders" became a tool for unveiling this psychological process which Cheng Tong had to undergo when working under politically restrictive and uncertain conditions. By describing various and uncertain views from labor NGOs and donors on the definition of what constitutes *mingan,* I showed how the ambiguity of *mingan* opens up an emergent problem space of intimacy which requires a type of tacit knowledge, skills, and discretion to navigate.

Focusing on the four-day workshop in Beijing where the NGOs and donors were brought together, I discussed how this space of intimacy is also productive by demonstrating how the notion of *mingan* is invoked, experienced, and utilized by different actors. By extending Herzfeld's concept of "cultural intimacy," I situated the local experiences, perceptions, and imagination of the state in the zone of intimacy embedded in the domain of uncertainty and laid bare by the politics of *mingan*. The politics of *mingan* illustrates how these actors try to navigate through the terrain of uncertainty and estimate an appropriate distance from the state by means of the reification of the state, which, according to Abrams, is a cultural process that makes the state deceptively tangible.

> The state is not the reality which stands behind the mask of political practice. It is itself the mask which prevents our seeing political practice as it is [...]. The state comes into being as a structuration within political practice; it starts its life as an implicit construct; it is then reified—as the *res publica*, the public reification, no less—and acquires an overt symbolic identity progressively divorced from practice as an illusory account of practice.
>
> (Abrams 1988 [1977]: 58, emphasis in original)

With the metaphor of the mask and its ability to conceal and obscure, Abrams implicates the state in the cultural processes and systems of signification that construct reality, which, in turn, is masked and inherently deceptive. According to Abrams, these processes, which are exercises of power and legitimation, provide ways to tease out the idea of the state, which is essentially "an ideological project" (1988 [1977]: 76). The interaction between the labor NGOs and donors at the workshop clearly shows the processes through which the Chinese state is envisioned, constructed, mocked, and sustained. It also demonstrates how these actors engage with the world of development where creative self-representations and strategic uses of essentialism can initiate a contact point and forge a relationship between actors where trust and solidarity become an effect rather than a precondition. It challenges the common notion of trust and solidarity as the ground on which relationships and networks are created and fostered, a popular discourse in international development where particularly the number of NGOs is used to measure the growth of civil society and thus democracy (Edwards & Hulme 1996; Mercer 2002).

Notes

1 References on the translation of the word *mingan* can be found at, for example, the Contemporary Chinese Dictionary (Chinese-English edition) and Baidu, China's biggest search engine: https://fanyi.baidu.com/translate#zh/en/%E6%95%8F%E6%84%9F accessed on June 20, 2015.
2 This conversation took place in July 2013.
3 The interview was conducted in May 2013.
4 Unnamed author. 2014. Thousands of China workers on strike. *BBC*, April 17. Available at: www.bbc.com/news/business-27059434 accessed September 19, 2014.
5 This conversation took place in March 2013.

6 I will talk more about this National Congress in Chapter 5, which deals with the subject of secrecy.
7 The interview was conducted in June 2013.
8 Fang, Lan. 2013. International humanitarian aid re-positioned (重新定位 国际援助). *Caixin*, February 22. Available at: http://m.magazine.caixin. com/m/2013-02-22/100493238.html accessed July 26, 2015.
9 The Chinese term *"tai lihai"* literally means "very good at or capable of doing something very well." Here, I have translated the term as "progressive" because that is what was referred to in this context. The focus was on the NGOs' capability for being progressive and critical of the government.
10 The interview was conducted in March 2013.

Bibliography

Abrams, Philip. 1988 [1977]. Notes on the difficulty of studying the state. *Journal of Historical Sociology* 1 (1): 58–89.

Appadurai, Arjun. 1996. *Modernity at large: cultural dimensions of globalization.* Minneapolis: University of Minnesota Press.

——— 1991. Global ethnoscapes: notes and queries for a transnational anthropology. In *Recapturing anthropology: working in the present*, edited by Richard Fox. Santa Fe, NM: School of American Research Press, pp. 48–65.

Berlant, Lauren. 1998. Intimacy: a special issue. *Critical Inquiry* 24 (2): 281–288.

Bourdieu, Pierre. 2000. *Pascalian meditations.* Stanford, CA: Stanford University Press.

Brandtstädter, Susanne. 2016. The rebel as trickster and the ironies of resisting in contemporary China. In *Irony, cynicism, and the Chinese state*, edited by Hans Steinmüller and Susanne Brandtstädter. New York: Routledge.

De Certeau, Michel. 1984. *The practice of everyday life.* Berkeley: University of California Press.

Douglas, Mary. 1975. *Implicit meanings: essays in anthropology.* London: Routledge.

Edwards, Michael, and David Hulme. 1996. "NGO performance and accountability: introduction and overview." In *Beyond the magic bullet: NGO performance and accountability in the post-Cold War world*, edited by Michael Edwards and David Hulme. West Hartford, CT: Kumarian Press.

Elyachar, Julia. 2010. Phatic labor, infrastructure, and the question of empowerment in Cairo. *American Ethnologist* 37 (3): 452–464.

Fassin, Didier, and Richard Rechtman. 2009. *The empire of trauma: an inquiry into the condition of victimhood.* Translated by Rachel Gomme. Princeton, NJ: Princeton University.

Ferguson, James. W. 1994. *The anti-politics machine: development, depoliticization, and bureaucratic power in Lesotho.* Minneapolis: University of Minnesota Press.

Fernandez, Aloysius Prakash. 2004. *NGOs and government in collaboration for development.* MYRADA Rural Management Systems Series: Paper 39. Bangalore: Myrada.

Fernandez, W. James, and Mary Taylor Huber. 2001. "Introduction: the anthropology of irony." In *Irony in action: anthropology, practice, and the moral imagination*, edited by James W. Fernandez and Mary Taylor Huber. Chicago and London: University of Chicago Press.

Fisher, William F. 1997. Doing good? The politics and anti-politics of NGO practices. *Annual Review of Anthropology* 26: 439–464.

Glaeser, Andreas. 2004. "Monolithic intentionality, belonging, and the production of state paranoia: a view through Stasi onto the late GDR." In *Off stage on display: intimacy and ethnography in the age of public culture*, edited by Andrew Skryock. Stanford: Stanford University Press.

—— 2000. *Divided in unity: identity, Germany and the Berlin Police*. Chicago: University of Chicago Press.

Hassid, Jonathan. 2010. *Pressing back: the struggle for control over China's journalists*. PhD dissertation, University of California, Berkeley.

—— 2008. Controlling the Chinese media: an uncertain business. *Asian Survey* 48 (3): 414–430.

Herzfeld, Michael. 2016. *Cultural intimacy: social poetics and the real life of states, societies, and institutions*. New York: Routledge.

—— 1992. *The social production of indifference: exploring the symbolic roots of Western bureaucracy*. Chicago: University of Chicago Press.

Hirschman, Albert O. 1995. *A propensity to self-subversion*. Cambridge, MA: Harvard University Press.

James, Erica Caple. 2010. *Democratic insecurities: violence, trauma, and intervention in Haiti*. Berkeley and Los Angeles: University of California Press.

King, Gary, Jennifer Pan, and Margaret E. Roberts. 2013. How censorship in China allows government criticism but silences collective expression. *American Political Science Review* 107 (2): 326–343.

Lash, Scott, and Jonathan Urry. 1994. *Economies of signs and space*. London: Sage.

Lewis, David, and David Mosse, eds. 2006. *Development brokers and translators: the ethnography of aid and agencies*. Bloomfield, CT: Kumarian Press.

Mercer, Claire. 2002. NGOs, civil society and democratization: a critical review of the literature. *Progress in Development Studies* 2 (1): 5–22.

Merton, Robert. 1972. Insiders and outsiders: a chapter in the sociology of knowledge. *American Journal of Sociology* 78 (1): 9–47.

Midgal, Joel S. 2001. *State in society: studying how states and societies transform and constitute one another*. Cambridge: Cambridge University Press.

Pitkin, Hanna Fenichel. 1972. *Wittgenstein and justice: on the significance of Ludwig Wittgenstein for social and political thought*. Berkeley: University of California Press.

Polanyi, Michael. 1966. *The tacit dimension*. Chicago: University of Chicago Press.

—— 1958. *Personal knowledge: towards a post-critical philosophy*. London: Routledge & Kegan Paul.

Riles, Annelise. 2001. *The network inside out*. Ann Arbor: University of Michigan Press.

Schuller, Mark, and David Lewis. 2014. Anthropology of NGOs. *Oxford Bibliographies*. doi:10.1093/obo/9780199766567-0090 accessed March 16, 2016.

Scott, James C. 1998. *Seeing like a state: how certain schemes to improve the human condition have failed*. New Haven, CT: Yale University Press.

—— 1990. *Domination and the arts of resistance: hidden transcripts*. New Haven, CT: Yale University Press.

Shryock, Andrew, ed. 2004. *Off stage on display: intimacy and ethnography in the age of public culture*. Stanford: Stanford University Press.

Spires, Anthony. 2007. *China's unofficial civil society: the development of grassroots NGOs in an authoritarian state*. PhD dissertation, Yale University.

Steinmüller, Hans. 2016. "Introduction." In *Irony, cynicism, and the Chinese state*, edited by Hans Steinmüller and Susanne Brandtstädter. New York: Routledge.

———— 2013. *Communities of complicity: everyday ethics in rural China*. New York: Berghahn Books.

Stern, Rachel E., and Jonathan Hassid. 2012. Amplifying silence: uncertainty and control parables in contemporary China. *Comparative Political Studies* 45 (10): 1230–1254.

Stevenson, Angus. 2010. ed. *Oxford dictionary of English*. Oxford: Oxford University Press.

Taussig, Michael. 1997. *The magic of the state*. New York: Routledge.

———— 1992. *The nervous system*. New York: Routledge.

Tsai, Lily L. 2010. "Quantitative research and issues of political sensitivity in rural China." In *Contemporary Chinese politics: new sources, methods, and field strategies*, edited by Allen Carlson, Mary E. Gallagher, Kenneth Lieberthal, and Melanie Manion. New York: Cambridge University Press.

Yang, Guobin. 2009. *The power of the Internet in China: citizen activism online*. New York: Columbia University Press.

———— 2008. "Contention in cyberspace." In *Popular protest in China*, edited by Kevin J. O'Brien. Cambridge, MA: Harvard University Press.

5 Intimating secrecy

In the winter of 2012, I started doing fieldwork at Shenzhen-based Wei Min Law Firm, a partner of the Hong Kong-based labor NGO Chinese Workers' Front (CWF). One day a few weeks into my fieldwork, I overheard that there was going to be a workshop organized by CWF in Hong Kong in December. Chen Yishen, founder of Wei Min Law Firm, was talking to his assistant Zhang Caoyuan while both of them were standing next to the water dispenser near my desk. I learned that all of CWF's partners in China were invited to attend and that the purpose of the workshop was to train these labor NGOs to train workers in collective bargaining.[2] I took the opportunity to ask Chen Yishen if I could go with him. Knowing the sensitive nature of such a workshop, I was not too hopeful that I would be given permission. To my surprise, his answer was positive. He said, "You can go as the intern of my law firm. You are with me so they won't say no." It shows the status and influence that Chen Yishen has in relation to CWF. He added, "But you need to make travel and living arrangements yourself." I agreed without any hesitation.

There was a palpable air of secrecy about the four-day workshop organized by CWF. The only information I was given was that it was scheduled to take place sometime in December 2012 and somewhere in Hong Kong. As December was approaching, I started to inquire about the workshop, but no one at the law firm was willing to give me any information. My questions were always met with a curt answer: "We don't know yet." After a few attempts, I stopped asking and hoped that they would inform me when it was time. One day in early December when I walked into the law firm, I saw Chen Yishen talking on his mobile phone and pacing back and forth in his office, which had a big glass window facing the entrance of the law firm. I went to my desk and turned on the computer, getting ready to start my work for the day. A few minutes later, Chen Yishen came out of his office and walked to his assistant Zhang Caoyuan, whose desk was about one-and-a-half meters away from mine, and said, "You will be staying with the NGOs. It's the same hotel as last time. You should go home and get ready. I'll leave a bit later." Zhang Caoyuan nodded without saying anything and started to pack his bag. Then Chen Yishen walked up to me and said, "The workshop is tomorrow so you should probably take the train tonight. Call me tonight when you are in Hong Kong. I will tell you about the venue then. My number also works in Hong Kong so just call the same number." I nodded. Chen Yishen went back to his office before I even had a chance to speak. I checked the time and realized that I didn't have much to spare, so I went home right away and packed. I boarded a train in the district of Luohu in Shenzhen[3] around six o'clock in the evening. As soon as I got on the subway on the other side of Luohu in Hong Kong, I called Chen Yishen and was given the venue for the workshop. It was to be held in the office of CWF, which is located in an office building in central Hong Kong. Chen Yishen instructed me to meet him at the entrance of the building at 8 o'clock the next morning.

Waiting at the entrance at the agreed-on time, I saw Chen Yishen across the street walking slowly toward me with another man. Chen Yishen was talking and gesticulating in a lively way while the other man, who was much taller than Chen Yishen, lowered and tilted his head and listened attentively. This man was the director of CWF, Li Jie. I recognized him from the pictures I had seen of him in the news media. When they arrived at the building, Chen Yishen introduced me to Li Jie, who was all smiles as he shook my hand and said, "Welcome to the workshop." On our way into the building, Li Jie was friendly and asked me what and where I was studying. The cordial conversation continued as we all stepped into the elevator. A few seconds later, we arrived at the designated floor and were greeted with a clean and carpeted hall with offices lining both sides. CWF's office was at the end of the hall. Following Li Jie and Chen Yishen, I was finally let inside the headquarters of CWF. Having heard so many stories about CWF as a highly politically sensitive organization that, according to rumor, collaborates with the CIA, I couldn't help but feel a sense of excitement as well as relief; it was as if I was let into a secret society (George 1993; Van de Port 2006). My journey from Shenzhen to the office of CWF in Hong Kong felt like a fictive initiation by which my trustworthiness was being tested.

Practicing secrecy

This chapter deals with secrecy and how secrets and the practice of secrecy are employed to manage relationships between the labor NGOs, both in mainland China and Hong Kong, and the donors, against the backdrop of state surveillance. In the previous chapter, I discussed how a site of intimacy predicated on the uncertain limits of state tolerance is manifested through the politics of *mingan* where the actors in the labor community strategically mobilize discourses and stereotypes in their self-representational practices in order to initiate and cultivate their relationships with the donors. These relationships show how the state is imagined and acted on, and how the workings of state power are manifested.

In Chapter 2, I described the ambiguously formulated state secrets, which can both expand and squeeze the political space for manipulation and interpretation depending on one's position and other circumstances such as timing, place, and personal relationship, which was discussed in Chapters 3 and 4. I have discussed how the labor NGOs have to operate under the knowledge that they are being monitored and under the threat that they can be arbitrarily accused of being connected to hostile foreign forces or of leaking state secrets to enemies, which, if convicted under China's Criminal Law and Security Law, would suffer penalties ranging from public surveillance and deprivation of political rights to life imprisonment, depending on the severity of the act. Placing secrecy at the center of this chapter, I go into depth to show how labor activists navigate through the ambiguous and risky terrains of Chinese politics while trying to be accountable to their foreign partners. The labor NGOs often talk about how they need to be careful and keep certain things secret when implementing projects so as to minimize interference from the state as mentioned in my meeting with Mandy, CWF's project coordinator, in the introduction. Hence, this chapter is about these "secret things" and the techniques of concealment used to maintain this intimate space of secrets, which also constitute the content of this shared intimacy.

As mentioned in the previous chapter, the notion of *mingan* is closely linked with the idea of secrecy, particularly because whatever is *mingan* can generate political risk and thus should be kept secret. It is worth reiterating that what constitutes *mingan* is often ambiguous, uncertain and arbitrary, which consequently has an impact on determining political risk and what should be kept secret. As such, to determine what constitutes *mingan* is to exercise a certain mode of observing risk, which highlights the contingent nature of risk (Luhmann 1993: 21–22). However, risk can also bring about secrecy as a way to manage precarious social relations. For example, Mariane Ferme (2001) shows how gender relations in contemporary Sierra Leone reflect a violent historical legacy of warfare and raiding in which secrecy and strategies of concealment have emerged as ways of managing conflict. The causal relationship between uncertainty, secrecy, and *mingan* can be difficult to unravel as the subjective experience and perception of risk and what is *mingan*, and the urgency of secrecy are coconstitutive. As such, it further compounds the ambiguity and arbitrariness of the political landscape in which these labor activists operate.

Moreover, using CWF as the ethnographic axis around which my discussions develop furnishes an analytical lens to explore the role of an intermediary NGO in the work of international development. As an intermediary, CWF serves as an important link between the grassroots labor NGOs in mainland China and funding agencies, particularly by facilitating the transfer of funds, skills, and knowledge. CWF operates in the grant economy (Boulding 1981; James 2010: 179) whereby it receives a grant from a Western donor to carry out projects. Some argue that grant economies are a type of economy that intersects with gift economies (Mauss 2002 [1950]; James 2010) and commodity economies (Appadurai 2006) in the sense that grant economies are "situated between direct and reciprocal exchange between givers and receivers in gift economies and the indirect transfer of currencies for crafted objects in commodity economies" (James 2010: 179).

Grants often demand greater formalization of the relationship between givers and recipients, and include the expectation that grant recipients will carry out specific tasks or goals over time at the individual, organizational, or governmental level. Grant economies are increasingly structured by an audit culture (Strathern 2000) in which aid grants are assessed by formal and informal audits in the hopes of attaining a greater degree of transparency and accountability, which are central issues in international development (West & Sanders 2003; James 2010; Jensen & Winthereik 2013). Hence, it becomes crucial to the survival of an organization, program, or project to demonstrate its ability to deliver and achieve expected outcomes as well as to demonstrate efficiency, productivity, innovation, and quality of services.

Situated between the NGOs and donors, CWF manages and supervises its NGO partners and accounts to the funding agencies, and facilitates communication between NGOs and the donors. A central part of CWF's work involves the maintenance and mediation of different sets of relationships: its relationship with the donors, its relationship with the mainland Chinese labor NGOs, and the relationship between the donors and Chinese mainland labor NGOs, which are usually put under the heading of "project management" by my interlocutors. To successfully manage and mediate these relationships, according to my interlocutors at CWF, often comes down to how to translate and communicate the goals of a certain project as mutually beneficial and collectively shared by all partners involved. An effective mediation allows for "the negotiation of common meanings and definitions and the mutual enrollment and cooptation into individual and collective objectives and activities" (Lewis & Mosse 2006: 14). Nevertheless, the oppressive political environment in which the Chinese labor NGOs operate has complicated this process of mediation and created one very crucial parameter for CWF's project management that cannot be ignored: the Chinese state. Nevertheless, CWF manages and mediates the potential tensions that can arise from the relationships among its collaborators, it cannot fail to attend to and pivot its day-to-day operation on how and what the Chinese state thinks and does.

As a link between the grassroots NGOs and donors, CWF occupies a middle ground where we can examine the tensions that arise from the process of mediation. These tensions are characterized particularly by the practice of secrecy: a constant interplay between concealment and revelation, exclusion and inclusion, and privacy and publicity. More importantly, it is through such an interplay that values such as trust, solidarity, and accountability are created, mediated, and contested. As much as the Chinese state has no doubt set up the parameters of how these NGOs work and communicate with one another, an ironic twist unfolds when examining the dynamics and micropolitics between these NGOs and their donors. I argue that the practice of secrecy, particularly public secrecy, in the labor community may not be as much about evading state surveillance, as the popular discourse has it, as it is about producing and consolidating trust and solidarity among these actors.

In early anthropological research, the concept of secrecy often carried negative, antisocial, and primitive overtones (Taussig 1999; Herdt 2003; Jones 2010), an approach that is characteristic of an implicitly social evolutionist stance in Western discourses since the Enlightenment. Under the influence of Georg Simmel (1906), anthropologists began to recognize secrecy's potential as a productive mechanism for constituting self, society, and culture (Herdt 1990; Jorgensen 1990) through the workings of exclusion and inclusion, concealment and revelation, as well as privacy and publicity. Recent work has explored the generative aspects of secrecy in a variety of different settings ranging from the "productive paranoia" of internalized surveillance (Masco 2006: 282), the parochial "moral autarchy" among nuclear weapon scientists (Gusterson 1998: 91) to how interactional secrecy enveloping derivatives formulae generates and structures financial products in an international bank (Lépinay 2011).

In line with this generative view on secrecy, I treat secrecy as a practice with a focus on its performative aspect (Herzfeld 2009), which is strategically employed to facilitate and manage the work of as well as the relationships between the labor NGOs and donors. More specifically, focusing on the practice of secrecy, I demonstrate how these labor NGOs and donors strategize to gauge the appropriate distance from the state by discussing the ways in which secrets travel (are kept, conveyed, and circulated), which, in turn, illustrates how relationships are transacted in the domain of uncertainty (Jones 2014).

The power of secrecy

Secrecy suffuses Chinese politics. This culture of secrecy has been an important part of the Chinese Communist Party's political practice since the Party was established in the early twentieth century (Teiwes & Sun 2007; Zhang 2009; Guo & Hickey 2010). Studies have shown that Chinese decision makers seem to prefer secrecy in the decision-making process as it helps maintain the public persona of decision makers and keep a psychological distance from their counterparts in other departments and the public (Gaenslen 1986). The legacies of such a political tradition and practice have resulted in a political and cultural aura in which secrecy breeds ambiguity while ambiguity amplifies secrecy; secrecy and ambiguity are considered important stratagems for gaining power, exerting control, and achieving victory (Zhang 2009: 80).

In Chapter 2, I described some information considered to be state secrets, such as the number of executions and strikes. During my fieldwork in 2012, a telling example of how secrecy abounds in Chinese politics was the fact that the specific date for the 18th National Congress of the Communist Party of China was kept secret. Speculation had run rampant for months over when the Congress was going to be held. Some reports put the date at mid-October as certain major events, like the Beijing Marathon and an exhibition on security equipment, were instructed to be delayed while hotels in Beijing were told to hold rooms empty to accommodate the 2,300-odd delegates.[4] In September, conjecture grew stronger and continued to point to the date at mid-October. However, the official announcement that the National Congress was to be held on November 8, 2012 did not come until October. The secrecy and delayed announcement of the specific date of the Congress had kept the labor NGOs on their toes and prolonged the uncertainty about the parameters of their work.

Describing secrecy as "one of the greatest accomplishments of humanity" (1906: 462), Georg Simmel foregrounds the role of secrecy in human societies and social relationships:

> Every relationship between two individuals or two groups will be characterized by the ratio of secrecy that is involved in it. Even when one of the parties does not notice the secret factor, yet the attitude of the concealer, and consequently the whole relationship, will be modified by it. The historical development of society is in many respects characterized by the fact that what was formerly public passes under the protection of secrecy, and that, on the contrary, what was formerly secret ceases to require such protection and proclaims itself.
>
> (Simmel 1906: 462–463)

Keeping secrets complicates social relationships and produces tensions, which, according to Simmel, works as a productive and regulating mechanism that not only sets the social boundaries between insiders and outsiders but also offers "the seductive temptation to break through the barriers by gossip or confession" (Simmel 1906: 466). Through the workings of concealment and revelation as well as exclusion and inclusion, secrecy marks "shadings and fortunes of human reciprocities throughout their whole range" (ibid.). In other words, secrecy produces value (Simmel 1906: 464; Jones 2014: 54), which, paradoxically, needs to be enacted and "performed in a public fashion in order to be understood to exist" (Herzfeld 2009: 135). Undeniably, the power and attraction of secrecy lies in the very possibility that it may be revealed. As such, the interplay between concealment and revelation can be conceptualized as a way of "socially mobilizing the secret as a form of sociocultural capital without dispersing restricted knowledge" (Jones 2014: 55). Fredrik Barth's comparative analysis of the ways in which knowledge is transacted in Southeast Asia and Melanesia provides an illustrative example of how the conjurer gives value to knowledge by successfully "veiling it and sharing it with as few as possible," with the means of secrecy and manipulation of cultural symbols (Barth 1990: 641).

In some ways, the kind of secrecy I have observed in the Chinese labor community resonates with both the productive view on secrecy in the sense that the practice of secrecy creates and strengthens trust relationships among the Chinese and Hong Kong NGOs as well as their Western donors. Here, trust can be deemed as a social and symbolic capital that is created, accumulated and maintained by the practice of secrecy among these organizations. And yet, the practice of secrecy by these actors does take on a strong performative character because they are fully aware of the powerful surveillance machine operated by the Chinese state. These NGOs and donors perform secrecy not so much that they are absolutely certain that by doing so they can evade surveillance as that they want to determine who they can trust in this already highly limited space of labor activism. As such, one can argue that the practice of secrecy in the Chinese labor community is both generative in creating trust among these actors and reproductive of consolidating the existing oppressive political conditions.

In Chapter 2, I described China's State Secrets System and the ambiguity surrounding what constitutes state secrets. I suggest that state secrets are not so much withheld knowledge as a kind of a "secrecy effect" that structures social and political relations between those who know and those who don't (Derrida 1994: 20). The secrecy effect is both constituted by and constitutive of the domain of uncertainty in which labor activists try to estimate the possible consequences of their action. As described in Chapter 2, one category of state secrets refers to "diplomatic activities, activities related to foreign countries, as well as commitments to foreign countries." Read in its broadest sense, "activities related to foreign countries" can cover a wide range of things that are left to the interpretation of the individual. As previously mentioned, the majority of the labor NGOs in China receive funding from abroad and hence they all have some sort of relationship with foreign countries, mostly via the link with Hong Kong.

This relationship is created and managed through predominantly project-based partnerships which entail a variety of activities such as transferring funds, receiving training, attending meetings and workshops, and documenting activities. Viewed against the backdrop of the State Secrets System, these activities can be easily seen as politically sensitive and can entail political risks for the labor NGOs. In other words, to manage and maintain partnerships between the NGOs and donors depends on how one negotiates and conducts these potentially risk-prone activities; it is also through such endeavors that trust is generated and mediated. In the following section, I will describe what techniques are employed to carry out some of these potentially perilous activities. The techniques of concealment are the channels of secrecy through which "relations of inclusion and exclusion or similarity and difference are modulated via communicative practices of concealment, revelation, revelation of concealment, and concealment of revelation" (Jones 2014: 56). More importantly, following

Simmel's generative view on secrecy, through the practice of secrecy, these dichotomous relations create and mediate such values as trust, solidarity, and accountability, which structure the rest of the analysis in this chapter. Nevertheless, I demonstrate in the discussion that follows, through the prism of secrecy, how these relations fraught with tension and contradictions ultimately challenge some of the core values that international development holds dear while reproducing and consolidating the existing political order.

Trust

In this section I discuss the practice of secrecy and draw on what media of secrecy are employed by the labor activists. I use "media" in its broadest sense to include not only the field of communication technologies but also all other materialities that people use to create and sustain social relatedness (Stasch 2009: 16–17; Jones 2014: 56). Attending to the ways secrets travel across different media provides a way to show the intertwined relationship between secrecy and risk as mentioned earlier and thus demonstrates how the perception and knowledge of secrecy is a recursive relationship (cf. Jones 2014: 54). As an analytical lens, it also offers the possibility of discussing how trust is created and forged under uncertain and ambiguous conditions and develops an alternative to the Parsonian theory of trust grounded on certainty and familiarity (Parsons 1978). With a focus on CWF, I have selected information and communication technologies, money, and informers (the body) to illustrate how CWF employs secrecy to manage and maintain their relationships with their partners in mainland China through the enactment of trust. As such, I argue that trust is not so much an ontological requisite, which is popularly viewed as the precondition of effective *guanxi* practices, as it is something that follows from relations. More importantly, in the face of government surveillance, trust is instrumentalized to create, shape, and maintain relationships in the labor community. Trust becomes a mode, rather than a basis of interaction.

Communication

As the project coordinator at CWF, Mandy is the main contact person with NGO partners in mainland China. She is always especially cautious and has developed some tactics for communicating with NGO partners. For example, in addition to the regular work phone shown on her business card, when communicating with the Chinese NGOs, Mandy usually uses prepaid phone cards so that she can constantly change her phone number. Chuckling when I asked whether this tactic works, Mandy replied,

> It doesn't seem to! Haha! A while ago, Wu Xiangjun [a labor NGO director] gave me a number that very few people knew about, which

really stressed me out. Then later he told me that the police knew about the conversation he had with me and asked him to come in for some questions The police asked him if he owned this number. We had no idea how that happened. At first, I thought my phone was tapped but I change my number all the time! Well, we don't know what happened. But of course, we are concerned about wiretapping. We can only do our best [to avoid saying anything sensitive or important].[5]

Control of information has been central to the governing strategy of the Chinese Communist Party. Under Mao Zedong's regime, the media system served the state by imposing ideological hegemony that fed the citizenry in every aspect of their daily lives with official information and interpretations of reality. The communication was vertically controlled by the central government, characterized by the media system that acted as a conveyer belt transferring Party thought from the leaders to the masses. The telecommunication network was only made accessible to elites and was supervised and monitored by the public security apparatus. Members of the public were discouraged from communicating with one another. However, with the beginning of economic reform in the 1970s, the role of the media started to change. The media organs were redefined and promoted as tools of economic and cultural development with an emphasis on business information and entertainment (Lynch 1999: 53–104). In the late 1980s, the Chinese population was given increased access to technology such as fax machines, telephones, and the Internet. In 1994, China was connected to the Internet for the first time, which ushered in an era of information revolution.

New information and communication technologies have no doubt played a role in renegotiating the boundaries between the Chinese state and society, but they have in no way dissuaded the Chinese government from wanting to keep a strict control over the flow of information. As a surveillance technology, wiretapping is a common practice used by the CCP to control members of society. A news story published by the Chinese outlet *Southern People Weekly* shows that wiretapping is even increasingly being used by Chinese officials to spy on their fellow colleagues.[6] Out of fear of wiretapping, it is not uncommon for some labor activists to request that everyone present switch off their mobile phones when convening a meeting of great importance. Mandy explained to me,

If your phone number is being tapped, the numbers that are near yours also fall within the range [of being tapped]. So, if you put your new number next to the number that is tapped, [they] should be able to find out that you have another number.

Against such pervasive surveillance, Mandy noted that she always assumed that her communication with the partners was tapped. "But wiretapping is really not that scary," added Mandy, waving her hand as if to dispel the dark clouds of surveillance that had been hanging over our conversation. Mandy explained,

> Unless he [the police] listens in twenty-four hours, he may miss [some information]. Sometimes we even reveal the time and venue [of an event] on the phone but they (the police) aren't fast enough [to react to the information heard]. For example, you and I are talking right now. If the person who is supposed to listen in happens to be away, maybe going to the bathroom or out for a cigarette, then he would have just missed some part of our conversation. So I am telling you that wiretapping is really not that scary. Unless it is during a specific and *mingan* period of time or unless both of us are very *mingan* [so sensitive that it entails political risk such as CWF's director Li Jie] we will not be monitored twenty-four hours. So if I make phone calls at irregular times, say, I call you at one o'clock today and three o'clock tomorrow, chances are they missed our conversation.[7]

Mandy's words indicate how state power can be exercised through the control of time, which was discussed in the previous chapter, and how she operated in two different time-maps. One is the concrete state-centric time-map. Operating on a state-led temporal modality is one of the ways in which labor activists measure the boundaries of state tolerance. Such a temporal modality provides a degree of certainty under uncertainty by avoiding *mingan* timing such as during major political events. In contrast to the concrete state-centric time, the act of constantly changing phone numbers and making phone calls at irregular times engages with a different time-map that is both abstract and tedious, similar to "attritional time, [which is] the mundane, repetitive, constant struggle that makes up political activism in the everyday" (Lazar 2014: 101). It is a tactic that "depends on time—it is always on the watch for opportunities that must be seized 'on the wing.' Whatever it wins, it does not keep. It must constantly manipulate events in order to turn them into 'opportunities'" (de Certeau 1984: xix, emphasis in original). Juxtaposed against the state-centric temporal modality, the everyday effort to keep attritional time, no matter how tedious it is, also offers a kind of certainty and day-to-day continuity due to the implicit understanding that the possibility of discontinuity and rupture always lurks in the background (Lazar 2014: 106). Operating under these different time-maps shows a constant consideration for the right timing (to determine whether a time is *mingan* or not) to reveal or conceal an activity, a conversation or a meeting. To shift skillfully between these different temporalities is crucial to the work of Mandy as well as other labor activists.

In addition to frequently changing her phone numbers, Mandy is also very careful with how she uses online communication. Mandy has a different email address for each partner. She sets up an email account for each of her partners. The username and password are only known to her and the partner, so no third party is involved. Mandy said that she is very certain that no one knows about these email accounts, unless the other person or she discloses the information. With the rapid spread and increasing usage of the Internet, the Chinese government faces an even greater challenge policing and supervising online information (Lynch 1999: 210–215). By the first half of 2008, the number of Internet users had reached 253 million; in just over ten years' time, about a quarter of the urban population had access to the Internet (Yang 2009: 2). As of 2018, China has more than 800 million Internet users and has become the world's biggest online community (Deng 2018).

One of the most concrete measures taken by the Chinese government is that Internet content providers have been separated from Internet service providers and are allowed different foreign ownership limits under the WTO (Kalathil & Boas 2003: 18). The reason for the division is that the Chinese government views Internet content providers as organizations having the power to interpret information and therefore qualifying themselves to be regulated in a different way from Internet service providers, which only provide connections to the Internet. Many observers have mixed views on the tension between economic modernization and political control that technology highlights. Some argue that China will no longer be able to control the flow of information (Kalathil & Boas 2003: 1–12; Yang 2003, 2009), while others note that the Chinese government has succeeded in minimizing the political impact of the Internet (Chase & Mulvenon 2002; Harwit & Clark 2003; Kalathil & Boas 2003: 13–46).

In 2000, the Ministry of Public Security established its Bureau for Supervising the Security of Public Information Networks (*gonggong xinxi wangluo anquan jiancha ju*). Its missions are to,

> monitor and control the Net-based activities of hostile organizations and individuals in and outside Chinese borders; report various information and trends regarding social and political stability in a timely manner; strengthen Internet patrol; [and] closely watch developments on the Internet.
>
> (MPS 2000 cited in Pei 2006: 86)

For example, CWF's website is banned in China. In 2000, the Ministry of Public Security issued a directive stating that Internet police must "step up the screening of domestic websites and home pages, conduct secure management of personal home pages, electronic bulletin boards, and free email accounts, and collect information on important websites in and outside China" (MPS 2000 cited in Pei 2006: 86). While how successful these measures undertaken by the Chinese government will be remains a debatable issue, they have no doubt had an impact on the ways in which the Internet and online communication are used by different social actors.

Regardless of the Chinese government's attempts to intercept and block email from overseas Internet service providers used by dissident groups, it has been noted that email and email publications are more difficult to block compared to websites (Chase & Mulvenon 2002: 70). There have been stories of dissident groups successfully overcoming the Chinese government's email blocking.[8] With the increasing accessibility of the Internet to the Chinese public, not only dissident groups but also individual Chinese citizens or netizens use the Internet to seek recognition, assert rights, and fight against discrimination. Some describe such contentious activities, which rely on the use of the Internet and other new communication technologies, as "online activism" (Yang 2009: 3). The issues touched on by online activism range from "consumer-rights defense to sexual orientation, from protests against harm inflicted on vulnerable individuals and disadvantaged groups to the expression and assertion of new lifestyles and identities" (ibid.: 3–4).

Nevertheless, to be able to successfully combat Chinese security services requires a certain level of knowledge and expertise in information and communication technology, which many labor activists in China do not have. Commenting on the issue of surveillance, Mark, development director of CWF, said,

> Frankly, we know for a fact that our computers are compromised. Our partners don't understand technology very well so I am sure their emails and clearly everything they have written on Weibo are read. It is impossible to defeat surveillance mechanisms. So given all their [the Chinese security services'] electronics, employees, their ability to intercept phone calls etc., there is really no way you can work under the assumption that you can evade surveillance. We work under the assumption that every email and document is read.[9]

When it comes to communicating with donors, CWF uses Hushmail, which is a web-based email service that offers PGP-encrypted email, file storage, and vanity domain services. To use Hushmail to communicate with funding agencies is a very common practice among the labor organizations in Hong Kong. Since Hushmail is not available in Mandarin and dealing with the Great Firewall[10] (Barmé & Ye 1997; cf. Thornton 2010: 179–198) is a rather daunting task for CWF's partners, Mark said,

> We really just use those popular free and anonymous email sites such as 163.net and 263.net. Then, of course, we also communicate on Weibo and QQ. These are really the most convenient for them. We don't use Gmail with them because Gmail is not only slow in China, it often gets cut off.

When asked about whether there is a more secure way of communicating with his partner in Hong Kong, Wei Peng, director of Blue Sky, said matter-of-factly, "There is no secret channel of communication. How do you keep secrets from the government?" Wei Peng noted that he doesn't like to use encryption not because it is difficult or complicated but because he doesn't want to attract attention from the government. Here, the use of encryption— an archetypal medium of concealment—is reasoned as potential liability that might increase the risk of police visits and questioning. In other words, it is potentially politically *mingan*. It shows that even when there are a range of media of secrecy at the NGOs' disposal, it is not always certain that they will avail themselves of these media. How much to reveal or conceal is a political question that often eludes a clear and accurate answer. Living with surveillance, these NGOs can at best navigate the spectrum of secrecy resorting to their previous experiences or guesswork or taking a chance.

What frustrates Wei Peng most is that sometimes his mobility is compromised because the state security agents read his email. "They found out about the workshop that I was invited to attend in Hong Kong and asked me not to travel," explained Wei Peng. Indignant about state surveillance infiltrating his email account, sometimes Wei Peng posts a screenshot of the login page of his email account on his WeChat account. The log-in page said, "There was some irregular login activity in your account. If it was not you who tried to login, your password might have been compromised." Underneath the screenshot, Wei Peng wrote, "God dammit! I have just changed my password!" The screenshot—a medium of revelation—posted by Wei Peng reveals what is normally concealed and articulates what is not openly talked about: a public secret that is both mundane and commonplace (Ashforth 1996: 1194), an important point that I will come back to later.

Money

Having a stable source of financial support is crucial to the survival and operation of these organizations. When working in a political environment where foreign funding is both politically sensitive and desperately needed, how do NGOs navigate the risky terrain of transferring and receiving money? How does money travel? According to the current regulations, a registered Chinese NGO needs to submit an application to ask for permission to receive foreign funds. The application includes a photocopy of the registration license of the applying NGO, a document that shows that the foreign funder is a legally registered entity, and an agreement between the NGO and foreign funders detailing how the money is to be used. Once the application is approved, the registered Chinese NGO is required to open a separate bank account which is solely designated to receive foreign funds. All transactions involving foreign funds need to be dealt with via this particular bank account. In 2009, the State Administration on Foreign Exchange announced a few changes to the regulations with regard to Chinese NGOs receiving foreign funds.[11] One of the most notable changes is that it requires registered Chinese NGOs and foreign donors to have notarized agreements. A notarized agreement must include details about how the money is going to be used. In the announcement, it also clearly states that the State Administration on Foreign Exchange monitors all transactions closely. The new regulations became effective on March 1, 2010. The requirement for notarized agreements is generally seen as the government's attempt to heighten its monitoring of foreign capital flow into the country and makes it even more difficult for NGOs to survive.[12]

One month into my fieldwork at CWF, I started to feel more comfortable asking sensitive questions concerning money. One day over lunch, I asked Mandy to tell me about how CWF sends money to their partners in mainland China.

> We transfer money to their personal account. There is no other way! Around 2009, there was this new policy on managing foreign funds. It says that individuals are only allowed to receive a certain amount [of foreign funds] every year. Many labor NGOs are not registered, or even if they are registered, they are afraid [of taking money directly from abroad] because they don't want other people to know. So they don't necessarily dare to let you transfer the money directly to the organization's bank account. This has to do with taxes but also the fear of government interference. So we usually just transfer the money directly to the [NGO] leader's private account.[13]

Not only does CWF take into account these labor NGOs' concerns by sending money directly to their leaders' private bank accounts, but CWF is careful with choosing the means through which the money is transferred. Mandy continued after washing down a mouthful of curry chicken rice with some iced tea.

> We use money exchange stores on the street. One of the advantages of going to such places is that it won't show who transferred the money. There will be records that there is money coming to this person's account but it doesn't show where exactly the money is coming from. Well, if the government really wanted to investigate, it could try but it should not be able to find any direct links with us.[14]

The use of money exchange stores clearly shows that CWF wants to veil its connection to its partners in mainland China in hopes that it might mitigate political risk for them. Depending on the size of the NGO in terms of the number of staff and size of the office, the amount of money transferred from CWF to each of its partners varies but usually falls between 20,000 RMB and 30,000 RMB a month, according to Mandy.

When I asked Mandy whether she was concerned about the risk of financial malpractice and corruption, she said that CWF tries to control and manage the funds by not transferring all the funds in one go but in installments. Mandy revealed to me that some years ago, the director of an NGO partner stole money from CWF, which led to the immediate termination of the partnership. In order to reduce the misuse of funds, Mandy noted that they now require the NGOs to submit a budget plan for the coming month so that CWF can review and decide whether or not to approve it. CWF will only reimburse expenses that are listed on the budget plan.

In addition to the reliance on money exchange stores, CWF also uses the simplest way of moving money across the border, that is, delivering cash in person. Sometimes when CWF's project coordinator or financial manager makes trips to visit their partners in China, they bring some funds with them and give them to the NGOs in person. Such a practice elicited a comment from a project manager at a North American funding agency who jokingly described the Hong Kong NGOs as the "white mafia." Sometimes when the NGOs come to Hong Kong for meetings and workshops, they also receive some funds for their organizations from CWF. As the labor NGO leaders in China joke, "We are here to collect money" (*lai lingqian le*).

I want to use one of CWF's partners as an example to specifically illustrate how trust and secrecy work between these NGOs. Little Flower Women Workers' Social Service Center (hereafter Little Flower) is one of CWF's partners in the program of collective bargaining. Distinct from most of CWF's partners, Little Flower is a registered civil non-enterprise institution and hence has an official bank account under the organization's name. The director of Little Flower is very concerned about her collaboration with CWF and wants to keep the partnership as secret as possible.[15] CWF has made some compromises and agreed to transfer their funds to Little Flower to a private bank account, but it is not the director's private bank account. "This person is a friend of the director (of Little Flower). We don't know this person's identity," said Mandy. Mandy explained that all the money designated for Little Flower is transferred from CWF to that private bank account. When Little Flower needs money, the director will ask her friend to withdraw it from the bank. "This is necessary so as to avoid the government's suspicion," stressed Mandy while acknowledging that this practice relies largely on the integrity of the NGO director and her friend. "If you want to work with them, you will have to trust them," said Mandy.

Transferring money to the bank account of a person who is unknown to CWF demands significant trust first and foremost on the part of CWF. In this case, the form of trust, as a particular mode of interaction in the context of uncertainty, goes against the common notion that *guanxi* practices are predicated on affective ties whereas trust is usually ascribed. In this case, trust is not an affective, neutral feeling or attitude based on familiarity as Parsons' theory of trust suggests (1978: 45–47). Here, trust presupposes a situation of risk; hence, a situation of risk is also a situation of trust. Such trust is predicated on the level of risk and the means through which this risk is conceptualized (Patterson 1999: 153–154). Having agreed to transfer money to a stranger's bank account, CWF can only bestow its trust and hope that the money will not be misused and will go to Little

Flower. CWF's trust only extends to eventualities which, if they do occur, would cause CWF to regret having made such a decision. Following Luhmann, trust always involves a critical alternative where the damage resulting from a breach of trust may be greater than the benefit to be gained from the bestowed trust (Luhmann 1979: 24). Therefore, one who trusts takes into account the possibility of damage resulting from others' actions and chooses a position which could lead to that possibility. "One who hopes simply has confidence despite uncertainty. Trust reflects contingency. Hope ignores contingency" (ibid.).

Travel

An important element in maintaining and enhancing the partnership between these labor NGOs is to take part in meetings, conferences, and training workshops. Due to Hong Kong's distinct political, economic, and administrative status, which was described in Chapter 2, there are special travel requirements for Chinese nationals. Chinese nationals traveling to the Special Administrative Regions of Hong Kong and Macau are required to secure a travel document called the People's Republic of China Exit-Entry Permit for Traveling to and from Hong Kong and Macau. It is colloquially known as the two-way permit (*tongxingzheng*). The two-way permit is the only travel document permitted for personal visits, family reunions, business and other nongovernmental purposes to and from Hong Kong and Macau. If traveling without a two-way permit, Hong Kong grants a stay of seven days to mainland Chinese who use their passports in transit through Hong Kong to and from overseas. The cost of applying for a two-way permit is 100 RMB and it is valid for ten years. Each time a Chinese national wants to make a trip to Hong Kong or Macau, they need to pay an additional 20 RMB to get an endorsement from the local police station and have this printed on their passport.

The purpose of the trip determines the length of time and thus the type of endorsement that a two-way permit holder can obtain when traveling to these special administrative regions. For individual visits, a two-way permit holder can usually get an endorsement for one visit or a maximum two visits within a period of three months and each visit should not be longer than seven days. The labor NGO workers who come to Hong Kong to participate in meetings and workshops usually fall into this category. To further complicate the regulations, different provinces in China have different rules concerning where the application for a two-way permit should be submitted. For example, if you are from Shandong Province, you are required to go back to your hometown and submit your application there.

Wu Xiangjun, director of a labor NGO, told me that he was taken away by the police when passing through customs in Luohu. He was on his way to a workshop organized by CWF I described in the beginning of the chapter when he was taken in for questioning, which lasted almost two hours.

Wu Xiangjun said that he had to travel with his passport[16] this time because his two-way permit had been taken away the last time he returned from Hong Kong. The reason given by the police was that he travelled too frequently. Wu Xiangjun shared with me his previous experiences with border crossings.

> Last year [2012], I was supposed to come to Hong Kong for a meeting. My two-way permit was still valid at the time. Then I was asked to drink tea and they took my permit. So I didn't get to go because they kept my permit until it expired. They probably read my email or listened in on my phone calls to find out that I was coming to Hong Kong so they took away my permit. Well, they can only prevent me from going to Hong Kong. If I am going to the U.S., they can't do anything about it because if you want to apply for a visa to the U.S., you go to the embassy. You don't go through the Public Security Bureau. It may sound ironic but it's easier for me to go to the U.S. than to Hong Kong. Whether you are going to Hong Kong or somewhere else, they can try to 'ka' [to compound and prolong the procedures] you so that you won't be able to make it to the event that you were planning on attending. So if I want to go to other countries it is easier [than going to Hong Kong]. Last time I pretended that I was going to Malaysia and Thailand and I had to transfer in Hong Kong. Nothing happened when I was leaving Chinese customs. It was when I entered the border of Hong Kong that they took me away for a talk. I had the travel agency take care of the plane ticket. When the thing was over, I canceled the ticket.[17]

I asked Wu Xiangjun to elaborate on what he meant by "taking care of the plane ticket." He explained how a Chinese citizen could travel with a passport to Hong Kong.

> When you go through customs, you need to show a round-trip plane ticket. The ticket shows that you are transferring in Hong Kong and you are going to a country like Indonesia or Thailand where you can get a landing visa. So this time, for example, I bought a return ticket to Indonesia. Of course, I am not really going to Indonesia. There are travel agencies that take care of such things for you. They will make a reservation for you so that if you do not pay [for the ticket] within a certain period of time, the reservation will be cancelled automatically. I got the reservation to show to staff at customs so I could come to Hong Kong.[18]

Wu Xiangjun revealed how purchasing a plane ticket for a trip that was never meant to occur can be used to negotiate his cross-border mobility with the Chinese state. The plane ticket here becomes a medium of secrecy that veils the true purpose and destination of his travel: a blank trip disguised to facilitate a certain degree of mobility. However, in contrast to

Wu Xiangjun's purposeful concealment of his real destination, Zhang Guoqi, a senior staff member at Green Grass Migrant Workers' Service Center, sometimes posts remarks like "Here I am again, Hong Kong" on WeChat as soon as he crosses the border. On his WeChat account, Zhang Guoqi often posts pictures of the places he visits, including Hong Kong, for trainings, workshops, and meetings. Once I casually commented on these and said jokingly that he had been very busy traveling around the country. He offered an amusing response imbued with irony: "I may as well just tell them where I have been," with the gesture of moving his head upward several times to indicate that he was referring to the police. It was a moment of intimacy in which we both shared an implicit understanding of government surveillance. Similar to Wei Peng's screenshot of how his email account was allegedly hacked, Zhang Guoqi's pictures—media of revelation—show an intentional revelation tinged with irony that lays bare the tension between the labor NGOs and the state, which is lived but rarely articulated openly. Moreover, his amusing remark, a discursive practice of humor, also figures as a medium of secrecy which is employed to make legible what cannot be expressed directly and openly (see also McCullough 2014).

That the secrecy surrounding cross-border activities has a clear temporal and spatial dimension shows how the presence of the state is evoked, embodied, and temporarily put aside. As soon as one crosses the border, secrecy ceases to exist. Instead of viewing the secrecy enveloping these social actors' cross-border mobility as a power struggle between the state and subaltern, secrecy here works more as a means to manipulate information in terms of what, how, and when information is revealed as well as concealed. In the face of state surveillance, to be able to determine the what, how, and when is crucial to the workings of the partnerships among these labor NGOs. Moreover, the labor NGOs that are willing to risk crossing the border to attend meetings and workshops held in Hong Kong are highly appreciated and described as having "*diqi*" (底气, the confidence and courage to face difficulties) by CWF. Such border-crossing activity demonstrates both the moral courage and the solidarity shared by these labor NGOs in their determination to push for the labor movement in China.

Informers

Regardless of how information and communication technology has revolutionized the ways in which the Chinese public communicate and access information, what lies at the heart of the communication infrastructure is that it provides a ground on which relationships can be created and facilitated. As such, the techniques of concealment described above are ultimately about dealing with people and estimating who is trustworthy and who is not. Mandy stressed that as a project manager, what she was concerned about most was not so much if her phone was tapped as if CWF's partners were trustworthy.

According to Mandy, when she comes across an interesting NGO that seems to have the potential and capacity for doing progressive work, she first simply asks around in the NGO sector to see what people say about a particular individual or organization. Mandy explained to me that she usually just focuses on the directors of the NGOs, as they are usually the most crucial people in the organization. In addition, Mandy also does a little "research on the Internet." By that, Mandy means that she visits a particular website called "the human flesh search engine" (*renrou sousuo yinqing*). The human flesh search engine is a website where self-organized Chinese netizens work collectively to investigate issues, individuals, or incidents of interest to them. The issues can range from incidents of animal abuse to adultery to corruption (Thornton 2010: 190–193). "I look up a person on this website as it can sometimes give you more detailed information about things and people. I'm really into gossip so I do this kind of thing," said Mandy laughingly. Availing herself of the gossip that she might find about a particular individual on the human flesh search engine, Mandy tries to learn about the reputation of a potential partner and thus assess his or her capability. Mandy's use of gossip shows that gossip is a communicative practice that "reports behavior; it rests on evaluating reputations" (White 2000: 60), which has the possibility of forming or disrupting relationships.

For Mandy, it is very important to investigate the people and organizations who contact CWF and show interest in collaboration. One reason is the concern of government infiltration. Mandy has heard from other NGOs that the Chinese state security agents would sometimes ask some Chinese mainland NGOs to come and work with CWF in order to obtain information about CWF or who CWF works with. In order to illustrate her point, Mandy related to me an incident that occurred in 2012 and caused a lot of trouble for a well-planned workshop.

> I know that one NGO leader gives information to the police. I am very *mingan*. When we had just begun our partnership, he asked a lot of questions and wanted a lot of information. The questions are not about me but about the projects and activities. He would ask these questions in advance, like way before the activities were to be held, and the questions were very specific. Well, I have been working at CWF long enough to know what he was up to.[19]

Mandy was talking about a labor NGO director with whom she had been having some issues related to trust. Describing herself as a *mingan* person, Mandy wanted to highlight that she was very quick to pick up anything that is slightly unusual. She told me that in 2012, she was organizing a training workshop here in Hong Kong and asked this NGO leader to bring workers over to share their experiences with collective bargaining. But then something happened. The NGO leader called her to say that *guobao* asked him to cancel the trip. This happened on the day when they were supposed to leave for Hong Kong. Mandy had booked the hotel and arranged everything for the workshop, so she was not pleased to be notified of the last-minute cancelation. Mandy proceeded with the workshop, but only five people turned up.

Still feeling somewhat agitated about the unsuccessful workshop, Mandy told me how she later tried to prove her suspicion that it was this NGO leader who had disclosed the information to the police. She pressed the NGO leader for an explanation when he came for meeting at CWF a few months later. Adamant to know about how the *guobao* found out about the workshop, Mandy demanded the Chinese NGO leader to give an explicit answer and quit being evasive. CWF's director (Li Jie) was present too; Mandy related to me what Li Jie said to the NGO leader:

> He said, 'You don't really have to report everything to them [*guobao*]. The thing is that if you report [the workshop] to them, whoever said yes [that you could attend] then knew about it and needed to take responsibility should anything happen. So they could only say no. But if you didn't tell them and just came to the workshop and they wanted to let you, they would pretend that they didn't know anything about it and thus wouldn't stop you.'[20]

Once again, Li Jie's words make plain an open secret that everyone is aware of but avoids bringing to explicit consciousness. Such a revelation shows how the labor NGOs perceive and imagine the state. While working under the assumption that the Chinese state can see everything, these labor NGOs need to grapple with another level of state-led uncertainty that hinges on complicity: What does the state care about? Does the state care about and respond to everything it sees? The uncertainty regarding the limits of state tolerance arises not so much out of what the state can see but rather what kinds of action would be seen as an affront to the state (cf. Scott 1998). This reminds us of Taussig's understanding of power, that it is "not that knowledge is power but rather that active not-knowing makes it so" (1999: 6–7). In other words, "knowing what not to know" (ibid.: 2) is an exercise of power that thrives on complicity. The words of Li Jie show that for the labor NGOs, determining the limits of state tolerance is more often than not about learning or guessing what things the state chooses not to know and see, and when.

In suggesting that his Chinese NGO partner not reveal everything to the police, Li Jie demonstrated his understanding of how such a mode of power works and his willingness to be attentive to and thus complicit in the rules of the game. What Li Jie was suggesting was also to encourage his NGO partners in the mainland to use some discretion. What is at work here is the interplay between what can be concealed and revealed, and the discretion required to make the judgment call (Mahmud 2014: 30; Herzfeld 2015: 25). What lies at the core of the assumption of the state's "knowing what not to know" is a mode of power exercised through generating a sense of contingency and the anxiety, fear, and worry among these labor NGOs trying to figure out what matters to the state in terms of when, what, why, and how the state chooses not to know. Not knowing what, why, and when the state cares becomes a function as well as a consequence (a means to an end) of these techniques of concealment, which are predicated on the admission of the omnipresence of state surveillance accompanied by occasional intentional revelations as political expressions of defiance. This is a specific illustration of how self-censorship works in this context. Here, power sustains itself by creating a recursive reality of speculation and imagination, a reality that is magnified by the practice of secrecy whereby these social actors make their decisions and employ different media, tactics, and techniques in order to form and sustain relationships while trying to keep the untrustworthy ones at bay.

Accountability

In the years leading up to the financial crisis in 2008, governments in Europe and North America started to decrease spending on humanitarian aid, including financial support for NGOs. There was also an increasing demand for governments and donors worldwide to be more transparent and accountable, which was manifested in the Paris Declaration on Aid Effectiveness in 2005. The Declaration outlines five main principles for making aid more effective: ownership, alignment, harmonization, results, and mutual accountability.[21] Central to this Declaration is the hope that the actions, plans, and strategies of the donors will be more transparent and accountable when they commit themselves to working toward standardized monitoring and evaluation systems and aligning funding strategies (Jensen & Winthereik 2013: xiv).

The changing discourse and practices of development work started to have an impact on the Hong Kong labor organizations around 2006–2007. Some donors came to Hong Kong to visit their partners and introduce new guidelines and practices for their partnerships. "They were very specific about what we need to do and how we do it," said one Hong Kong labor NGO worker, noting that "one of the main changes is that they want us to start to design, manage, and implement our projects by using the logical framework approach (LFA)." Designed as a tool to enhance transparency and accountability, the LFA is used to plan, manage, monitor, and evaluate international development projects. It is widely used in major donor organizations such as the U.S. Agency for International Development Aid (USAID), United Nations Development Program, European Commission, Swedish International Development Cooperation Agency (SIDA), and Norwegian Agency for Development Cooperation (NORAD). Faced with the demand for transparency and accountability and the politically restrictive conditions of China, how does CWF, straddling between the donors and the grassroots labor NGOs in mainland China, negotiate the seemingly conflicted relationship between publicity and secrecy as well as accountability and secrecy? In the section that follows, I will discuss this issue by focusing on a central element of CWF's work: paperwork, an important bureaucratic technology, and tease out the tension inherent in their relationship with the donors.

Secrecy and publicity

A key characteristic of the LFA is that it requires clearly defined objectives and indicators that can be used to monitor and evaluate the success or failure of a project, which, in turn, can enhance the management and thus accountability of a project. The LFA puts emphasis on information that is quantifiable so that it can be used to track and assess the progress of a project in specific numeric terms. As such, an important part of the work of the labor NGOs is to translate their work into numbers and document the data. For example, a labor NGO takes note of how many legal leaflets are distributed every month and how many phone calls as well as visits from workers seeking help and advice are received every day. If the labor NGO holds an activity, it is required to specify the number of participants, the gender distribution of the participants, the length of the workshop, the budget of the activity, and whether the activity receives any publicity in the media including social media such as Weibo, which is then measured by how many shares and comments are shown. Similar to the use of hashtags on Twitter, the use of the "@" sign is a common practice among the labor NGOs when posting on Weibo. One labor NGO even has a list of people and organizations printed out and stuck it on the wall in their office; the director of this labor NGO instructs his staff to make sure to "@ these people" when they post on Weibo. "The more people you @, the more may share the post. Then it looks like a lot of people are paying attention to us," explained the NGO director.

These reports from the grassroots labor NGOs in mainland China are sent to Mandy and Mark at CWF, who then compile, edit, and translate these reports and turn them into mid-term and yearly reports for the donors. Commenting on the reporting, Mark noted that different funders have different requests and "sometimes the reporting can get really intense. Once we had at least 30 matrices to report on and that was just for one donor!"

These numbers are used to measure the success of a project and assess whether the project has achieved its intended goals such as an increase in workers' consciousness or solidarity. Admitting that issues like workers' consciousness are hard to measure, Mark said that when CWF submits a project proposal using the LFA, they need to think about strategic objectives and intermediary objectives, and what activities should be designed to achieve these objectives. More importantly, "You also need to think in quantitative terms. You need to know how you are going to measure your objectives," explained Mark. He continued to say,

> When it comes to raising workers' consciousness, it is very easy to more or less make stuff up. You know you can say that they did such and such

activity and they have raised workers' consciousness or they have improved that. Does giving out flyers outside the factories raise workers' consciousness? It may. It depends on who is reading it [the report] and what interaction goes on between the distributor and the workers. But because you hand out 10,000 or 100,000 flyers can you then prove that workers' consciousness was raised? I think that's the question that a lot of organizations [funding agencies] want to preempt. Nowadays they [funding agencies] want to see more concrete proof of how their money is spent.[22]

With the rapid growth of online activism, some funding agencies are investing more resources in encouraging the use and spread of social media in China, which is increasingly viewed as a way to measure the growth of civil society. CWF encourages its partners to use social media for advocacy and has organized a few workshops to teach the labor NGOs how to use social media such as Weibo and a video camera so that they can record some of their training meetings with workers. During my fieldwork with the grassroots labor NGOs in mainland China, the staff always made sure someone was in charge of taking photographs when the NGO was holding an activity, especially a training workshop in which migrant workers were invited to participate; "so we have something to post on Weibo," said the staff. When I participated in the second workshop on the topic of collective bargaining and the role of the ACFTU organized by CWF, I was asked to help CWF post remarks on Weibo as the workshop proceeded during the day. The only instruction from CWF's director was that I should not mention any names out of respect for the privacy of the participants. Mark likes to make use of the media, including social media, not only because it can be an effective way to carry out advocacy work but also because it provides a better way to verify the work of CWF's NGO partners. "When it is posted on Weibo or printed in the newspaper, you can be sure that this thing did happen. The NGO didn't make it up. It is just a better method of verification," said Mark. Nevertheless, how does CWF resolve the potential tension between the deployment of risk-reducing secrecy and the publicity that comes with the use of the media? In other words, how does CWF weigh accountability against secrecy?

As described earlier, the staff at CWF basically work under the assumption that the Chinese government can read and hear everything in their email and phone conversations with their partners in mainland China. Therefore, when writing and submitting reports to the donors, Mark, who is in charge of written and verbal communication with CWF's funders, tries to be careful with what he puts into the reports. Mandy works closely with Mark on reporting. As the project coordinator, Mandy receives and follows up on the written reports from CWF's partners in mainland China. Mandy edits and compiles all the reports from one labor NGO into one single document, which contains information on what the NGO has done in the past six months. Then Mandy will send this document to Mark, who will translate the document from Mandarin into English. This process of putting together an English report (compiling, editing, and translating) for one funding agency is time consuming and can take from six to eight weeks.

During my fieldwork, I had access to these written reports and saw that Mandy kept all the names and personal information in the compiled and edited document. Mark has to make decisions on what information he should conceal or can reveal due to security concerns. For example, he doesn't include the full names of the people in the reports. But for some donors, Mark noted, this is not good enough. Mark said that some donors want more information so he often gets questions like, Where are the workers from? Which factories? What sector are they in? Looking Frustrated, Mark told me that he has tried to communicate with CWF's donors and explain to them why CWF didn't want to give too much specific information in the reports. But one funding agency, a trade union, told him that they work with workers in the car and metal industries so they can give CWF more support if they know which sectors the workers are in. However, another frustrating situation that arises is that when Mark does send in detailed information, he still gets questions from donors. With a wry smile on his face, Mark explained,

> Sometimes we send them attachments that are twenty, thirty pages of case details. I clearly get the impression that they have not read those attachments. They ask the most basic questions about the case, which clearly indicates that they didn't read the documents we sent them. Tremendously annoying! It takes me weeks to translate all that! They ask questions like: What happened in the factory? How many trainings did they have? There is a case chronology detailing every meeting that they have.[23]

When commenting on the issue of privacy and publicity, Mandy doesn't have the same kind of concerns as Mark. She said, "Well, they [the labor NGOs] are not really doing anything *mingan* anyway so there is no need to worry that somebody else is reading the reports." By "somebody else," Mandy was referring to the state security agents. However, her comment and the act of keeping all of the names in her reports is once again the divulgence of a public secret widely shared in the labor community. More crucially, it is through such a disclosure that Mandy comes to terms with the tension between secrecy and publicity. Together with the other media of secrecy and techniques of concealment discussed in this chapter, Mandy's comment, which expressed a sentiment shared by some of the other staff members at CWF, is one example of the occasional admission and disappointment expressed by CWF's staff about the effectiveness of doing these secret things, and some even questioned the need to be this "secretive." So the question is, Why the secrecy? I will discuss this question in the conclusion.

Conclusion

In this chapter, I illustrated some media of secrecy and techniques of concealment employed by the labor NGOs, which, according to them, are meant to circumvent government surveillance and reduce government inference in their work. However, from time to time, intermittent revelations of the target of their concealment, that is, the Chinese state, are made public and accompanied by ironic and sometimes defiant remarks. These comments reveal the different levels of epistemological articulations between what people say they do, what they actually do, and what they think about what they do, and raise an apparent question about secrecy: Why do they invest so much labor in manufacturing a secret undertaking that is known and seems to negate itself? It is as if they were keeping a public secret: "that which is generally known, but cannot be articulated" (Taussig 1999: 5). What is the value of the unproductive labor? More importantly, what is the power of secrecy?

Taussig describes public secrecy as the basis of social institutions constituting "the most interesting, the most powerful, the most mischievous and ubiquitous form of socially active knowledge" (Taussig 1999: 3).

> We all 'knew' this, and they knew' we 'knew,' but there was no way it could be easily articulated, certainly not on the ground, face-to-face. Such 'smoke screens' are surely long known to mankind, but this 'long knowness' is itself an intrinsic component of knowing what not to know, such that many times, even in our acknowledging it, in striving to extricate ourselves from its sticky embrace, we fall into even better-laid traps of our own making. Such is the labor of the negative, as when it is pointed out that something may be obvious, but needs stating in order to be obvious. For example, the public secret. Knowing it is essential to its power, equal to the denial. Not being able to say anything is likewise testimony to its power. So it continues, each negation feeding the other ....
> (Taussig 1999: 6, emphasis in original)

More crucially, the power of public secrecy is exercised by way of maintaining "[the] verge where the secret is not destroyed through exposure, but subject to a quite different sort of revelation that does justice to it" (Taussig 1999: 3). In *Phenomenology of Spirit*, Hegel accentuates that understanding or experience cannot be achieved without recognizing the logical principle that the negative is as decisive as the positive when confronted by a contradiction. Hegel underscores that negative experience is the authentic experience of a world of contradictions, antagonism, and alienation where the individual's desire for self-realization is repressed while the collective means of attaining it is shifted to an objective process and effectively revoked. The struggle with ambiguities and contradictions is the labor of the negative that works to attain the greatest power of all: understanding (Hegel 1977: 18).

The relationships between the Chinese labor NGOs, CWF, and their donors form different layers of reality underpinned by how these labor activists perceive and act on the capriciousness of the state. The occasional acknowledgment and complaint of state surveillance, in the example of the secret practices adopted by CWF, as well as Zhang Guoqi's and Wei Peng's pictures on social media, are intended to reveal the secret without destroying it. They reveal truth, which is "not a process of exposure which destroys the secret, but a revelation which does justice to it" (Benjamin 1977: 31). The practice, perception, and evaluation of secrecy in the labor community are an illustration of the workings of power where the notion of the state is constantly invoked, enacted, articulated, and negotiated. As Taussig aptly points out, "[...] it is precisely the role of secrecy, specifically public secrecy, to control and hence to harness the great powers of contradiction so that ideology can function" (Taussig 1999: 268). The discrepancies between what these labor activists say, do, and think about what they do in relation to the state demonstrate their understanding of what secrets are and how they keep and mediate these secrets in order to manage relationships among themselves.

Contextually invoked, secrecy becomes a channel to create and facilitate these relationships. Trust and solidarity are generated and mediated when the partners demonstrate their knowledge of when and how to reveal and conceal information. This is in no way to make light of the infiltration of Chinese security services and the state's iron grip on freedom of speech and association in the country. On the contrary, it is precisely this political reality that makes the relationships between the donors and the labor NGOs in Hong Kong and mainland China imaginable, and without which it would be difficult to insert the labor NGOs in Hong Kong into the international division of doing development work. Therefore, the practice of secrecy is not so much about dealing with the Chinese state as it is about managing the relationships between these labor NGOs. By employing secrecy, these social actors are not only estimating their distance from the state but also among themselves. Against the backdrop of uncertainty about state surveillance, the discrepancy among the talking, thinking, evaluating, and practicing of secrecy discloses a social world where secrecy is practiced contextually and strategically, and is predicated on the guesswork of what the state cares to see. As such, the strategic use and practice of secrecy offers a different entry point to consider the workings of state power. In the next chapter, I go further to illustrate how state power is manifested and negotiated when labor NGOs apply the skills and knowledge discussed in this chapter and in Chapter 6 in a particular development program. With this development program, I demonstrate how labor NGOs struggle to carve out a space for activism yet still mired in the uncertainty of state tolerance.

Notes

1 It is worth mentioning that at this stage in my fieldwork I had not been in any contact with CWF. Having heard so much about CWF through their partners in

China and how sensitive it is to work with CWF according to the Chinese labor NGOs, I had been waiting for such a meeting. The workshop presented a great opportunity for me to meet CWF.

2 In the next chapter, I will talk more about the meaning and application of collective bargaining in China and how it is different from mainly Western contexts.

3 Shenzhen and Hong Kong share a border, so it is very convenient to travel between these two cities. One can go by airplane, train, bus, or ferry. Taking the train is one of the most popular ways and it takes about one hour and a half. There are a number of entry points between these two cities depending on one's destination within the city. When traveling from Shenzhen to Hong Kong, many people take the subway to the district of Luohu, cross customs and take the subway again, which goes all the way to downtown Hong Kong.

4 Subler, Jason. 2012. Ready, steady, go for China Congress, not marathon runner. *Reuters*, September 5. Available at: www.reuters.com/article/us-china-congress-idUSBRE8840FS20120905 accessed March 31, 2016.

5 The passage was taken from an interview I had with Mandy in June 2013.

6 Unnamed author. 2013. Wire-tapping wars: the world of official espionage. *China Digital Times*, February 17. Available at: http://chinadigitaltimes.net/2013/02/wiretapping-wars-the-world-of-official-espionage/ accessed March 29, 2016.

7 The passage was taken from an interview I had with Mandy in June 2013.

8 A famous example is the spamming campaigns of *Xiao Cankao* (*VIP Reference*), a Washington D.C.-based Chinese-language online publication. Founded in November 1997, *Xiao Cankao* publishes articles from Hong Kong, Taiwan, and Western news sources that are not available to the public in China. As a countermeasure to protect readers and obstruct the Chinese government's efforts to prevent users in mainland China from accessing their publication, *Xiao Cankao* provides a degree of "plausible deniability" to their subscribers by spamming numerous copies to recipients who have not requested them (Chase & Mulvenon 2002: 31). Moreover, the editors of *Xiao Cankao* frequently change web addresses and use a different email address every day to thwart Chinese security services' attempts to block the electronic distribution of their publication (ibid.).

9 The passage was taken from an interview I had with Mark in June 2013.

10 The term was coined by Geremie R. Barmé and Sang Ye in their article titled: "The Great Firewall of China," *Wired* 5.06, June 1997. Available at: http://archive.wired.com/wired/archive/5.06/china.html accessed April 7, 2015.

11 More information on receiving foreign funds is available here: www.safe.gov.cn/safe/glxx1/index.html accessed January 29, 2019.

12 Richburg, Keith B. 2010. China's crackdown on non-profit groups prompts new fears among activists. *The Washington Post*, May 11. Available at: www.washingtonpost.com/wpdyn/content/article/2010/05/10/AR2010051004801.html accessed April 1, 2015; Jackson-Han, Sarah. 2010. NGOs face tighter curbs. *Radio Free Asia*, April 21. Available at: www.rfa.org/english/news/china/ngo-04212010124252.html accessed April 1, 2015.

13 The passage was taken from an interview I had with Mandy in June 2013.

14 The passage was taken from an interview I had with Mandy in June 2013.

15 One staff member of Little Flower didn't know that her organization was in partnership with CWF after having worked there for almost a year.

16 Traveling with his passport meant that Wu Xiangjun was only passing through Hong Kong en route to somewhere else. According to the regulation, he was allowed to stay in Hong Kong for seven days during transit.

17 The passage was taken from an interview I had with Wu Xiangjun in April 2013.

18 The passage was taken from an interview I had with Wu Xiangjun in April 2013.

19 The passage was taken from an interview I had with Mandy in June 2013.

20 The passage was taken from an interview I had with Mandy in June 2013.

21 From: www.oecd.org/dac/effectiveness/45827300.pdf accessed February 10, 2020.
22 The passage was taken from an interview I had with Mark in June 2013.
23 The passage was taken from an interview I had with Mark in June 2013.

Bibliography

Appadurai, Arjun. 2006. The thing itself. *Public Culture* 18 (1): 15–21.
Ashforth, Adam. 1996. Of secrecy and the commonplace: witchcraft and power in Soweto. *Social Research* 63 (4): 1183–1234.
Barmé, Geremie R., and Sang Ye. 1997. "The Great Firewall of China." *Wired* 5.06. June 1997. Available at: http://archive.wired.com/wired/archive/5.06/china.html accessed April 7, 2015.
Barth, Fredrik. 1990. The guru and the conjurer: transactions in knowledge and the shaping of culture in Southeast Asia and Melanesia. *Man, New Series* 25 (4): 640–653.
Benjamin, Walter. 1977. *The origin of German tragic drama*. Translated by John Osborne. London: New Left Books.
Boulding, Kenneth E. 1981. *A preface to grants economics: the economy of love and fear*. New York: Praeger.
Chase, Michael, and James Mulvenon. 2002. *You've got dissent! Chinese dissident use of the Internet and Beijing's counter-strategies*. Santa Monica, CA: RAND Corporation.
De Certeau, Michel. 1984. *The practice of everyday life*. Berkeley: University of California Press.
Deng, Iris. 2018. "Chinese internet users surge to 802 million in test of government's ability to manage world's biggest online community." *The South China Morning Post*. August 21. Available at: www.scmp.com/tech/china-tech/article/2160609/chinese-internet-users-surge-802-million-test-governments-ability accessed on 20190919.
Derrida, Jacques. 1994. To do justice to Freud: the history of madness in the age of psychoanalysis. *Critical Inquiry* 20 (2): 227–266.
Ferme, Mariane C. 2001. *The underneath of things: violence, history, and the everyday in Sierra Leone*. Berkeley: University of California Press.
Gaenslen, Fritz. 1986. Culture and decision-making in China, Japan, Russia, and the United States. *World Politics* 39 (1): 78–103.
George, Kenneth M. 1993. Dark trembling: ethnographic notes on secrecy and concealment in highland Sulawesi. *Anthropological Quarterly* 66 (4): 230–239.
Guo, Baogang, and Dennis V. Hickey. eds. 2010. *Toward better governance in China: an unconventional pathway of political reform*. Lanham, MD: Lexington Books.
Gusterson, Hugh. 1998. *Nuclear rites: a weapons laboratory at the end of the Cold War*. Berkeley: University of California Press.
Harwit, Eric, and Duncan Clark. 2003. Shaping the Internet in China: evolution of political control over network infrastructure and content. *Asian Survey* 41 (3): 377–408.
Hegel, Georg Wilhelm Friedrich. 1977. *Phenomenology of spirit*. Translated by A. V. Miller. Oxford: Oxford University Press.
Herdt, Gilbert. 2003. *Secrecy and cultural reality: utopian ideologies of the New Guinea men's house*. Ann Arbor: University of Michigan Press.

————— 1990. Secret societies and secret collectives. *Oceania* 60 (4): 360–381.

Herzfeld, Michael. 2015. Anthropology and the inchoate intimacies of power. *American Ethnologist* 42 (1): 18–32.

————— 2009. The performance of secrecy: domesticity and privacy in public spaces. *Semiotica* 175: 135–162.

James, Erica Caple. 2010. *Democratic insecurities: violence, trauma, and intervention in Haiti.* Berkeley and Los Angeles: University of California Press.

Jensen, Casper Bruun, and Brit Ross Winthereik. 2013. *Monitoring movements in development aid: recursive partnership and infrastructures.* Cambridge, MA: MIT Press.

Jones, Graham M. 2014. Secrecy. *Annual Review of Anthropology* 43: 53–69.

————— 2010. Modern magic and the war on miracles in French colonial culture. *Comparative Studies in Society and History* 52 (1): 66–99.

Jorgensen, Dan. 1990. Secrecy's turns. *Canberra Anthropology* 13 (1): 40–47.

Kalathil, Shanthi, and Taylor C. Boas. 2003. *Open networks, closed regimes: the impact of the Internet on authoritarian rule.* Washington, DC: Carnegie Endowment for International Peace.

Lazar, Sian. 2014. Historical narrative, mundane political time, and revolutionary moments: coexisting temporalities in the lived experience of social movement. *Journal of the Royal Anthropological Institute* 20 (S1): 91–108.

Lépinay, Vincent Antonin. 2011. *Codes of finance: engineering derivatives in a global bank.* Princeton, NJ: Princeton University Press.

Lewis, David, and David Mosse, eds. 2006. *Development brokers and translators: the ethnography of aid and agencies.* Bloomfield, CT: Kumarian Press.

Luhmann, Niklas. 1993. *Risk: a sociological theory.* New York: Aldine de Gruyter.

————— 1979. *Trust and power.* Translated by Howard Davis, John Raffan, and Kathryn Rooney. Chichester: Wiley.

Lynch, Daniel C. 1999. *After the propaganda state: media, politics, and "thought work" in reformed China.* Stanford: Stanford University Press.

Mahmud, Lilith. 2014. *The brotherhood of Freemason sisters: gender, secrecy, and fraternity in Italian Masonic lodges.* Chicago: University of Chicago Press.

Masco, Joseph. 2006. *The nuclear borderlands: the Manhattan Project in post-Cold War New Mexico.* Princeton, NJ: Princeton University Press.

Mauss, Marcel. 2002 [1950]. *The gift: the form and reason for exchange in archaic societies.* Translated by W. D. Halls. London and New York: Routledge.

McCullough, Megan, B. 2014. The gender of the joke: intimacy and marginality in Murri humor. *Ethnos* 79 (5): 677–698.

Parsons, Talcott. 1978. *Action theory and the human condition.* New York: Free Press.

Patterson, Orlando. 1999. "Liberty against the democratic state: on the historical and contemporary sources of American distrust." In *Democracy and trust*, edited by Mark E. Warren. Cambridge: Cambridge University Press, pp. 151–207.

Pei, Minxin. 2006. *China's trapped transition: the limits of developmental autocracy.* Cambridge, MA: Harvard University Press.

Scott, James C. 1998. *Seeing like a state: how certain schemes to improve the human condition have failed.* New Haven, CT: Yale University Press.

Simmel, Georg. 1906. The sociology of secrecy and of secret societies. *American Journal of Sociology* 11 (4): 441–498.

Stasch, Rupert. 2009. *Society of others: kinship and mourning in a west Papuan place.* Berkeley: University of California Press.

Strathern, Marilyn, ed. 2000. *Audit cultures: anthropological studies in accountability, ethics, and the academy.* London: Routledge.

Taussig, Michael. 1999. *Defacement: public secrecy and the labor of the negative.* Stanford: Stanford University Press.

Teiwes, Frederick C., and Warren Sun. 2007. *The end of the Maoist era: Chinese politics during the twilight of the Cultural Revolution, 1972–1976.* Armonk: M. E. Sharpe.

Thornton, Patricia M. 2010. "Censorship and surveillance in Chinese cyberspace: beyond the Great Firewall." In *Chinese politics: state, society, and the market,* edited by Peter Hays Gries and Stanley Rosen. London: Routledge.

Van de Port, Mattijs. 2006. Visualizing the sacred: video technology, "televisual" style, and the religious imagination in Bahian Candomblé. *American Ethnologist* 33 (3): 444–461.

West, Harry G., and Todd Sanders, eds. 2003. *Transparency and conspiracy: ethnographies of suspicion in the new world order.* Durham and London: Duke University Press.

White, Luise. 2000. *Speaking with vampires: rumor and history in colonial Africa.* Berkeley: University of California Press.

Yang, Guobin. 2009. *The power of the Internet in China: citizen activism online.* New York: Columbia University Press.

———— 2003. The co-evolution of the Internet and civil society in China. *Asian Survey* 43 (3): 405–422.

Zhang, Enyu. 2009. "Contextualizing the practice of regionalization in China's foreign policy." In *China and the global politics of regionalization,* edited by Emilian Kavalski. Farnham: Ashgate Publishing.

6   Collective action

In August 2012, unsatisfied with their working conditions, a group of bus drivers and ticket attendants lodged complaints with their employer and the local labor authorities in a city in Guangdong. These workers' demands included the payment of delayed wages and social security and receiving a copy of their employment contracts and a written statement of the wages that each employee received every month. At first, a total of 75 bus drivers and ticket attendants signed the petition, which was delivered to the local labor authorities. The employees' complaints fell on deaf ears and two of the leading employees were asked to stop working indefinitely. More bus drivers and ticket attendants joined the petition and the group expanded to 150 people. In late September 2012, these workers took the protest a step further and stopped coming to work. They gathered outside the company, holding up a banner with the following text: "Give back our legal working conditions. Defend our legal labor rights. Fairness. Openness. Justice" (*huan women hefa de laodong daiyu, weihu women hefa de laodong quanyi, gongping gongkai gongzheng*).

A volunteer at South Mountain Migrant Workers' Center (hereafter South Mountain) saw the news about these protesting workers on QQ and told Liao Yumin, director of South Mountain. Together with Wen Xue, another staff member at South Mountain, Liao Yumin went to visit these workers outside the bus company in order to gain a better idea of their demands. They also handed out leaflets introducing South Mountain as a labor NGO devoted to strengthening workers' rights and improving working conditions. A few days later, some of the protestors came to South Mountain seeking advice since the company was not responding to the workers' requests and refused to meet with them. After the meeting, Liao Yumin and Wen Xue returned to the bus company and met with the protesting workers. Liao Yumin convened a meeting with the workers on the spot and offered a few strategies to push for their demands. He told them that they needed to stay together and try to get more workers to join them. He helped the workers make a few more banners with more eye-catching text so as to attract attention from the media and exert pressure on the company. Liao Yumin also advised the workers to petition (*xinfang*) labor authorities on both the municipal and provincial levels.

A few hours later, a manager from the company came out and told the workers to come to the conference room inside for a meeting. The workers told the manager that they wanted Liao Yumin and Wen Xue to be present at the meeting. At first, the manager rejected their request because he said that the matter was "internal affairs." The workers were not happy with this and refused to have the meeting. A few more hours went by and the management finally gave in and agreed that South Mountain staff could be present at the meeting with the workers. But the management insisted that South Mountain not videotape, tape record, or talk during the entirety of the meeting. It was under these conditions that Liao Yumin and Wen Xue were allowed to attend the meeting.

In addition to the employer and top management from the company, the chief of the local labor bureau, the party secretary of the township, and the chief of the township were also at the meeting. This meeting between the company and the workers lasted for a few hours and was futile as the two parties failed to reach a consensus and none of the issues raised by the workers were addressed by the management. After the meeting, the tug of war between the workers and the company continued for another month. The bus company continued to offer "incentives" for a settlement. For example, the boss told the workers that they could get the delayed wages only if they agreed to give up on obtaining a copy of their employment contracts. Many workers were indignant but felt helpless in the face of their employer's attitude. This workers' collective action lasted for three months. During these months, many workers caved in, took the money from the company, and signed a new employment contract without keeping a copy for themselves. In the end, only eight bus drivers and two ticket attendants did not accept the company's conditional offer. After three months of collective action, the remaining 10 workers decided that they didn't want to continue fighting and left the company, thus putting an end to their collective action.

NGOs and workers

The story of the bus workers illustrates a form of social resistance to the consequences of China's state socialist system's incorporation into global capitalism as well as the role that a labor NGO can play in the workers' collective organization and struggle to make their claims and assert their rights. It shows that when resorting to acting collectively, Chinese workers have to undergo a time-consuming and often frustrating process of dealing with the management and labor authorities as well as confront the risk of, for example, the loss of employment. More pertinent to this study, the story reveals the lack of legitimacy and thus the ambiguous status of the labor NGO in its attempt to assist the workers in their collective action against their employer. As mentioned in Chapter 3, the Chinese government is particularly cautious with regard to collective cases as they have the potential to transform into mass incidents that can threaten the legitimacy of the political regime as well as social stability.

This chapter addresses the ambiguous and uncertain role of labor NGOs and discusses how they deal with such ambiguity, and particularly the risk and repercussions that engaging in workers' collective action can entail. To illustrate this, I discuss the implementation of a specific development program, a collaboration between Hong Kong-based Chinese Workers' Front and its NGO partners in mainland China, South Mountain Migrant Workers' Center and Green Grass Workers' Service Center. I describe and analyze how these two NGOs carried out the program, and the consequences of their respective approach. In Chapters 2 and 3, I discussed the constraints within which these labor NGOs have to negotiate when carrying out their work, such as state surveillance and coercion. In Chapters 4 and 5, I talked about the knowledge and skills involved in negotiating the politics of *mingan*, and the techniques of concealment that these labor NGOs acquire, employ, and perform in order to navigate through the uncertain political landscape. In this chapter, I demonstrate how labor NGOs employ the knowledge, skills, tactics, and techniques discussed in Chapters 3, 4, and 5 to gauge the appropriate distance from the state while implementing the collective bargaining program.

Drawing on a specific development program—collective bargaining—designed by CWF, this chapter aims to concretely demonstrate how such knowledge, skills, tactics, and techniques were applied when the labor NGOs in mainland China tried to implement this program, which was generally regarded as politically sensitive and risky. Furthermore, by concentrating on the specific process of implementing the program, I also include the role of the workers, the ultimate target of the development program, in my analysis and address the general lack of discussion on workers in the existing literature of labor NGOs in China (Franceschini 2014). Juxtaposing two of CWF's NGO partners in Guangdong, I discuss how "success" and "failure" at the grassroots level are perceived and articulated by the labor NGOs so as to illustrate the tangible precariousness of their work. These two NGOs show how they embody, manage, and negotiate the uncertainty about the boundaries of permissible activism. More generally, the juxtaposition also makes visible the juncture and disjuncture between the local and the global in international development.

Collective bargaining with Chinese characteristics[1]

In 2011, Green Grass formed a partnership with CWF, as did its two other branch offices. One of them was South Mountain. Since 1994, CWF has been advocating for workers' rights, promoting democratically run trade unions in China and working to connect China's labor movement with the international labor movement. With an annual budget of approximately two million dollars, CWF has 14 full-time employees based in Hong Kong. The employees come from mainland China, Hong Kong, Europe, and North America.[2] Compared to other labor groups in Hong Kong, CWF is significantly bigger both in number of employees and operating budget. CWF's financial support comes predominantly from foundations and trade unions in North America and Europe (Pan in Durrenberger 2017: 135–160).

Currently, CWF has two main programs in their advocacy work: labor rights litigation and collective bargaining. Both are designed, according to CWF's website, "to empower, enable and further inspire the workers' movement in China." CWF has been running its labor rights litigation program since 2004, working with law firms, labor rights lawyers, and labor NGOs in China to provide legal advice and financial support. Its collective bargaining program, launched in 2008, offers collective bargaining training for workers and labor NGOs in China. The term "collective bargaining" has only recently appeared in China; the predominant and official expression has always been "collective consultation." The term "collective bargaining" implies the presence of conflicting labor relations (Chan & Hui 2014: 225), something the Chinese government does not wish to acknowledge. However, in recent years some local officials have started to use the term "collective bargaining" in their official documents. In 2008, the Shenzhen government was the first local government in the country to officially adopt the term in the amended version of its Shenzhen Implementation Measures for PRC Trade Union Law. In January 2010, while deliberating on the Shenzhen Collective Consultation Ordinance, many standing committee members of the Shenzhen Municipal People's Congress suggested using "collective bargaining" instead of "collective consultation" as a means to strengthen workers' confidence in their legal rights (Chan & Hui 2014: 225).

In Western societies, where trade unions are considered legitimate bargaining representatives, the mechanism of collective bargaining is deemed to further workers' interests. In China, the only trade union allowed to represent workers' interests is the All China Federation of Trade Unions (ACFTU), which is, as we have seen, crippled by its political subordination to the CCP. Therefore, the Western understanding of the role of trade unions differs greatly from the reality in China. Workers in China strike in order to initiate negotiations, similar to a type of "collective bargaining by riot," a term introduced by Eric Hobsbawm (1968) to describe the widespread problem of machine-wrecking by British workers in the eighteenth and nineteenth centuries. This is very different from other countries, where strikes are the last resort.

Recruited by CWF in 2010, Douglas works both as a researcher and collective bargaining instructor. He travels frequently between Hong Kong and mainland China to train CWF's NGO partners and workers, but training materials largely come from foreign trade unions. "We do need to make some adjustments so that the training works in the Chinese context. For example, in most foreign trade unions, union members are required to pay a membership fee so when negotiating on behalf of the workers, the unions will do their best to help the workers; they don't want to lose members. But in China, the union (the ACFTU) 'automatically' gets financial contributions from the employers. There is no incentive for them to work for the workers," explained Douglas. "So we adopt a foreign framework but try to localize the content. This is called 'collective bargaining with Chinese characteristics,'" he said laughingly, playing with Deng Xiaoping's famous phrase "socialism with Chinese characteristics."

Although the right to strike is included in neither the Chinese constitution nor in the Labor Law, Trade Union Law or Labor Contract Law, strikes are not criminalized (Chan 1998: 142), which puts strikes in China in legal limbo. "It's like crossing the road. Even though the light is red, you can go ahead and cross as long as there are no cars coming," said Douglas, describing the contingent nature of the collective action that is occurring across China. This is not to say that there is no risk for workers who go on strike. They still risk being discharged by their employers, especially workers who lead and organize a strike. Striking workers also face the risk of arrest on charges of disturbing social order, which will be shown in one of the examples to be discussed in this chapter.

CWF's collective bargaining program was designed to be implemented in collaboration with CWF's partners in mainland China, including six labor NGOs, each of which receives an annual budget between 200,000 RMB and 300,000 RMB, and one law firm in mainland China. These training sessions are devised to provide participants with the skills they need to initiate and engage in collective bargaining. One specific strategic objective is to create successful models of worker-led collective bargaining, which "can gain widespread acceptance among the public and serve as reference points for legislation and policy design," according to CWF's program description in their funding proposal.

Under CWF's supervision and management, CWF's NGO partners are responsible for finding potential collective cases through media reports, Internet forums, Weibo, hotlines, worker trainings and the NGOs' existing networks. Once the labor NGOs come into contact with workers who have issues with their employers, the NGOs will offer coaching. This includes legal education, collective bargaining training, factory analysis, the formation of factory-specific bargaining requests, instructions on how to democratically elect worker representatives, and how to bargain with management. The way in which CWF's collective program is designed suggests that labor NGOs that have a good number of volunteers and extensive contacts with workers make ideal partners. As described in Chapter 3, since the late 1990s, Green Grass has been offering migrant workers the service of drafting legal documents and bringing workers' grievances and disputes to court. The staff at Green Grass creates a paper and digital file for each worker who seeks help from the organization; this documentation has formed a good pool of potential volunteers and worker activists, which are crucial to its operation. When Green Grass organizes an event, they use their database to contact and mobilize workers. While conducting my fieldwork at Green Grass, there were three full-time employees and an intern and the organization had to rely on volunteers to carry out its work. This model of operation was applied to the other branch offices of Green Grass, including South Mountain. These NGOs have a solid base of volunteer and worker support, which proves to be crucial when they start to engage in workers' collective action. South Mountain's involvement with the workers in the bus company was indirectly facilitated by a volunteer who happened to see the news about these protesting workers.

Finding collective cases

South Mountain was set up in 2008 and had been registered as a private enterprise since.[3] It was located in a city about one hour by train from Guangzhou. At the time of my fieldwork, South Mountain had two full-time staff: director Liao Yumin and an intern. The director of Green Grass, Yang Haiqin, had regular contact with South Mountain. Sometimes the two organizations would hold activities and training workshops together. While South Mountain needed to report its day-to-day work and activities regularly to Green Grass, the organization enjoyed a certain degree of autonomy when it came to the specifics of carrying out its work in the area where it was located. Since its establishment, the work of South Mountain had predominantly consisted of providing legal aid and consultation for migrant workers who were injured at work. Liao Yumin and his staff made themselves known and gained access to the migrant worker community mainly through visiting hospitals in the area.

Starting in 2011, the focus of their work had shifted to promoting collective bargaining on the factory floor because of the new partnership with CWF. "What can you do? We just have to go with the funding (*genzhe jingfei zou*)," said Liao Yumin to me when I visited him in his office. It was obvious that Liao Yumin was anxious about the new direction that his NGO was taking. He said that in its prime, when the NGO was mainly targeting injured or individual workers, they would receive about 70 workers every month who came to seek advice and help. "We used to go to the hospitals and talk to the workers. That was easy and you could send the volunteers to do it, too. But now we need to try to get into the workers' community and find out what kind of problems they have and try to identify who has the capability to organize and mobilize workers. It is much more difficult," he explained.

According to Liao Yumin, it is a challenging task to help the workers initiate collective bargaining and be part of the process. "It is like a test to see if you have solid support and trust from the workers." He explained to me that it was difficult to organize workers and build solidarity when working with injured workers because "they don't stay." Helping injured workers get financial compensation from their employers is usually a long process; it can sometimes take a few years. During this process, Liao Yumin said, "You do get to know the workers quite well. But once they get the money, they leave.

They go back to their hometowns and open a small business there or do something else. They don't stay."

The walls of the South Mountain office were filled with red pennants from workers who were grateful for South Mountain's assistance in claiming financial compensation from their employers. Liao Yumin's words indicate the general trend toward focusing on donor-funded projects, which has been one of the primary factors driving the growth of NGOs since the 1980s (Mercer 2002: 14). Many studies have noted and are critical of how this funding approach tends to finance service provision projects at the expense of political activities (Farrington & Lewis 1993; Hojman 1993; Arellano-Lopéz & Petras 1994; Feldman 1997; Clarke 1998a, 1998b). In the case of labor NGOs, such a project-based mentality has been criticized as working against the goal of building workers' solidarity (Froissart 2005; Lee & Shen 2011).

Although the coordinator for the collective bargaining program in Hong Kong didn't require their partners to take on a certain number of collective bargaining cases each year, Liao Yumin said, "The pressure is there. You just can't not have any case at all, can you?" He worked hard to make progress on the new collective bargaining program. Instead of visiting the hospitals, Liao Yumin and his staff began to pay more frequent visits to places where migrant workers live and gather and distributed labor law-related leaflets. They went to industrial areas and handed out leaflets to workers leaving their shifts. "Now we need to work in a more targeted manner. More strategically. I first try to contact a worker, talk with him and see what kind of problems he has with his factory. Then I try to see if I can use him to recruit more workers and expand to the entire factory," explained Liao Yumin, adding that such an approach requires much more of an investment of time and energy in building trust with the workers. The prefatory story of the workers from a local bus company is one example of how Liao Yumin tried to get involved with the workers. Nevertheless, his involvement never went as far as to help the workers initiate collective bargaining with their employer. On the contrary, his involvement led to some repercussions that greatly alarmed and affected both South Mountain and Green Grass.

Emergency meeting

One morning in early November 2012, a few days after the bus workers' collective action had ended, three *guobao* came to visit South Mountain and asked Liao Yumin to come with them to the police station for a few questions. Liao Yumin went with the officers and made a phone call to the director of Green Grass, Yang Haiqin, to inform him of the visit. This incident caused quite a stir in the office of Green Grass, where I was doing fieldwork at the time. Yang Haiqin was very concerned and called the other staff at South Mountain several times that day to ask why Liao Yumin had been taken to the police station. Yang Haiqin was told that it had to do with his involvement with the bus workers. Liao Yumin was kept at the police station for almost a day. When he was released in the evening, he phoned Yang Hai-qin to let him know that he was okay. As soon as Yang Haiqin had talked with him on the phone, he summoned an emergency meeting and asked the staff of South Mountain to come to Green Grass the next day.

When I arrived at the office of Green Grass the next day, I saw Liao Yumin and Wen Xue chatting with Zhang Guoqi, a senior staff member at Green Grass, and Mei Yue, the worker-turned-intern. We exchanged some greetings and Liao Yumin made a joke about him still being alive as if he was trying to lighten the tense atmosphere in the office. As soon as Yang Haiqin walked into the office, he summoned everyone to the conference table and asked Liao Yumin to brief everyone on what exactly happened at the police station. Below is an excerpt of the emergency meeting:

YANG: How many were there [public security officers]?
LIAO: Three.
YANG: Were they interrogating you?
LIAO: They tried to trick me first. They asked if I knew why I was there.
YANG: They always ask that first [Laughter from the staff].
LIAO: He [one of the police officers] said, 'Think! What you have done?' I said, 'No, I didn't do anything' [Liao's reply caused some giggling around the conference table]. He said, 'Think again.' I said, 'No, I can't think of anything' [More laughter from the staff].
ZHANG: This is taught by the same teacher [Everyone at the conference table laughed out loud].
LIAO: He asked me if I had been to X district [where the bus company was located] recently. I said, 'Yes, I have.' Then he said, 'What were you doing there?' I told him frankly why I was there. I know this is what he was after. So I said, 'I heard that in X district some bus drivers stopped working and were defending their rights. They were affecting the traffic. So we went there to understand the situation.' [...] He said a lot of things and asked me a lot of questions, like what my status[4] is and my past work experiences. So I told him about my past work experiences. Then he said, 'You guided the workers to defend their rights but did you instruct the workers to do anything too aggressive [guoji 过激]?' I said, 'No. I just guided them to defend their rights according to the law.' But he tried to trick me again by saying, 'Did you know that two workers have already bought their train tickets to Beijing?' I said I didn't know any of that. I called them [the workers] and they said there was no such a thing. If they were going on their own, I wouldn't be surprised. I can't stop them, either. Then he tricked me again by saying, 'If they [the workers] trust you so much, why didn't they listen to you?' I said, 'They [the workers] didn't trust me very much [...]. We went there [X district] and gave them someone to talk to. It's like they found a lifesaving straw to clutch at! [zhua dao yi gen jiuming de daocao].'
YANG: Did they make a report?

LIAO: Yes. I even signed!

YANG: It's an interrogation then [the staff laughed].

LIAO: I even signed with my fingerprint. On the written report, they wrote 'strike' [bagong 罢工] but I changed it to 'work stoppage' [tinggong 停工]."

YANG: What was the atmosphere like? Were they polite or harsh [xiong 凶]? Or not very friendly?

LIAO: Sometimes polite, sometimes harsh. They were trying to make you relax for a while and then make you scared.

The emergency meeting described above is illustrative of a number of things. First, the purpose of the meeting was for Yang Haiqin to estimate the gravity of the repercussions in the wake of Liao Yumin's involvement in the bus workers' collective action; in other words, it was to evaluate what the state was thinking about this incident. As the general director of both Green Grass and South Mountain, Yang Haiqin was responsible for the operation of his offices. Should anything happen during any operation, he was to be held accountable, which was why he was very concerned and quick to hold the meeting to find out as much information as possible about the incident. This is illustrated by the detailed questions that Yang Haiqin raised during the meeting ranging from the number of *guobao* to the presence of a written report to the atmosphere of the questioning. These questions were used by Yang Haiqin to judge whether the meeting was just another tea-drinking session or was, in effect, an interrogation. With a signed report, Yang Haiqin established that it was an interrogation. The implication of this is crucial. According to Yang Haiqin, this meant that the *guobao* treated Liao Yumin as the suspect of a crime, which was to instigate the workers to go on strike. This crime or even the mere allegation of a crime could cost Liao Yumin greatly, with the potentially severe consequences including imprisonment or the shutting down of South Mountain entirely. More importantly, it could have further implicated Green Grass. It is worth noting that before signing the report, Liao Yumin changed the wording of "strike" to "work stoppage," whereby he, on the record, tried to lessen the severity of his involvement with the workers. Although a work stoppage is a form of strike, in the labor community in China it is commonly referred to as a more spontaneous and less organized form of protest by workers whereas a strike is considered to be both more organized and often initiated and led by workers in a more concerted manner.

Second, the laughter that occurred during the meeting stands in stark contrast to the agitation, fear, and nervousness palpable in the office of Green Grass before the meeting started and thus demands some analytical attention. In order for the audience to enjoy the humor, they must get the joke. This means that the audience "must be capable of analyzing the cognitive frames presented by the actor and following the process of the creation of the humor" (Beeman 1999: 103). During the meeting, the comments on the *guobao* elicited the most laughter from the staff. For example,

Yang Haiqin's remark "they always ask that first" indicates that he was very familiar with the standard procedure when dealing with the *guobao*, and the laughter that ensued shows that most of the people at the meeting understood this as well. That Liao Yumin's response to that question drew even more laughter was even more suggestive that such familiarity was generally shared by those at the conference table. In response to Liao Yumin's reply to the *guobao*, Zhang Guoqi made a joke, commenting "this is taught by the same teacher," which made everyone in the room burst into laughter. It should be pointed out that by "the same teacher," Zhang Guoqi was not referring to any specific individual but to the knowledge of how one should behave and respond when dealing with the *guobao*. Such knowledge commonly circulated among labor activists, legal experts, and workers is a form of self-help in a political system where state coercion and violence often take place in a seemingly random and unpredictable manner.[5]

Yet, what is so funny about state coercion? In her study on the performance of humor in the Australian aboriginal group Murri, Megan McCullough analyzes how humor operates as a way for women to temporarily disrupt the moral policing and governance that has constituted the marginality of Murri women entrenched in the gendered relationships of their everyday lives (McCullough 2014: 678). McCullough argues that Murri women use humor to "imaginatively and subjectively play with their marginality in ways that make legible that which cannot be expressed directly about stigma, sexuality and violence, especially to non-indigenous people" (ibid.). As such, humor allows the women to talk about an "open secret" (ibid.: 682) and creates a space in which Murri people can talk to each other and counter stereotypical assumptions and misconceptions about Murri life (ibid.).

In a similar vein, the humor and laughter that occurred during the emergency meeting in the office of Green Grass lay bare the institutional risk of being a labor activist in an authoritarian regime and gave expression to a form of state violence that is commonly known but is not supposed to be openly discussed. Making humor out of hurtful realities (Goldstein 2003), the joking comments made by Yang Haiqin and Zhang Guoqi allude to state control, state repression, and the ambiguous and marginalized status of labor NGOs. The laughter from the labor NGO staff is a response to this specific form of state control that they are subjected to that doesn't unsettle the status quo. Zhang Guoqi's joke is a "hidden transcript" where the joke both reinforces state control, the target of the joke, and defies it at the same time (Scott 1990). Hence, the laughter is corrective (Seizer 2005: 271–272), and yet it is also a refusal to be viewed as victims. This was distinctly illustrated by Liao Yumin when he explained how the state agents tried to trick him but he was able to keep with the script as tellingly manifested in Zhang Guoqi's joke.

Having worked in the NGO community for more than a decade, Yang Haiqin is used to handling political risks and threats. However, no matter how experienced he is, each time something goes wrong, the situation needs to be handled on a case-by-case basis because "no one really knows what they are thinking," said Yang Haiqin, commenting on China's state security system. Labor activists in China typically form judgments and make decisions "based on their best guess of likely consequences and these hunches are continually updated to reflect new information" (Stern & O'Brien 2012: 177). The information is usually generated either through direct experiences with the state agents or through indirect communication from official speeches, regulations, policies, and stories of repression. The questions asked during the emergency meeting were intended to gather as much information as possible so that Yang Haiqin could attempt to evaluate the severity of the situation and figure out whether Liao Yumin's questioning was also an intentionally communicative gesture on the part of the police officers, and if so, what message they were trying to convey to him. When the limits of the permissible are unclear, acquiring different types of information is a common way for activists to not only determine what is appropriate behavior, that is, to gauge the proper distance from the state, but also to assess the damage and conduct damage control should a line be crossed. In a political system where censorship and warnings typically occur after the fact, "people discover the presence of a line only by crossing it" (Stern & O'Brien 2012: 179). The incident involving Liao Yumin is a clear example of this.

As a veteran labor activist, Yang Haiqin was very critical of Liao Yumin's behavior. Toward the end of the emergency meeting, Yang Haiqin stressed that Liao Yumin made a major mistake: Liao Yumin got involved after the workers had already taken collective action and stopped working. "We don't need you to be paratroopers (*sanbing*)!" stressed Yang Haiqin to the staff of South Mountain. Yang Haiqin noted that it was highly *mingan* for a labor NGO to try to parachute into a position when the workers had already organized and mobilized themselves to take action against the employers. The reason for the caution was obvious. "You should avoid giving the *guobao* any reason to arrest you," said Yang Haiqin.

Yang Haiqin continued to emphasize that Liao Yumin's intervention failed to lead to any solid and positive result. Clearly upset, Yang Haiqin told Liao Yumin, "Nothing concrete came out of your involvement. The workers went their separate ways in the end. No workers' group was formed and sustained. Your involvement led to nothing but trouble." Yang Haiqin added, "It is not a bad thing to try to have more contact with the *guobao*. Try to communicate with them more." For Yang Haiqin, it is necessary to cultivate a good relationship with the public security officers and a regular and open communication channel is beneficial.

The situation between public security officers and Liao Yumin could be seen as having been resolved for the moment. Yang Haiqin knew that it could have gone much worse. Toward the end of the emergency meeting, Liao Yumin tried to lighten up the mood by making a joke, "If I were to be detained, I would get free meals. It's on the government. What's the big deal?" As the head of both Green Grass and South Mountain, Yang Haiqin couldn't help but express his anger and worry, and scolded Liao Yumin. "Are you aware that we are wiping your ass (*women shi zai bang ni ca pigu!*)?!" What Yang Haiqin meant was that Green Grass had to clean up after Liao Yumin's careless behavior. Yang Haiqin criticized Liao Yumin for his lack of "political sensitivity" (*zhengzhi mingan du*) "What were you thinking? The 18th National Congress is about to convene. Instead of staying low, you went and made trouble!" Yang Haiqin implied that there would be visits from the police to inquire more about the incident. He said he would have some explaining to do.

With the example of South Mountain, I have presented and discussed what repercussions a labor NGO could face when engaging in workers' collective action. In this particular case of the bus workers, I showed how and why things went wrong and how Green Grass tried to estimate the political damage afterward. This example clearly illustrates one of the main themes that runs through this study: How does one act or not act when the limits of state tolerance are unclear and when the pressure of executing a funded project is tangible? In other words, how does one gauge the appropriate distance from the state while being accountable to the donors? The story of Liao Yumin, according to Yang Haiqin, shows that he was at the wrong distance from the state at the wrong time, which also led to the failure of his involvement. In the next section, I will present a contrasting story where Green Grass tried to negotiate the uncertainty of the permissible and calculate a proper distance from the state. According to Green Grass and CWF, the following example is an illustration of how a labor NGO successfully intervened in a collective case.

The successful case[6]

When I started my fieldwork in the office of Green Grass, one thing that caught my attention was a bright red banner hanging next to six framed photos to the left of the entrance (Pan 2017). The photos showed past activities and organization's outreach services to workers. In the middle of the banner ran the following text: "*Workers' Solidarity Has Power, Collective Bargaining Yields Results*" (*gongren tuanjie you liliang, jiti tanpang you chengguo*). On the upper right-hand side it read "To Green Grass Workers' Service Center" and on the lower left "From the 199 Workers of Bao Han Electronics Factory." It was dated September 2012. Zhang Guoqi proudly told me the story of these workers and said it was their very first successful case assisting the workers in collective action.

In 2011, a few dozen workers at Bao Han Electronics Factory wanted to recover social insurance payments their employer had not paid over the years and demanded the employer start making payments to the social insurance system for them. The social insurance program places the responsibility on the employer, requiring it to register for participation and make regular contributions, both on behalf of the workers (deducted from wages) and on behalf of the firm (as a share of payroll).[7] Zhang Guoqi told me that one of the main problems with labor protection in China is not that there is no legal framework to regulate labor relations but that labor policies and regulations are unevenly implemented at the local level, resulting in labor protection measures that are seldom enforced. The issue of social insurance is one such example.

The Bao Han workers heard about Green Grass through a volunteer at the NGO and sought the organization's advice. Green Grass told them to recruit as many workers as possible and "make a list of things that need to be addressed in the factory. It is not very smart to just have one issue [demanding social insurance payments]," in the words of Zhang Guoqi. After several meetings with Green Grass, the workers listed four things they wanted their employer to address:

1 all workers should receive a copy of their employment contracts;
2 workers should be paid high temperature allowances;
3 workers should be entitled to annual paid leave; and
4 the employer should make payments to social insurance.

With the additional issues now included, the initial group of workers managed to mobilize their co-workers to participate in collective action. Nearly two months later, the number of workers on board had increased from 38 to 128, and in the end 199 workers came together to participate in the nearly year-long battle of asserting their rights and claiming their entitlements. In the process, Green Grass helped the workers organize and elect 13 workers' representatives whose primary task was to communicate with the management on behalf of the workers. They exchanged information and participated in negotiations with the management. Green Grass also helped the workers set up a solidarity fund with contributions from each worker involved in the collective action. Zhang Guoqi explained that the solidarity fund was used to cover expenses that may have been incurred during the workers' collective action, such as those related to dealing with labor authorities. The workers decided how much each worker should contribute to the fund.[8]

"It was a very long process and the management treated the workers very badly," said Zhang Guoqi, citing one incident that seriously damaged the morale of the workers. "During their negotiations with the management, two workers' representatives were arrested and detained by the police. They were accused of instigating the workers to cause disturbance at work and illegally detaining the manager," said Zhang Guoqi. The workers were demanding a response to their requests but the manager refused so the workers gathered outside the manager's office and waited. The standoff lasted for two days. When the police came, the two workers' representatives were taken away and detained for 25 days. Three days into their detention, the two workers' representatives were dismissed by the factory because, according to the management, they had failed to show up for work.

Zhang Quoqi stressed that the arrest was a turning point that brought the workers even closer and inspired more people, including some lawyers, to get involved. With the encouragement of Green Grass, many Bao Han workers donated money to help the families of the two arrested workers' representatives. Lawyers who represented the pair met with local labor authorities and explained the unfounded allegations. After the lawyers' intervention, the two workers were released on probation after 25 days in the detention center. The arrest of the workers' representatives made the workers even more determined to stake their rights claims. After numerous visits and phone calls to the labor authorities, the Bao Han workers, encouraged by Green Grass, continued to negotiate with the management. It took nearly a year to reach an agreement with the management, who finally agreed to pay their social insurance. After their collective action had come to an end, the workers at Bao Han donated the remaining 1500 RMB in their solidarity fund to Green Grass as a token of their gratitude and trust.

ACFTU passing the buck

A few weeks into my fieldwork at Green Grass, I was invited to a dinner with the workers from Bao Han celebrating their successful negotiation. I was sitting next to A Tai, one of the workers' representatives from Bao Han who told me that they had invited the ACFTU officials to the dinner.

> We knew they wouldn't come but Qi Ge [a nickname for Zhang Guoqi] told us that we have to invite them to express our gratitude to them. We want to make them feel that they have helped us greatly. But we knew they wouldn't come. The invitation was really just a formality.

In their nearly year-long battle to defend their rights, the Bao Han workers submitted their petitions to the ACFTU several times but the ACFTU didn't take them seriously. "They were just passing the buck to each other (*huxiang ti piqiu*)," noted A Tai. He described how the local officials were indifferent to the workers' grievances. More than one month had passed since the workers submitted their written demands to the factory, but they still hadn't heard any response from the management. The workers decided to send the petition to the ACFTU at the district level. A few days later, the ACFTU sent someone to the factory to investigate and, after another week had passed, an ACFTU district official organized a meeting between the workers and the management. "But the meeting was pretty useless. The ACFTU official seemed to side with the management and kept saying that they would start the investigation as soon as possible and wanted us to wait patiently," noted A Tai. A few days after the meeting, the workers called the ACFTU's district office to follow up on the case. But they were merely given the response that the ACFTU was working on it and, again, that the workers should just wait patiently. Dissatisfied, the workers called the provincial office of the ACFTU and the response was, 'We care very much about this case and your demands but we should follow the procedures,' said A Tai, recounting the conversation he had with the provincial-level ACFTU official, who asked the workers to contact the district office. Later on the same day, A Tai received a phone call from the district office. "He (the person from the ACFTU) sounded upset and told me that we shouldn't have called the provincial office of the ACFTU before we knew anything. It made it look like we were complaining about them [to the provincial ACFTU]," noted A Tai. According to A Tai, many workers had been really frustrated with the inefficiency of the ACFTU.

After calling the district ACFTU for a month, the workers finally got a response. The district ACFTU held a meeting with the workers' representatives and informed them of the results of a meeting between the ACFTU and the management. After the intervention of the ACFTU, the factory agreed to give a copy of the employment contract to the workers, pay high temperature allowances, and provide paid annual leave. As for the payment of social insurance, which was the main demand of the workers, the ACFTU official suggested they resort to legal measures and deal with the management directly.

Giving officials credit

Despite the often-expected indifference and sometimes contempt from the labor authorities when dealing with workers' problems, Green Grass always encouraged the workers to first seek support and help from the local ACFTU and other labor authorities such as the Labor Supervision Group (*laodong jiancha dadui*) and Human Resources and Social Security Bureau (*renli ziyuan shehui baoxian ju*). Even knowing that such visits can be futile, Green Grass still stressed the necessity of going through the legal procedures and trying all the legal channels. There are obvious reasons for doing so. First, it gives the workers' collective action legitimacy so that, when challenged, they can say they tried every legal channel before resorting to collective action such as a strike. Second, having tried all the legal channels in vain, the workers can hold the concerned authorities accountable for not doing anything. When coaching workers on how to submit their petition to local labor authorities, Zhang Guoqi always instructs workers to send their petitions, relevant documents, and applications as registered mail. "When you send it as registered mail, you will get a receipt. The recipient has to be signed upon receiving the mail. Then you will have evidence showing that you indeed sent the document so they (the local labor authorities) can't say that they didn't receive anything from you," explained Zhang Guoqi. While coaching the Bao Han workers on following the formal legal procedures for reporting grievances, Green Grass continued to informally organize and mobilize them, instructing them on how to negotiate with their employer. In order to protect themselves from being labeled as "attempting to instigate disturbance," the staff at Green Grass kept in close contact with the workers via mobile phone, Weibo, and QQ.

After the Bao Han workers had completed their negotiations with their employer, Green Grass went further to make sure that the relationship between the labor authorities, the ACFTU, the workers, and the NGO was not damaged. They instructed the workers to give a complimentary red banner to the ACFTU, and to arrange for the media to take photographs so as to publicize the good work done by the ACFTU. At the dinner, A Tai showed me a photo on his mobile phone of the workers standing with the ACFTU officials. In the photo, the four workers' representatives from Bao Han and the chairman of the ACFTU were in the center of the photo holding the red banner together. The banner says: *"Workers' Rights are Protected. Trade Unions Support Workers (gongren quanyi you baozhang, gonghui zuzhi shi houdun)."* Also in the photo were two ACFTU officials and Zhang Guoqi. This photo was posted on Green Grass's Weibo page. The photo was accompanied by the following text:

> Today, four workers' representatives from Bao Han on behalf of 199 workers visited the local chapter of ACFTU to hand in a banner. The banner says: 'Workers' Rights are Protected. Trade Unions Support Workers.' The workers want to express their gratitude that the ACFTU was behind the workers in their battle to defend their rights. The workers have faith in the ACFTU because it speaks for the workers and defends workers' rights.

This post was shared widely among Green Grass's network, including the ACFTU officials, scholars, labor NGOs, and workers. A Tai said that both the banner and the dinner invitation for the ACFTU are like "putting up a show." The workers agreed to go along with the act because they were grateful for how Green Grass had helped them along the way.

The banner, the dinner invitation, and the media publication of the picture are performative practices carefully designed and employed by Green Grass to publicly give the ACFTU full credit for the outcome of the Bao Han workers' collective action regardless of the fact that the ACFTU had been passive and indifferent to the workers' claims, and biased toward the employer most of the time during the workers' struggle. By giving the ACFTU credit for the workers' collective action, Green Grass was also enacting a performance of complicity in that the NGO and the workers had to take matters into their own hands because the authorities had vested interests and failed to defend and protect the workers' rights. Green Grass was fully aware that to expose and publicly criticize the authorities' failures would gravely jeopardize its existence and development; more importantly, for Green Grass to continue the collective bargaining program, it would need to have a good relationship with the authorities. As a result, Green Grass decided to put on a show and give credit to the ACFTU and thus was complicit in covering up the state's failure to help the workers.

During the process of assisting the Bao Han workers, Green Grass went to great lengths to ensure that the NGO was only coaching and guiding the workers, and whenever possible, made the organization invisible to the authorities. But this widely circulated picture also brings up the issue of secrecy and publicity discussed in Chapter 6. It shows the paradoxical incongruity between the practices of secrecy and the NGO's need to publicize its work in the labor community, which clearly illustrates the workings of the power of public secrecy. That the Chinese state fails to protect and defend workers' rights is an open secret that cannot be openly discussed. A fickle being, the Chinese state is always lurking in the background. This discrepancy arises from yet functions to resolve the arbitrariness of and uncertainty about the limits of state tolerance, which can sometimes be contradictory.

By actively giving credit to the ACFTU for assisting with the workers' collective action, Green Grass hoped to give their involvement with the workers some kind of legitimacy. By having a picture taken with the local ACFTU officials, Green Grass could publicly show that they had the support of the ACFTU in their assistance with the workers' collective action. According to Green Grass Director Yang Haiqin, this tactic benefited both parties: the ACFTU got the credits while Green Grass could continue to operate as a labor NGO without too much harassment from the state security agents. Yang Haiqin stressed, "This is how we protect ourselves." This self-preservation technique is a political move that requires great deliberation to strike a good balance in cultivating the relationship between the NGO and the local authorities. Failure to do so can lead to some serious consequences for the NGO, which I will discuss in the next section.

The case of the Bao Han workers had been discussed in the labor community as a successful example of how a labor NGO assisted workers in collective action from the beginning to the end. Green Grass had managed to stay in the background, guiding and coaching the workers without implicating themselves by attracting allegations that they were instigating the workers to cause social disturbance. "One important principle is that we don't get involved when the workers have already initiated some kind of collective action. It's too risky," noted Zhang Guoqi. The case of the bus workers described in the beginning of the chapter is an example that violates this principle, which led to Liao Yumin being questioned by the Public Security Bureau. Zhang Guoqi continued,

> Many of the cases we have handled started from scratch so we could help organize, cultivate, and mobilize the workers. It is okay for us to guide and coach from the side [...]. In this way, you can manage the exterior risks.

By "exterior risks," Zhang Guoqi referred not only to the risk of workers being arrested but also to the political risk that his organization could face when involved in collective action.

Spreading risk

Soon after the Bao Han case, Green Grass began to take on more and more collective cases. One day in early October 2012, I was sitting at the office conference table with Zhang Guoqi and Mei Yue, the worker-turned-intern at Green Grass. Yang Haiqin walked in looking upset and stressed. He had just come from drinking tea with the *guobao*. According to the director, some people at the Public Security Bureau were not happy that Green Grass was helping workers push for collective bargaining on the factory floor. Yang Haiqin was told to stop the collective bargaining program, but Green Grass received all of its funding through its collaboration with CWF, which required Green Grass to engage in collective bargaining. Had Yang Haiqin succumbed to the pressure from the Public Security Bureau, his organization would have faced immediate financial hardship. Yang Haiqin told those of us sitting at the table that the 18th National Congress was going to be held in early November so "if we are just doing the collective bargaining program, it is too risky. We need to start visiting injured workers again so we can spread the risk." Later at the staff meeting, Yang Haiqin instructed Mei Yue to start visiting injured workers in the hospital and distributing leaflets introducing Green Grass as a labor organization that helps injured workers claim financial compensation from their employers.

Yang Haiqin also developed another strategy for spreading the risk that created tension among the staff and difficulty implementing the collective bargaining program. I didn't learn about it until after I had left Green Grass and started doing fieldwork with CWF when I met Zhang Guoqi at a workshop organized by CWF. During the tea break, Zhang Guoqi told me that it had become increasingly difficult to carry out the collective bargaining program because of "the spectacled," which was his nickname for Yang Haiqin. Zhang Guoqi explained,

> Once I was going to meet Chen Yishen [lawyer from Wei Min Law Firm] in a hotel where we were going to meet with some workers to discuss our plans. As soon as I arrived at the hotel, the police came. I thought it was strange that they [the *guobao*] knew and had even shown up so quickly. The spectacled must have told them [the *guobao*]. Then it happened again with another meeting. I was meeting a group of workers in a restaurant. As soon as we arrived, 20 police officers were outside the restaurant. What a show! It must be him [the spectacled]. No one else! They knew the place and time. There is no other way that they could have found out so fast. Now Wei Qiang [the other full-time staff member at Green Grass] and I are concerned that he [the spectacled] will sell us

out to the *guobao*. When he [the spectacled] gets a phone call [from the *guobao*] telling him that he shouldn't take a certain case, he will assign the case to either me or Wei Qiang. But the thing is: If the case goes well, for example, the workers successfully receive compensation without causing too much or any disturbance then he has no problem taking credit for it. But if something goes wrong, he says that he didn't handle the case, it was us.[9]

The fact that Yang Haiqin might have been giving the *guobao* too much information also concerned Mandy, CWF's project coordinator, who, as mentioned earlier, once complained to me that she had to cancel a workshop last minute because Yang Haiqin told the *guobao* about it. Toward the end of my fieldwork, Yang Haiqin had lost the trust of his colleagues and partners in Hong Kong. By feeding the *guobao* more and more information about what collective cases Green Grass had heard about or were handling, Yang Haiqin appeared to have carved out a space for his organization at the expense of his partners, or in the words of Mandy, "he has sold out a lot of people!" CWF decided they would not renew their partnership with Green Grass after the current contract expired.

Conclusion[10]

In this chapter, I juxtaposed two labor NGOs and demonstrated how their different approaches to implementing the collective bargaining program led to very different outcomes. These two examples bring into view the dynamics between the grassroots labor NGOs, the intermediary NGO, the labor authorities, and the employers. They illustrate the risk as well as the knowledge and skills required to avoid, negotiate, and mitigate the political repercussions of engaging and organizing collectively in a politically restrictive environment where the space for carrying out activism is not only limited but contingent.

The analysis presented here is not intended to dismiss the role that Green Grass and South Mountain played in assisting the workers but to call into question the models under which these labor NGOs operate and whether Green Grass, South Mountain, and CWF do contribute to the labor movement in China as they claim. The stories of Bao Han and the bus workers show that while there is some formal representation for the workers in the Chinese system, it does not do much to help workers resolve issues they have with their employers. Labor NGOs in China have emerged to try to bridge this gap but they have to negotiate economic, political, and institutional constraints. As shown in the cases of South Mountain and Green Grass, the labor NGOs' survival depends on foreign donors whose funding is predominantly project-based with specific goals. In their partnership with CWF and the Western donors, South Mountain and Green Grass were required to look for potential cases and help workers in their collective action. However, due to their precarious legal status, South Mountain and Green Grass were not able to be directly involved in the workers' collective action, such as negotiations, strikes, and work stoppages nor were they able to engage in any substantial negotiations with the state. By adopting informal tactics such as giving credit to union officials and actively reporting to the public security officers, Green Grass, for example, managed to carve out a temporary space for its survival and operation but it did so at the cost of its partnership with CWF.

In their report to the foreign donors, CWF described the case of Bao Han as a successful example of collective bargaining because the workers came together and got what they wanted. The development officer at CWF told me that the collective bargaining program was much better than other programs they have initiated in the past because,

> it is easier to show concrete results. With a case like Bao Han, we are able to show what the workers gained in the process, the social security payments, for example. It is so much easier from the perspective of reporting. With these concrete results, we can tell the donors that the workers' consciousness has been raised. It's better than telling them how many copies of the Labor Contract Law we have printed and distributed.

What this development officer did not mention is that all Bao Han workers who participated in the collective action eventually left the factory and had to look for employment elsewhere, which led to the disintegration of the workers' group. Furthermore, the emphasis on concrete results in terms of material concessions from the state runs the risk of upholding the institutional conditions and arrangements that allow labor exploitation. "Material gain has become the linchpin of subordination" (Lee & Zhang 2013: 1504). Viewed as such, it explains why "the majority of social unrest in China seldom challenges the legitimacy and system of one-party rule but has mostly focused on issues of livelihood and material interest" (ibid.). From my conversations with the workers, there is no doubt that a consciousness of rights and solidarity had been cultivated. Nevertheless, a sense of powerlessness was also prevalent. The momentum built during their collective efforts failed to sustain itself after their action and bring about more substantial transformation in their workplace, such as a worker-elected workplace union. It calls into question whether CWF's collective bargaining program and its implementation strategy did fulfill its stated goals of creating a sustainable model of worker-led collective bargaining, influencing legislation and policy design, and contributing to the labor movement in China.

A labor activist based in Hong Kong described CWF and its partners this way:

> They are like firemen. They go where the fire is and try to put it out. They are just chasing after fires rather than doing something about the root of the problem that causes all these fires in the first place.

This comment lays bare the problematic relationship between the NGOs, the state, the donors, and the community they try to serve. The "success" of the Bao Han workers framed and trumpeted by CWF illustrates how a labor NGO tried to work on a particular issue using a particular strategy, while at the same time also exhibiting how the NGO lost perspective on the larger goals of its work, which is inherently undermined by the fundamental issues of state authoritarianism, unaccountable governance, and pervasive worker powerlessness.

The two examples discussed in this chapter illustrate how the labor NGOs tried to navigate through the uncertainty of the political terrain and negotiated the risks entailed by their labor activism. Both examples paint a gloomy picture and show that the labor NGOs do not have much power in determining or defining their relationship with the state. In the domain of uncertainty, the NGOs have creatively devised tactics and practices to carve out a space for their activism. But to a large extent, these NGOs still have to operate on the terms laid down by the state. While engaging informal and performative practices may temporarily help the labor NGOs operate, in the long run, with the perplexing vagaries of Chinese politics characterized by its culture of secrecy, it does raise the question of whether the labor NGOs in China are able to accumulate political momentum so as to become a progressive political force of change in society. The labor community may very well end up building a "fractured movement rather than mass-based movements for social change" (Smith in INCITE! 2007: 11).

Notes

1 This section was published in "Agents of change or status quo? Labor NGOs in South China." In *Uncertain times: anthropological approaches to labor in a neoliberal world*, edited by E. Paul Durrenberger. Boulder: University Press of Colorado, pp. 135–160.
2 The distinction between mainland China and Hong Kong is made to illustrate the difference between Chinese people who have settled in Hong Kong for a generation or more and Chinese people who have just come to Hong Kong to study or work. The latter group is popularly called "new immigrants" by the residents in Hong Kong.
3 South Mountain was closed down as a result of government repression in 2015.
4 "Status" refers to Liao Yumin's residence permit. The police wanted to know if Liao Yumin had official permission to live in the city.
5 Advice on how to deal with state security agents when one is arrested is popularly disseminated on the Internet, especially on social media. The link below is an example: A lawyer posted the standard procedures for dealing with the police and what rights a person has when being taken to the police station. http://mp.weixin.qq.com/s?__biz=MzA5NTMxNjcxMQ==&mid=200365043&idx-=1&sn=3f3df913a0b87eae9050be0886aca2f8&scene=2&from=timeline&isappinstalled=0&key=d7e970edec361a55a624b29bb08a5e7b69247767ab65c83b-d82a8cdf405824868afbd3108cf4416b6d756a2a7b845188&ascene=2&uin=M-jI2NDEwNTE1OA%3D%3D accessed April 15, 2016.
6 Some discussions of this successful case have been published in "Agents of change or status quo? Labor NGOs in South China." In *Uncertain times: anthropological*

approaches to labor in a neoliberal world, edited by E. Paul Durrenberger. Boulder: University Press of Colorado, pp. 135–160.

7   Contributions need to be made over a number of years in order to grant eligibility for benefits: 15 years for the pension program, and at least one year for unemployment insurance.

8   It can be 50 RMB or 100 RMB per person. The fund is managed by a worker selected by the workers themselves.

9   The passage was taken from an interview I had with Zhang Guoqi in May 2013.

10 Some parts of the conclusion have been published in "Agents of change or status quo? Labor NGOs in South China." In *Uncertain times: anthropological approaches to labor in a neoliberal world*, edited by E. Paul Durrenberger. Boulder: University Press of Colorado, pp. 135–160.

Bibliography

Arellano-Lopéz, Sonia, and James F. Petras. 1994. Nongovernmental organizations and poverty alleviation in Bolivia. *Development and Change* 25: 555–568.

Beeman, William O. 1999. Humor. *Journal of Linguistic Anthropology* 9 (1–2): 103–106.

Chan, Anita. 1998. "Labor relations in foreign-funded ventures, Chinese trade unions, and the prospects for collective bargaining." In *Adjusting to capitalism: Chinese workers and the state*, edited by Greg O'Leary. New York: M. E. Sharpe, pp. 122–149.

Chan, Chris King-chi, and Elaine Sio-leng Hui. 2014. The development of collective bargaining in China: from "collective bargaining by riot" to "Party state-led wage bargaining." *The China Quarterly* 217: 221–242.

Clarke, Gerard. 1998a. *The politics of NGOs in Southeast Asia: participation and protest in the Philippines*. London: Routledge.

——— 1998b. Nongovernmental organizations (NGOs) and politics in the developing world. *Political Studies* 46 (1): 36–52.

Farrington, John, and David J. Lewis, eds. 1993. *Nongovernmental organizations and the state in Asia: rethinking roles in sustainable agricultural development*. London: Routledge.

Feldman, Shelley. 1997. NGOs and civil society: (un)stated contradictions. *The Annals of the American Academy of Political and Social Science* 554: 46–65.

Franceschini, Ivan. 2014. Labor NGOs in China: a real force for political change? *The China Quarterly* 218: 474–492.

Froissart, Chloé. 2005 The rise of social movements among migrant workers: uncertain strivings for autonomy. *China Perspectives* 61: 1–15.

Goldstein, Donna M. 2003. *Laughter out of place: race, class, violence, and sexuality in a Rio shantytown*. Berkeley: University of California Press.

Hobsbawm, Eric. 1968. *Laboring men: studies in the history of labor*. London: Weidenfeld and Nicolson.

Hojman, David E. 1993. Nongovernmental organizations (NGOs) and the Chilean transition to democracy. *European Review of Latin American and Caribbean Studies* 54: 7–24.

Lee, Ching Kwan, and Yuan Shen. 2011. "The anti-solidarity machine? Labor nongovernmental organizations in China." In *From iron rice bowl to informalization: markets, workers, and the state in a changing China*, edited by Sarosh Kuruvilla, Ching Kwan Lee, and Mary E. Gallagher. Ithaca, NY and London: Cornell University Press.

Lee, Ching Kwan, and Yonghong Zhang. 2013. The power of instability: unraveling the microfoundations of bargained authoritarianism in China. *American Journal of Sociology* 118 (6): 1475–1508.

McCullough, Megan B. 2014. The gender of the joke: intimacy and marginality in Murri humor. *Ethnos* 79 (5): 677–698.

Mercer, Claire. 2002. NGOs, civil society and democratization: a critical review of the literature. *Progress in Development Studies* 2 (1): 5–22.

Pan, Darcy. 2017. "Agents of change or status quo? Labor NGOs in South China." In *Uncertain times: anthropological approaches to labor in a neoliberal world*, edited by E. Paul Durrenberger. Boulder: University Press of Colorado, pp. 135–160.

Scott, James C. 1990. *Domination and the arts of resistance: hidden transcripts*. New Haven, CT: Yale University Press.

Seizer, Susan. 2005. *Stigmas of the Tamil stage: an ethnography of special drama artists in South India*. Durham, NC: Duke University Press.

Smith, Andrea. 2007. "Introduction: the revolution will not be funded." In *The revolution will not be funded: beyond the non-profit industrial complex*, edited by INCITE! Women of Color against Violence. Cambridge, MA: South End Press.

Stern, Rachel E., and Kevin J. O'Brien. 2012. Politics at the boundary: mixed signals and the Chinese state. *Modern China* 38 (2): 174–198.

Conclusion
Laboring through uncertainty

After I finished my fieldwork in Hong Kong in early September 2013, I went back to Guangzhou to visit my NGO friends and bid my farewell as I prepared to return to Sweden. I was particularly concerned about one person, Wei Peng, director of Blue Sky, because I had heard that he had been "grounded" (*jinzu*) by the *guobao*. Wei Peng had been one of my key interlocutors, and he has become a good friend with whom I still keep in contact. "I can't go anywhere. I can't go to Hong Kong or Beijing. I can't even go home and visit my family.[1] I have to be here [in the city of Wuhua]," he told me as we met for noodles at his favorite restaurant in Wuhua, which was located in an alley hidden from the main street. I asked Wei Peng about the reason why he was grounded. He explained that based on information from his friend working at the local newspaper, he believed that it was most likely because he got involved in a collective action in which a group of street sanitation workers were demanding better working conditions. "I have consulted some media friends and labor scholars. They suggested I talk to the local ACFTU and say that I should not be involved in this case anymore. So I have stopped meeting with the workers. [I need to] lay low for a while. Taking on collective cases is really difficult," he said, shaking his head with a helpless grin on his face. Instead he planned to focus on the children of migrant workers, which he believed would be less *mingan*.

As we finished our meal and got ready to leave the restaurant, Wei Peng, looking somewhat demoralized, let out a sigh and said,

> I really don't understand. Last month, CWF and its [NGO] partners had a big dinner party here to celebrate their success in helping the sanitation workers [in Guangzhou] claim delayed wages and social security. Chen Yishen [lawyer from Wei Min law firm] was there too. A lot of people and workers came to the dinner. Why did I run into trouble when I got involved in this collective case but they didn't?

Wei Peng's question was legitimate, and I was as confounded as he was. "Obviously, not just anyone can handle collective cases and it seems that it does not have as much to do with whether it is a collective action as who is handling it," he noted as we slowly walked back to his office. Wei Peng was doing what most labor activists would do in a situation like this: evaluate the facts and deduce some kind of logical explanation so as to estimate the government's motive and thus guide his future action. I discussed this subject in Chapter 3 in which the labor NGOs developed several theories about the motives behind the 2012 crackdown. Nevertheless, Wei Peng's plausible explanation was challenged by the question that immediately followed: "But it is CWF we are talking about! How can the government not know that CWF is supporting these NGOs engaging in collective action? How can they [the government] not know?"

Given that CWF has been portrayed as a highly sensitive organization by the Chinese government and official media, I fully understood Wei Peng's confusion and frustration. "A labor activist in Hong Kong told me that CWF has some sort of agreement with the ACFTU," said Wei Peng in a low voice, indicating the politically sensitive nature of this information. "What kind of agreement?" I asked as we stood outside his office. He shook his head and said,

> No one knows. Maybe they [CWF] were collaborating with the ACFTU to help [the ACFTU] reestablish trust with the workers. But I really don't know what's going on with these NGOs [that were involved with the collective bargaining program with CWF].

Sharing Wei Peng's frustration and his uncertainty about the future of labor NGOs in China, I told him that I would also be grappling with these questions after I had returned to Sweden. Lastly, before I reluctantly said goodbye to him, Wei Peng asked me, "How are you going to write your book with all the information you have collected?" I gave him a smile that was mixed with frustration and embarrassment, and said, "I honestly have no idea."

Writing uncertainty

During my fieldwork, several interlocutors asked me how I was going to write my book, especially when I seemed to be more interested in collecting gossip and digging into the secrets of the labor community than in the "more substantial work of labor activism," as one of the labor scholars pointed out to me. By "more substantial work of labor activism," this Chinese labor scholar referred to the strategies adopted by labor NGOs and activists to organize and mobilize workers so as to bring about important policy and institutional change for Chinese workers. Having discussed how two labor NGOs implemented the program of collective bargaining in Chapter 6, I did address the concern raised by this labor scholar, but my analytical focus was on the operational model adopted by the labor NGOs in mainland China and Hong Kong through which I raised questions about the role of the labor NGOs in bringing about significant institutional change for the workers of China.

Mandy, the project coordinator at CWF, once said to me jokingly, "If you were to write a novel based on what you have heard about the labor NGOs here, I bet it will be a bestseller!" To these comments, my response was usually one of self-deprecation, which was not only an admission of the nervous conditions of my fieldwork (Cerwonka 2007: 1–40) but also an acknowledgment of the ethos of ambiguity, uncertainty, and insecurity that runs through my field. Mandy's joke about writing a novel poignantly lays bare the challenge of honoring the trust that my research participants have bestowed on me and being truthful to what I have heard and experienced, and yet producing a scholarship of engagement that involves collaboration between the researcher and the researched community. In other words, Mandy's joke and Wei Peng's question also express their concern about my own production of knowledge about the labor community in South China.

In this study, I did not assign myself the task of educating a largely Western audience about China, yet my scholarship still inserts itself in a field that is commonly examined through the divide between undemocratic China and the democratic West. The rationale behind such a divide is that international development work is distinctly characterized by the Western political philosophy of liberalism in which democracy is often treated as a coproduct of the market economy (Paley 2008: 13). The common expectation is that the market is seen as a key road to freedom and thus some version of equality (Appadurai 2007: 31). Hence, that the freedom of market opportunity is to be followed by political liberalization is captured by the phrase "free market democracies" (Paley 2008: 13). While acknowledging this general philosophy of the development industry, I am not interested in assessing the political impact of specific development projects. Rather, I want to understand how the dynamics of state power are manifested and reconfigured locally against international development and describe what reconfigurations of power relations and forms of engagement are made possible in the margins of the Chinese state.

In this study, I am pursued by a feeling that I may not have completely grasped everything that was happening around me in the course of my fieldwork. My task and goal are to describe how this ethnographic process of trying to know yet ending up with more of the unknown has unfolded. It is a process of writing an ethnography about the limits of knowing and acting, which, in turn, become the conditions as well as constraints of the ethnographer's knowing, acting, and writing. Even as I was grappling with my own confusion, it was clear to me that many of my research participants were similarly confused as distinctly illustrated by Wei Peng's words above as well as in the preceding ethnographic chapters. Ethnographic writing is like sculpture: "some parts are fine-tuned, polished, and attentive to every conceivable detail, while other aspects of social life appear as a sketchy presence [...] according to the author's focus as well as the available data and the recording techniques used" (Herzfeld 2014: 4). The challenge I set up for myself was to describe things that are vague. Throughout this study, I have described truthfully what I have experienced. Many of my experiences had to do with situations of uncertainty that were manifested in circumstances of ambiguities, paradoxes, indeterminacy, and incoherence that my research participants and I had to wrestle with. These experiences were often vague and inchoate. The vagueness or "unevenness" (Herzfeld 2014: 4) that has marked my experiences captures the "messiness" or "indeterminacy" distinctive of social interaction (Malaby 2003; Herzfeld 2014: 4). I have tried to write in such a way as to keep that indeterminacy and incoherence that have characterized the social world of my research participants.

To write about the indeterminacy of these people's stories also implicates my own act of writing in a state of uncertainty and vagueness. This may seem to work against the logic of good scholarly writing, which is expected to be clear and coherent. Yet, paradoxically, this seems to be the only way to do justice to the stories I have collected. Writing uncertainty through this book is also a recognition and exploration of "the serendipity of the writing process" (Herzfeld 2014: 4). In a sense, my act of writing resonates well with what Taussig calls "Nervous System writing" (Taussig 2015).

> Nervous System writing aims at being one jump ahead of the rules of rulelessness but knows at the same time that this is a doomed pursuit. If it is true that there is a mythology deposited in our language, Nervous System writing aims not at exposing that mythology but at conniving with it.
>
> (Taussig 2015: 10)

In Chapter 1, I discussed my own role of complicity when using gossip as an ethnographic practice to learn about the social world of my research participants. I learned how to gossip like the locals do. Consequently, my own investigation became complicit in understanding and depicting how a mode of knowing is developed and articulated by my interlocutors. Hence, gossip is not only a practice of complicity in this ethnography but also a conceptual exercise through which I examine how knowledge is created, mediated, and circulated among these actors. After the fieldwork was completed, my complicity continued to be at work in the very act of writing. The labor NGOs in my study tried to carve out a space for their activism by guessing and gauging the appropriate distance from the state in a complicit way. In order to capture and analyze their endeavors, I had to admit and lay bare my own epistemological uncertainty, which, paradoxically, forms the basis for a certain understanding of the Chinese state that is achieved not through demystifying the state but through describing what sustains the mystification as well as demystification of the state. The productivity of the notion of uncertainty, both analytically and methodologically, is manifested through its capacity to resolve such a paradox by arriving at a contested degree of certainty in the midst of uncertainty.

Engaging in complicity

This study is an ethnography in the margins of the state in which I have explored how uncertainty constitutes and is constitutive of the social and political life of a group of labor NGOs dependent on foreign funds. Pivoting on the notion of uncertainty, I have examined how certain relationships, practices, and subjectivities are imagined, generated, negotiated, and sustained in situations of ambiguity, paradoxes, and contingency. This, in turn, illustrates how uncertainty about the state's tolerance for labor activism fosters different ways of engaging in complicity between the state and the labor NGOs, which reproduces and sustains the political order of things. Pertinent ethnographic examples are described and discussed in Chapters 3 to 6, following Chapter 2, in which I described the economic, social, legal, and institutional conditions under which labor NGOs in China have emerged. Chapter 3 addresses how uncertainty is played out, experienced, and managed by the labor NGOs by focusing on two specific ethnographic examples. One deals with the labor NGOs' responses to and theories on the large-scale crackdown in 2012, while the other illustrates how one specific labor NGO mobilized social relationships and employed tactics to manage the perplexing vagaries of Chinese politics. Both Chapters 4 and 5 go further to illustrate and discuss how the relationships between the labor NGOs, the Chinese state, and foreign donors are situated, organized, and mediated in the domain of uncertainty, a fertile ground on which a complicit intimacy/intimate complicity is fostered. In Chapter 4, "The Politics of *Mingan,*" using the example of a workshop in Beijing, I showed how the labor NGOs and foreign donors constitute and share an intimate space mapped out by various articulations and representations, including discursive practices of irony and humor, of what is perceived to be *mingan* by these actors. I discussed how something or someone becomes *mingan* at the point when the "institutional intimacy" (Herzfeld 2016: 1–44) of the state is threatened, or when that intimacy, conversely, converges with the self-defense of the labor NGOs and activists. Most institutions develop institutional cultures and those cultures often contain secrets that are sources of comfort and amusement for their members but are not shared with outsiders because, if leaked, they would cause great embarrassment for the members of the institutions. Guarding these secrets constitutes an institutional intimacy. How to navigate through a wide range of *mingan* issues, people, organizations, places, and timing, or guard this institutional intimacy, is what I called the politics of *mingan*. Phrased differently, the politics of *mingan* also speaks to the constant struggle of these labor NGOs to gauge the appropriate distance from the state and thus perform their complicit role in sustaining the existing political order.

Like the notion of *mingan*, secrecy works in a similar way to demarcate and maintain the bounds of this institutional intimacy. In Chapter 5, "Intimating Secrecy," I considered the notion of secrecy against pervasive state surveillance by describing several techniques of concealment employed by the labor NGOs both in mainland China and Hong Kong. To perform secrecy is intimately connected with the actors' knowledge and skills of negotiating the politics of *mingan*. Discerning what is *mingan* requires discretion in order to determine the concealment of the whens, whats, whos, and hows. Trust is generated, mediated, and reinforced when the actors demonstrate their will and collaborate to exercise discretion and perform secrecy. Nevertheless, by treading the landscape of *mingan* politics with care and tact, these labor NGOs' performance of secrecy also engages with the Chinese state in a complicit way by being discrete about what they do. By discussing how the actors themselves perceived and evaluated their own endeavor of keeping secrets, I underscore the power of public secrecy (Taussig 1999) and argue that these actors' performance of secrecy is not so much an attempt to evade government surveillance as it is an effort to negotiate trust among these NGOs. This is made even more explicit by the common admission from the labor activists that it is very difficult to trick state surveillance, as demonstrated by Wei Peng's words above.

The ideas of *mingan*, secrecy, and intimacy are further crystalized through complicity when I discussed the development program of collective bargaining in Chapter 6, which was a collaboration between the Hong Kong labor NGO CWF and a few labor NGOs in mainland China. The politically sensitive nature of collective action in the Chinese context makes the implementation of this development program a revealing illustration of how the knowledge, skills, tactics, and techniques discussed in Chapters 3, 4, and 5 were applied to assess the appropriate distance from the state. For my discussion, I drew on two different labor NGOs: Green Grass and South Mountain, both of which were CWF's partners, explained how they respectively implemented the program, and discussed why one succeeded while the other failed. Green Grass's successful implementation of the collective bargaining program led to some trade-offs with the state security agents that had eventually jeopardized its trust relationship with CWF. With these two contrasting examples, I portrayed how the grassroots labor NGOs in mainland China were mired in a political and economic quandary, and presented a critique of the ways in which these labor NGOs collaborated with international development.

Uncertain future

Situating my study in the domain of uncertainty, I have described how a group of people and organizations placed in a difficult situation tried to negotiate trust with one another and make the best out of the situation that they could but were unable to control the larger forces of the state and international development that pushed them in that direction. By discussing the different modes of complicity employed by the labor NGOs and the Chinese state specifically in relation to the notions and practices of *mingan* and secrecy, I illustrated how complicated and painful this situation, in which state power is constantly speculated, gauged, and negotiated, is. Through the examples provided in this study, it is clear that these various ways of engaging in complicity are a necessary precondition not only for the labor

NGOs but also for the Chinese state to function. One of the reasons that the state does not imprison these activists and close down the NGOs is that the state is very aware that the labor NGOs are doing things that it has failed to do but which need to be done in order to keep moving. The inactive national trade union ACFTU is a clear example of this. Extending Herzfeld's theory of cultural intimacy and complicity, I show that complicity works in both directions in the Chinese context: By doing the things that the state has failed to do, the labor NGOs conspire with the Chinese state to protect its reputation in order to safeguard the country's financial interests and global competitiveness, while the labor NGOs shield the state from being embarrassed by being perceived as somehow culturally inferior.[2] I argue that by achieving complicity with the labor NGOs, the Chinese state is able to hide the shortcomings that often arise from its pragmatic, opportunistic, and sometimes ad hoc way of governing. As such, the kind of complicity discussed in this study becomes a means of dealing with the discontent that arises from the state's inadequacies and failures, which does sound a little like Herzfeld's articulation of "secular theodicy" (Herzfeld 1992: 5–7).

In addressing the question of how to explain a system or a world that is flawed, Herzfeld suggests that secular theodicy serve the more pragmatic goal of providing "people with social means of coping with disappointment" (ibid.: 7). According to Herzfeld, grumbling against a flawed system is a means whereby people manage to reconcile with the imperfection and contradiction. The main point of Herzfeld's theory of secular theodicy is basically that people complain when confronted with the mismatch between what people expect from an ideal planning system and the system people actually experience. It is tempting to attribute the kind of complicity employed by the Chinese labor NGOs to one of such means to grumble against the Chinese state. Doing so, however, would fail to adequately capture and grasp what is really going on between the Chinese state and the labor community. What these NGOs are up against is not merely a system that is flawed but a state that is fundamentally oppressive. What these NGOs are doing is more than just to reconcile with the mismatch or complain about the system that is not working properly. They engage complicity with the Chinese state because the state has failed to do what it is obligated to do and because this seems to be the only way to slowly realize their goals while minimizing the risk of their own safety. What the Chinese case illustrates is because this kind of complicity is something that the state cannot admit to, it gives rise to the conditions imbued with uncertainty under which these labor NGOs have to operate. Working in both directions between the Chinese state and the labor NGOs, the kind of complicity discussed here is productive in helping the functioning and protection of the state while leaving room for NGOs to maneuver, which is not fully captured in Herzfeld's theory of secular theodicy. As such, the complicity and the subsequent uncertain conditions—the complicity of uncertainty—ultimately reproduce the existing political order of things.

These NGO actors are uncertain largely because they have no way of knowing how each individual who represents the state will interpret the mandate and keep things running while knowing that things are still imperfect but not being able to admit that the imperfections still exist. The uncertainty and the subsequent complicity make it very difficult, if not impossible, for my research participants to fathom and describe the situation not just for me but mostly for themselves. The fact that they have not been able to talk about this directly creates the conditions under which they are able to operate. In fact, the labor NGOs depend on a certain degree of uncertainty where there are no explicit rules. It is not in their interest to make things too clear because if they do, not only will they be liable to prosecution, but they will also place the people who collude with them in the government at equal, if not higher, risk. More importantly, the constant insistence on not understanding what was going on and thus not being able to talk about it very directly is itself part of the ongoing mystification that is illustrated in all the examples of paradoxes, incoherence, and ambiguities throughout this study. The productivity of uncertainty reveals its force in these situations of indeterminacy and feelings of incompleteness that are actually the mask that these actors have to use to keep things going. For these labor NGOs and activists, the future seems rather uncertain and gloomy. But as shown in Wei Peng's efforts to find new projects for his NGO, these labor NGOs still have to keep going.

By studying the development of labor NGOs in South China and their relationships with intermediary labor NGOs in Hong Kong and foreign donors, I have demonstrated how the Chinese state operates and exercises power through uncertainty. Predicated on the capriciousness of the Chinese state, the uncertainty of the permissible boundaries of activism is a fertile and intimate ground on which social relationships are created, negotiated, and managed. My study illustrates how the ambiguous and unstable boundary between state and society is an exercise of state power that has consequences (Mitchell 1991: 90). Focusing on the uncertainty at the margins of the Chinese state, I explore political practices and the processes that legitimize domination in opposition to those who reify the state as an invisible structure that shapes existing institutions (Mitchell 1991; Sharma & Gupta 2006: 46). It is in the domain of uncertainty that I trace and examine how this legitimation proceeds and how it is consolidated. My study shows that the domain of uncertainty is a productive space where implicit knowledge and practices are cultivated, learned, and circulated in order to navigate through the unclear boundaries of the state's tolerance of activism while at the same time generating modes of complicity that maintain the political order of things. As such, with the example of labor NGOs, I analyze how politically organized social subjection is carried out through complicity and show how intimacy as a contingent space for political contention and engagement is an entry point for understanding state power.

Paradoxically, the processes of legitimation described in this study also illustrate the limits of state reason and intervention. The Chinese state exercises control over its population effectively largely because it skillfully obscures its inability to know everything about its population through the construction of a reality where the rules of conducting acceptable political behavior are unclear. It is a form of government that takes advantage of the limits of state reason and intervention by making the population constantly guess and gauge the appropriate distance from the state, which, in turn, leads to effective self-censorship and subsequent modes of complicity that sustain state power. The effectiveness and productivity of Chinese state power are precisely predicated on its adroit management and manipulation of uncertainty. This study is a modest attempt to think about the state and describe ethnographically how the state operates. Moreover, locating and studying the Chinese state in the domain of uncertainty contributes to the ongoing discussion on whether China can continue its economic growth without significant political reform, and the larger issue of democratization.

Since 2013, the Chinese government has further stepped up its clampdown on labor activists. Some rights groups say the government's increasing hostility toward labor activism largely has to do with China's slowing economy and a concomitant surge of labor disputes (Pan in Wright 2019: 162). The most recent and notable incident was the arrest of six labor rights activists in Guangzhou in the winter of 2015. These activists had been active in the labor rights movement in Guangdong and had assisted workers in negotiating better working conditions with their employers. They were formally arrested on charges such as disturbing social order and embezzlement. In 2016, these activists were all released, with three receiving suspended sentences for "gathering a crowd to disrupt social order." The opaque circumstances of their detention and possibly coerced confessions have raised questions of access to defense lawyers, treatment in detention, and unexplained intimidation of family members (ibid.).

Following the intensified suppression of labor activists in 2015, some of the labor NGOs that I worked with in 2012 and 2013 either disintegrated completely or shifted their focus to social service provision for migrant workers' children (ibid.). These new developments suggest that the future of labor activism in China will be even more uncertain and gloomy than it has been in past decades. The skirmishes between labor NGOs and the Chinese state are most likely to continue and to be accompanied by new forms of knowledge and practices to navigate through the uncertain terrain of Chinese politics. Future research is needed to further explore the variations and reconfigurations of the politics of engagement and contention.

Notes

1 Wei Peng is from the province of Hebei, where his wife and daughter still live.
2 I am indebted to Professor Michael Herzfeld for suggesting that I make these two kinds of intimacy explicit in my writing.

Bibliography

Appadurai, Arjun. 2007. Hope and democracy. *Public Culture* 19 (1): 29–34.

Cerwonka, Allaine, and Liisa H. Malkki, eds. 2007. *Improvising theory: process and temporality in ethnographic fieldwork*. Chicago: University of Chicago Press.

Herzfeld, Michael. 2016. *Cultural intimacy: social poetics and the real life of states, societies, and institutions*. New York: Routledge.

———— 2014. Serendipitous sculpture: ethnography does as ethnography goes. *Anthropology and Humanism* 39 (1): 3–9.

———— 1992. *The social production of indifference: exploring the symbolic roots of Western bureaucracy*. Chicago: University of Chicago Press.

Malaby, Thomas M. 2003. *Gambling life: dealing in contingency in a Greek city*. Urbana and Chicago: University of Illinois Press.

Mitchell, Timothy. 1991. The limits of the state: beyond statist approaches and their critics. *The American Political Science Review*, 85 (1): 77–96.

Paley, Julia. ed. 2008. *Democracy: anthropological approaches*. Santa Fe: School for Advanced Research Advanced Seminar Series.

Pan, Darcy. 2019. "Thinking like a state: doing labor activism in South China" In *Handbook of Protest and Resistance*, edited by Teresa Wright. Cheltenham, UK: Edward Elgar Publishing, pp. 151–165.

Sharma, Aradhana, and Akhil Gupta, eds. 2006. *The anthropology of the state: a reader*. Oxford: Blackwell Publishing.

Taussig, Michael. 2015. *The corn wolf*. Chicago and London: University of Chicago Press.

———— 1999. *Defacement: public secrecy and the labor of the negative*. Stanford: Stanford University Press.

Index